FORMATIONS OF CLASS AND GENDER

Theory, Culture & Society

Theory, Culture & Society caters for the resurgence of interest in culture within contemporary social science and the humanities. Building on the heritage of classical social theory, the book series examines ways in which this tradition has been reshaped by a new generation of theorists. It will also publish theoretically informed analyses of everyday life, popular culture, and new intellectual movements.

EDITOR: Mike Featherstone, *Nottingham Trent University*

SERIES EDITORIAL BOARD
Roy Boyne, *University of Teesside*
Mike Hepworth, *University of Aberdeen*
Scott Lash, *Lancaster University*
Roland Robertson, *University of Pittsburgh*
Bryan S. Turner, *Deakin University*

THE TCS CENTRE
The Theory, Culture & Society book series, the journals *Theory, Culture & Society* and *Body & Society*, and related conference, seminar and postgraduate programmes operate from the TCS Centre at Nottingham Trent University. For further details of the TCS Centre's activities please contact:

Centre Administrator
The TCS Centre, Room 175
Faculty of Humanities
Nottingham Trent University
Clifton Lane, Nottingham, NG11 8NS, UK
e-mail: tcs@ntu.ac.uk

Recent volumes include:

Spatial Formations
Nigel Thrift

The Body and Society
Explorations in Social Theory
Second Edition
Bryan S. Turner

The Social Construction of Nature
Klaus Eder

Deleuze and Guattari
An Introduction to the Politics of Desire
Philip Goodchild

Pierre Bourdieu and Cultural Theory
Critical Investigations
Bridget Fowler

Re-Forming the Body
Religion, Community and Modernity
Philip A. Mellor and Chris Shilling

FORMATIONS OF CLASS AND GENDER

Becoming Respectable

Beverley Skeggs

SAGE Publications
London • Thousand Oaks • New Delhi

First published 1997

Published in association with *Theory, Culture & Society*,
Nottingham Trent University

SAGE Publications Ltd
1 Oliver's Yard
55 City Road
London EC1Y 1SP

SAGE Publications Inc.
2455 Teller Road
Thousand Oaks, California 91320

SAGE Publications India Pvt Ltd
B-42, Panchsheel Enclave
Post Box 4109
New Delhi 110 017

British Library Cataloguing in Publication data
A catalogue record for this book is available
from the British Library
ISBN 13: 978-0-7619-5511-5

Library of Congress catalog record available

Typeset by M Rules
Printed in Great Britain by The Cromwell Press Ltd,
Broughton Gifford, Melksham, Wiltshire

Contents

To Mary Mullaney

To the women who gave me access to their lives, made this book possible and really questioned me. I will remain grateful always to Mary Mullaney, Karen Smith, Angela Shatwell, Jane Capewell, Sarah Hart, Sue Cliffe, Jane McDowell, Alison Jane Scholtze, Jo Harrap, Michelle Murphy, Julie Dodd, Sue Callary, Marie Allen, Janet Winton, Caroline Brammeld, Michelle Powell, Catherine Tilley, Beverley Vaughan, Diane Gilbert, Michelle Davies, Michelle Kidson, Lynette Hughes, Alicia Drinkwater, Debbie Snell, Pam Clarke, Jackie Hargrove, Carol James, Amanda Jefferies, Babs Naylor, Wendy Owen, Yvonne Worrall, Sharon Worrall, Rachel Cooke, Sue Cottrell, Darren Eyes, Darren Fowles, Ann-Marie Egerton, Kerry Gandy, Kate Evans, Lynne Astles, Andrea Berry, Julie Preen, Louise Potts, Diane Ratcliffe, Andrea Read, Julie Shallcross, Kate Townsend, Shirley Tracey, Elizabeth Wilson, Janice Worrall, Louise Williams, Karen Welch, Sheila Bailey.

Enormous thanks to those who have read and greatly improved this work – Joe Bristow, Alex Callinicos, Rosemary Deem, Lynne Pearce, Mairtin Mac an Ghaill, Andrew Sayer, Jackie Stacey, Alan Warde, Alison Young. They are amongst the most stimulating, rigorous, generous and enjoyable colleagues and friends any person would ask for. Especial thanks to Celia Lury who not only read and made invaluable contributions but who also covered all my work when I was seriously ill and has been an inspiration and a great friend. To Sara Ahmed, Sarah Franklin and Maureen McNeil for coming to Women's Studies at Lancaster and making it even better. Thanks also to Ann Gray, Christine Griffin, Joanna Hodge, Ellen Seiter, Kathleen Reeve, Jackie Cook and Karen Jennings for great international discussions and information.

I owe lots to Val Atkinson, Nickie Whitham, Jean Grugel, Pat Kirkham, Joy Castleton, Paula Davis and George Scully for inspiration, sustenance and friendship over a long period of time. Mary Maynard and Denis Gleeson enabled my access to and movement through academia, always providing rigorous critique and inspiration, as did my first colleagues Erica Stratta, Kate McDonald and Catherine Neal at Worcester. My students have sustained me over time and helped me to clarify my thoughts. Special thanks to Suzanne Thomas. Thanks also to Robert Rojek at Sage who rescued this project. My very respectable parents have always provided support of many different varieties and I will always be grateful. Amos Zamorski provided the backing track that sustained the isolation of writing – thanks.

1

Introduction: Processes, Frameworks and Motivations

I think my clothing says I'm respectable. [Mary, 1992]

All my life I've wanted to say 'look I'm as good as you', well now I think this house says it. It says 'I've made it, I'm respectable and you can't put me down'. [Yvonne, 1992]

Respectability is one of the most ubiquitous signifiers of class. It informs how we speak, who we speak to, how we classify others, what we study and how we know who we are (or are not). Respectability is usually the concern of those who are not seen to have it. Respectability would not be of concern here, if the working classes (Black and White) had not consistently been classified as dangerous, polluting, threatening, revolutionary, pathological and without respect.[1] It would not be something to desire, to prove and to achieve, if it had not been seen to be a property of 'others', those who were valued and legitimated. If respectability had not been one of the key mechanisms by which some groups were 'othered' and pathologized it would not be the subject of this study. It is rarely recognized as an issue by those who are positioned with it, who are normalized by it, and who do not have to prove it. Yet for those who feel positioned by and position themselves against the discourse of respectability it informs a great deal of their responses. For the 83 White working-class women of this longitudinal ethnographic study, set in the North West of England, respectability is always an issue.

Feminist (and) cultural theory proliferates with theories of identities and subjective constructions, but few of these theories explore the processes by which 'real' women negotiate and understand them'selves'. This book contextualizes theoretical debates through closely detailed ethnographic research. It is based on research conducted over a total period of 12 years including three years' full-time, in-the-field participant observation. It began when the women enrolled on a 'caring' course at a local college and it follows their trajectories through the labour market, education and the family. In this sense, it is part of what Marcus (1992) defines as modernist ethnography which concentrates on how subjectivities are constructed across a range of different sites, across time, enabling long-term analysis of movements, investments and positionings. It is part of the British Cultural Studies tradition in that theoretical, methodological and political concerns are worked through empirical understandings and that careful attention is paid to the historical legacies which inform contemporary representations. The book draws on a range of cultural and feminist theorists to engage with the lived experience of how the women inhabit different social positions and cultural representations.

There has been a marked tendency in recent years to move away from talking and listening to those outside of academia. This book shows how theory can be radically transformed if others are let in on the conversations. The women of this study are not just ciphers from which subject positions can be read-off; rather, they are active in producing the meaning of the positions they (refuse to, reluctantly or willingly) inhabit. The methodological debates about the production of knowledge are central to the book which engages in the more general debates within epistemology about reflexivity and methodology whilst also making explicit the processes through which the theories are constituted and reconstituted over time.

Whilst this book draws on the attempts of a specific group of women to negotiate class, gender, hetero/sexuality, femininity, caring and feminism, it does have a more general address. That is to question how feminists, cultural theorists and sociologists have generated frameworks to understand how women live and produce themselves through social and cultural relations. The ramifications of the particular analysis provide a grounded framework which is applicable to other groups (who are always positioned in proximity to respectability).[2] Respectability contains judgements of class, race, gender and sexuality and different groups have differential access to the mechanisms for generating, resisting and displaying respectability.[3] By using respectability as an analytical tool this book aims to reinstate class in feminist (and) cultural theory. This is because class as a concept and working-class women as a group have almost disappeared from the agendas of feminism and cultural theory. Yet, as this book will show, the category 'woman' is always produced through processes which include class and classifying produces very real effects which are lived on a daily basis.

This introduction maps the centrality of respectability to the development of class categorizations. It then makes an argument for reinstating class and establishes a framework for doing so. The final section provides an outline and documents the motivations for the book.

Respectable Distinctions

Respectability was a central mechanism through which the concept class emerged. Finch (1993) shows how the categorization of social groups in the UK and Australia occurred through the interpretation of the behaviour of women of urban slums and the classification of them into respectable and non-respectable. This division, she argues, came to be seen as a reasonable way of relating to, and intervening in, the lives of people defined as working class; and Nead (1988) shows how judgements about respectability were central to nineteenth-century visual representations of femininity and moral judgements about women's appearance. Judgements of respectability were also central to the organization of women's homes, their childcare practices and the control they exercised over members of their family. These judgements persevere, as Susan notes in response to visits by a Health Visitor:

> You know they're weighing you up and they ask you all these indirect questions as if you're too thick to know what they're getting at and you know all the time they're thinking 'she's poor, she's no good, she can't bring her kids up properly' and no matter what you do they've got your number. To them you're never fit, never up to their standards. [Susan, 1992]

> All the time you've got to weigh everything up: is it too tarty? will I look like a right slag in it? what will people think? It drives me mad that every time you go to put your clothes on you have to think 'do I look dead common? is it rough? do I look like a dog?' [Anne, 1992]

Respectability has always been a marker and a burden of class, a standard to which to aspire: Engels, in the nineteenth century, described the ideal of respectability as 'a most repulsive thing', 'a false consciousness bred into the bones of the workers' (1953: 522–3). The classification by and of the working classes into rough and respectable has a long history (see Stacey, 1975): many attempts – often through religion – were made to 'rescue' White working-class women from the clutches of non-respectability. To not be respectable is to have little social value or legitimacy.

Respectability was also central to the development of the notion of Englishness. It was a key characteristic of what it meant to belong, to be worthy and to be an individual. As Strathern (1992) notes, respectability was the means by which morality was made public and seen to be an object of knowledge. Respectability embodies moral authority: those who are respectable have it, those who are not do not. But only some groups were considered to be capable of being moral, others were seen to be in need of control. Strathern argues 'the first fact of English kinship is the individuality of persons'; this individuality was only available to the genteel middle classes. They were defined against the lack of individuality of the masses. 'Individuals' were the respectable, the moral, the worthy, the English, the White and the non-working class, who could sit in judgement of others. Respectability became a property of middle-class individuals defined against the masses. This early mapping of class relationships onto what it meant to be a worthy, moral individual provides a legacy and framework for this study and for understanding the desires for respectability today. Whilst class relations have clearly been refigured through different historical periods, certain central features remain. The working classes are still 'massified' and marked as others in academic and popular representations where they appear as pathological: the cynical use of single mothers in the UK to represent a threat to social order to generate support for Conservative party policy on law and order (at the 1995 Party Conference) and the use of 'Welfare Mothers' and 'Crack Babies' in the US shows how easily historical constructs can be recycled. Similarly, a recent magazine fashion spread in the UK edition of *Marie Claire* entitled 'Council Estate Slags' suggests that working-class women are still represented through their 'deviant' sexuality.[4]

The women of this study are aware of their place, of how they are socially positioned and of the attempts to represent them. This constantly informs their responses. They operate with a dialogic form of recognition: they recognize the recognitions of others. Recognitions do not occur without value judgements and the women are constantly aware of the judgements of real and imaginary others. Recognition of how one is positioned is central to the *processes* of subjective construction. Throughout the book I show how experiences of being positioned and classified (as working class, as heterosexual, as feminine, as caring, as vulgar, as feminist) produce different responses which impact upon subjective construction. These recognitions enable the women to navigate themselves through classificatory systems and measure and evaluate themselves accordingly. One central feature of the research is how the positions they occupy are rarely accommodated with comfort. They live their social locations with unease. The book explores the uneasy sense of standing under signs to which one does and does not belong (Butler, 1992).

The central themes which are used throughout the book are as follows: first, *processes of identification* and differentiation, including recognition, disidentification, dissimulation and subjective construction; second, *issues of location*, positioning and movement through social space and place – here special attention is given to issues of *access*; third, *interrogation and applicability of concepts* and categories used here and in feminist theory more generally, and fourth, the *deployment of different forms of capital*. This chapter first makes an argument for reinstating class into feminist and cultural theory. It then sets out frameworks, used in the rest of the book – on metaphors of capital and processes of subjective production – ending with chapter outlines and a brief discussion of my motivation to study respectability.

Reinstating Class

Finch (1993) examines how 'the working class' as a category came into effect through middle-class conceptualizations. These conceptualizations were produced from anxiety about social order and through attempts by the middle class to consolidate *their* identity and power by distancing themselves from definable 'others'. The middle class, Finch shows, came to recognize themselves through difference: a difference they produced through the generation and distribution of representations of different 'others': as McClintock notes:

> The degenerate classes, defined as departures from the normal human type, were as necessary to the self-definition of the middle-class as the idea of degeneration was to the idea of progress, for the distance along the path of progress travelled by some portions of humanity could be measured only by the distance others lagged behind. (1995: 46)

The conceptualizations of the middle classes were enabled by particular Enlightenment technologies, such as social surveys, observation, photography and ethnography, which were part of a project to constitute 'reason' through the classification of observable behaviour, what Finch defines as the 'classing gaze':

The range of chosen concerns through which middle-class observers made sense of the observed, included references to: living room conditions . . . drinking behaviour . . . language (including both the type of things which were spoken about, and the manner in which they were referred to – literally the types of words used); and children's behaviour . . . These were *moral*, not economic, references. (1993: 10; emphasis added)

By the end of the nineteenth century 'the working class' had become a knowable, measurable and organizable category. They could be recognized and they could learn to recognize themselves through categorization: a categorization which initially had no meaning for them. The importance of the use of moral categories, Finch argues, is that it placed women at the centre of the discursive construction because it was women who were predominantly observed. At the core of all articulations of the working class was the discursive construct of the modern, that is middle-class, family in which the behaviour of women was interpreted in relation to their role as wives and mothers and based on their responsibility, the control of their sexuality, their care, protection and education of children and their capacity for the general surveillance of working-class men. Observation *and* interpretation of the sexual behaviour of working-class women on the basis of their appearance was central to the production of middle-class conceptualizations.

The cult of domesticity was central to the self-defining of the middle classes and to the maintenance of ideas of an imperialist nation. Yet the labour involved in its production was often made invisible by the use of 'downstairs' domestic servants (McClintock, 1995). The self-defining of the middle classes also produced, McClintock (1995) argues, the categorizations of race. These categorizations were interlocked with those of class through the generic definition of 'dangerous classes'. Domestic servants, for instance, were often depicted by the racialized iconography of degradation – of contagion, promiscuity and savagery. As Engels (1844/1958) notes of the working class: 'a physically degenerate race, robbed of all humanity, degraded, reduced morally and intellectually to bestiality' (p. 33) who are 'a race wholly apart' (p. 361). Depictions of domestic degeneracy, McClintock shows, were widely used to mediate the contradictions in imperial hierarchy.

It is these historical productions of class into which any representation of class is located: class is a discursive, historically specific construction, a product of middle-class political consolidation, which includes elements of fantasy and projection. The historical generation of classed categorizations provide discursive frameworks which enable, legitimate and map onto material inequalities. Class conceptualizations are tautological in that positioning by categorizations and representation influence access to economic and cultural resources. The discursive constructions are recognized as a form of positioning; which is why attempts to classify the women as working class generated such negative responses (as shown in Chapter 5). They have been positioned by the historical discursive construct of class and this has an effect on how they understand themselves and others.

The long and continual process of representing the working class did not have its history in the re-presentation of an original, of a real; yet the continual re-presentation of representations, which some theorists would identify as a process of reiteration (where representations continually reference themselves through daily reproduction) does have real effects in the responses that people make to them. Representations, however, as this study shows, are not straightforwardly reproduced but are resisted and transfigured in their daily enactment. Categories of class operate not only as an organizing principle which enable access to and limitations on social movement and interaction but are also reproduced at the intimate level as a 'structure of feeling' (cf. Williams, 1961, 1977) in which doubt, anxiety and fear inform the production of subjectivity. To be working-classed, Kuhn (1995) argues, generates a constant fear of never having 'got it right'.

Without understanding the significance of class positioning many of the women's movements through social space, through education, families, labour markets and in particular, in the production of their subjectivity, could not be understood. Yet class has almost disappeared from feminist analyses, even those claiming a materialist feminist position (see, for instance, Hennessy, 1993).[5] This may be because in the past the majority of feminist debates on class have focused on very detailed Marxist analysis of the family, the labour market and the value of domestic labour (Breugel, 1979; Brenner and Ramas, 1984) or it may be that it has disappeared because class itself is so hard to define. For instance, do we mean class structure, identity, consciousness, action, and so on when we speak of class? Other difficult questions are also raised: how does class relate to the sexual division of labour, and is it a cause or an effect ? Have feminists avoided class because it is impossible to measure accurately? (see Crompton, 1993, for a summary of the debates). Or is it that for those who now get to write and represent feminist (and) cultural theory class is not experienced or felt as immediately as gender? It may not be recognized as a problem for those who have the privilege to ignore it.[6] The retreat from class in feminist theory, McRobbie (1982) argues, has had an important function of enabling other spheres of women's lives to be investigated such as the state and the law. But it seems that the baby has been thrown out with the bath water. To abandon class as a theoretical tool does not mean that it does not exist any more; only that some theorists do not value it. It does not mean the women would experience inequality any differently; rather, it would make it more difficult for them to identify and challenge the basis of the inequality which they experience. Class inequality exists beyond its theoretical representation. The movement in feminist theory from a Marxist perspective into more literary informed influences parallels a class movement, whereby feminist theory becomes more 'up-market', drawing on the cultural capital of those who have had access to 'high culture' and higher education: in some cases feminist theory has become a vehicle for displaying 'cleverness' and masking the inequalities that enable 'cleverness' to be produced and displayed.

The retreat from class has occurred across a range of academic sites. Retreatists either ignore class or argue that class is 'an increasingly redundant issue' (for instance, Holton and Turner, 1989, 1994). This is consolidated by publishers who tell me that 'class doesn't sell'. The retreat, Crompton (1993) defines as the sociological equivalent of the 'new individualism', a movement highly evident in many postmodern theories (Callinicos, 1989; Skeggs, 1991c). Interestingly race is not dismissed as a structural dinosaur. A great deal of postmodernist theorizing dismisses class as a structural concept, a relic from modernism which has no applicability to the supposed ability to travel through differences unencumbered by structure or inequality. The concept of difference has, in many places, come to stand in for inequality (see Maynard, 1994). Harvey (1993) notes the irony of this at a time when business interests are operating as classes and using the state as a class instrument (Edsall, 1984).[7] Others make retreats from class analysis by using empirical evidence to suggest that the significance of class has declined. They usually use social mobility, educational opportunity and electoral behaviour studies to 'demonstrate' the decline of class. Goldthorpe and Marshall (1992), however, argue that exactly the same empirical data can be used to show class is still significant as a major means of social differentiation, and Warde (1994) notes that the 'decline of class' thesis is usually a matter of speculation with little substantive evidence.

The search for a more appropriate label, however, draws attention away from exploitation. Also, when a retreat is mounted we need to ask whose experiences are being silenced, whose lives are being ignored and whose lives are considered worthy of study.[8] We also need to think about the relationship between responsibility and knowledge: to ignore or make class invisible is to abdicate responsibility (through privilege) from the effects it produces. To think that class does not matter is only a prerogative of those unaffected by the deprivations and exclusions it produces. Making class invisible represents a historical stage in which the identity of the middle classes is assured. There was a time when the concept was considered necessary by the middle classes to maintain and consolidate differences in power: its recent invisibility suggests that these differences are now institutionalized, legitimated and well established. So rather than abandon the concept of class as a reactionary configuration I want to re-nuance it to show how it is a major feature of subjectivity, a historical specificity and part of a struggle over access to resources and ways of being. Class informs not only the production of these women's subjectivity but also how it is central to us all, even if we do not feel impeded by it or choose not to recognize it, or to avoid it through disidentifications and dissimulations.

The next section on metaphors of capital provides the general theoretical framework that informs each chapter of the book. This framework is chosen because it provides the greatest explanatory power to understand the intersections of class and gender in subjective production. It enables an analysis which can understand contradiction and investment across space and time. The framework is established here so that each chapter can work through the nuances of it in practice in relation to each different formation of caring, femininity, class, feminism and sexuality. Each chapter modifies the framework though the specificity of its analysis but ultimately it is the archaeological foundation on which the book is built.

Framework: Metaphors of Capital

Bourdieu (1979, 1986, 1987, 1989) suggests a model of class which is based on 'capital' movements through social space. The structure of this space is given by the distribution of the various forms of 'capital', by the distribution of their properties, properties which are capable of conferring strength, power and consequently profit on their holder. This also enables an analysis of the micropolitics of power. From this model we can see how class formation operates between abstract structures and concrete specifics of everyday life, noting that because of constant change, class formation is necessarily partial (Sayer and Walker, 1992). Class, for Bourdieu, is neither an essence or an indeterminate set of fluctuating signifiers, but an arbitrarily imposed definition with real social effects (Moi, 1991). He identifies four different types of capital: economic, cultural, social, symbolic:

1 Economic capital: this includes income, wealth, financial inheritances and monetary assets.[9]

2 Cultural capital: this can exist in three forms – in an embodied state, that is in the form of long-lasting dispositions of the mind and the body; in the objectified state, in the form of cultural goods; and in the institutionalized state, resulting in such things as educational qualifications. The discourses of femininity and masculinity become embodied and can be used as cultural resources. This is not to say that gendered relations are purely cultural. They are not. Cultural capital only exists in relation to the network of other forms of capital. Gender carries different amounts of symbolic capital in different contexts (Moi, 1991).[10]

3 Social capital: resources based on connections and group membership. This is capital generated through relationships.[11]

4 Symbolic capital: this is the form the different types of capital take once they are perceived and recognized as legitimate. Legitimation is the key mechanism in the conversion to power. Cultural capital has to be legitimated before it can have symbolic power. Capital has to be regarded as legitimate before it can be capitalized upon. All capitals are context specific. Thus people are distributed in the overall social space according to: the global *volume* of capital they possess; the *composition* of their capital, the relative weight in their overall capital of the various forms of capital and evolution in time of the volume and composition according to their *trajectory* in social space.

The social space we occupy has been historically generated. If the transmission of capital over time, hence in families over generations, is introduced we can see how when we are born, we enter an inherited social space from which comes access to and acquisition of differential amounts of capital assets. From being born into gender, class and race relations we occupy the associated social positions such as 'woman', 'Black', 'working class' (Moi, 1991). We also inherit ways of understanding; we inherit the meanings associated with social positions and positions in knowledge. Each kind of capital can only exist in the interrelationships of social positions; they bring with them access to or limitation on which capitals are available to certain positions. They become gendered through being lived, through circulation, just as they become classed, raced and sexed: they become simultaneously processed. The social relations of capitals into which we are born and move have been constructed historically through struggles over assets and space. Gender, class and race are not capitals as such, rather they provide the relations in which capitals come to be organized and valued. Masculinity and Whiteness, for instance, are valued (and normalized) forms of cultural capital.[12] Our social locations influence our movement and relations to other social positions and hence our ability to capitalize further on the assets we already have. For instance, if born into a White working-class family with only small amounts of historically designated legitimate cultural capital (say, for example, the cultural capital of the 'lads' studied by Willis (1977) which was macho physical hardness, or the working-class femininity of the women of this study) the ability to trade with this asset will be circumscribed by the division of labour and the values already ascribed to particular assets generated through historical symbolic struggle. The 'lads' find their physicality to have little worth in a predominantly service economy. Yet despite their inability to trade this masculinity in the division of labour they are able to use it to gain power (but not capital) in relationships with women. In the same way, the women (as is shown in Chapter 4) had by the age of 16 only limited capital to trade – their feminine cultural capital – and this was only convertible on a diminishing labour market or as unpaid labour in voluntary caring or in the family. When they traded their femininity and appearance on the marriage market (see Chapters 6 and 7) they were able to negotiate more power but only in interpersonal terms rather than gaining access to wider institutional power. The trading of femininity, however, also involves them as the object of the exchange. The women had only limited resources to trade; their ability to increase their capital assets, to convert them to gain material reward, was severely limited. 'Family' factors which influence all forms of capital also imposed limitations as a substantial proportion of the young women (28 per cent) have had to contend with abusive fathers, children's homes, foster parents, separated or divorced parents, which severely disrupted their ability to accrue capital across various sites. This means that they never enter a level playing field.

Bourdieu's economistic metaphors are useful for understanding how access, resources and legitimation contribute to class formation. For instance, we can understand why those with a small volume of cultural capital will have difficulties increasing its composition and will subsequently have a circumscribed trajectory. To avoid relativizing the different forms of capital we need to understand the mechanisms by which the different forms of capital are enabled or curtailed. We need to know how the structures historically generated from previous movements of capital such as the labour market and the education system institutionalize (that is provide spaces for the capitalization of the different forms of capital). Embodied capital, such as physical appearance, can be capitalized upon in labour and marriage markets (as Chapter 6 shows). Class positions are not just relative forms in social space, they are institutionalized positions: the cultural capital of the middle classes can offer substantial rewards in the labour market. Chapter 3 charts the symbolic and historical struggles which institutionalized caring as a form of working-class femininity with limited access to economic capital and Chapter 4 sets out how these symbolic struggles become institutionalized through the provision of limited subject positions to inhabit.

But, we need to remember that the different forms of capital Bourdieu identifies are essentially metaphors, they are not descriptors of empirical positions.[13] They are useful, Moi (1991) argues, because they enable us to identify the interests and benefits of particular groups. However, Bourdieu's (1986) *Distinction*, an analysis which develops these metaphors, does ultimately code behaviour in a cold and mechanical classificatory manner which does not bring out the pleasures and pain associated with gender, class and sexuality. This book does not hide these affective aspects of inequality.

It is the symbolic struggles that enable inequalities in capital to be reproduced. Analysing access and legitimation of cultural formations enables us to see how cultural capital is or is not converted into symbolic capital and hence how inequalities are generated and systematic disempowerment engendered. Symbolic capital is powerful capital: it brings power with it. If one's cultural capital is delegitimated then it cannot be traded as an asset; it cannot be capitalized upon (although it may retain significance and meaning to the individual) and its power is limited. Femininity, for instance, can be seen as a form of cultural capital. It is the discursive position available through gender relations that women are encouraged to inhabit and use. Its use will be informed by the network of social positions of class, gender, sexuality, region, age and race which ensure that it will be taken up (and resisted) in different ways. Whereas it is possible to trade masculinity more readily and for greater reward in the labour market (men still hold the majority of jobs in the primary labour market, for instance), the ability to capitalize on femininity is restricted. It provides only restricted access to potential forms of power.

Femininity can be used socially in tactical rather than strategic ways. De Certeau (1988) distinguishes between strategies and tactics: strategies, he argues, have institutional positioning and are able to conceal their connections with power; tactics have no institutional location and cannot capitalize on the advantages of such positioning. Rather, tactics constantly manipulate events to turn them into opportunities; tactical options have more to do with constraints than possibilities. They are determined by the absence of power just as strategy is organized by the postulation of power.[14] Femininity brings with it little social, political and economic worth. It is not a strong asset to trade and capitalize upon. As McCall (1992) notes, rarely is femininity exclusively profitable for women as implied in Bourdieu's definitions. This argument is developed in Chapter 6.

Most representations of working-class people contribute to devaluing and delegitimating their already meagre capitals, putting further blocks on tradability, denying any conversion into symbolic capital. When conversion is blocked positions of inequality are maintained. The allocative function of education plays a role in delegitimating and limiting the value of the cultural capital of working-class groups. The blocking of conversion also occurs at the cultural and discursive level whereby the symbolic capital of one group enables it to use its power to culturally and economically exploit another. The classic case is the symbolic representations of Black women and men as atavistic, animalistic and inhuman in order to legitimate the practices of slavery and colonial exploitation (Fryer, 1984). Likewise, the representational denigration of White working-class women blocks their capacity to convert their cultural capital into symbolic capital to gain other capitals and ensure material security.

The space for contestation over cultural and symbolic forms of capital occurs at local as well as national and global levels. The local is the site where de-legitimacy is resisted. Yet the ability to counteract the de-legitimation of their own cultural capital at a local level does not mean that already devalued capital can be capitalized upon. Rather it suggests momentary refusals of powerlessness. To challenge powerlessness does not mean that one automatically shifts into positions of power. It means, straightforwardly, that one is refusing to be seen as powerless or be positioned without power.

To stretch economic metaphors even further it may be useful to think of the value of the arenas in which different forms of capital are traded. The structure of the field of power, argues Waquant (1993), depends at every moment on struggles over the respective weight of different forms of capital within the structure. *Not* being middle class is certainly valued in many working-class social groups. In fact careful monitoring for pretensions often takes place, evidenced through the long-standing clichés , such as 'too big for your boots', 'full of airs and graces' or 'stepping out of line'. Clichés as Walkerdine and Lucey (1989) note have the useful purpose of reminding us who we are. The women of the study 'know their place'. Yet, the display of working-classness, such as strong regional accent or critique of pretensions, may be devalued in different arenas (markets) such as education or the media in which the exchange rate is rarely established by the working class. Different arenas have different powers.[15] The media as an institutional site for symbolic capital is able to legitimate the symbolic power of the middle classes, whereas local working-class resistance has no powerful institutional site to distribute its claims to legitimacy – its 'right to be'. The media as an institution can produce symbolic violence against the working classes. It is these different market values (themselves historically developed from the division of labour, from resistance to it, from struggles against exploitation and delegitimacy) that may give local cultural value to certain dispositions but which have little trading value on the markets that matter for economic survival. The women constantly enter implicit trading arenas where their sexuality, femininity and respectability are judged in terms of value in which the rate is established by others.

Just as metaphors of capital provide a framework for understanding power and exchange in the reproduction of inequality, metaphors of space have a similar explanatory value for understanding movement through social space and restrictions on it. Metaphors of spaces and places such as location and positioning enable distribution and allocation of resources and peoples to be framed.[16] There is also a real physical aspect to the women's movement through space (social mobility), especially in the areas to which they are denied entry.

Access to knowledge, capitals and movement is a key feature of the study. Whereas postmodernist theories imply that there can be a voluntary free fall through the social positions that are available to people to inhabit, this study demonstrates how restriction on access is central to subjective constructions. Economic positions, institutional positions, subject positions and discursive positions are not equally accessible. Being an 'individual', for instance, is rarely available as a discursive means for knowing themselves as working-class women. This links into Foucault's (1988) later work where he acknowledges that subjectivity can only be constructed from positions within social relations and structures.

I now set out how I use certain concepts throughout the book. Subjectivity is used to mean the conditions of being subjected to frameworks of regulation, knowledge and discourse and constructing subjectivity in the process. This is developed from Henriques et al. (1984) who use the French *assujettir* to mean both to produce subjectivity and to make subject. These processes are investigated by exploring the women's experiences of what it is *to be* through categorization, such as 'woman' , 'feminine', 'heterosexual'. And I use subject positions to investigate the specificities of how women become particular subjects, especially respectable subjects. Subject positions are the effects of discourse *and* (organizational) structures.[17] They are part of wider discourses (for instance, caring can apply to a wide range of activities and occupations). How particular discourses inform subject positions depends on how they are organized through institutional structures (such as education and the media). Discursive positions are less specific than subject positions. Respectability is a discursive position which informs the take-up and content of subject positions. Institutional organization influences the form discourses are able to take and which discourses are available for distribution. The particular shape subject positions take depends not only upon their position within wider discourses and institutions but also on how they are taken up. Some subject positions may not produce subjectivity if they are not occupied or invested in. Subject positions are also different from social positions. Social positions are based on structural organization such as class, race and gender which circumscribe and access movement into certain subject positions. These structurally organized social positions enable and limit our access to cultural, economic, social and symbolic capital and thus the ability to recognize our-selves as the subject positions we occupy. (Dis)identifications from/with and (dis)simulation of these social and subject positions are the means by which identities come to appear as coherent.

Outline

Chapter 2 sets out the processes involved in doing the research and in pro-ducing this book. It engages in wider debates in feminist theory, methodology and epistemology about the meaning of experience, the role of interpretation, the responsibility and accountability involved in knowledge production. It questions the authority of the researcher and examines the power relations laid bare in the production of the research. It explores how the social posi-tioning and subjectivity of the researcher impact upon and necessarily inform the production of situated knowledge. Chapter 3 provides a historical frame-work which also contributes to the underpinning of the book. It maps out how contemporary legacies, discursive frameworks and subject positions were produced. Showing how working-class women were always seen to be both a problem and a solution to national crisis in social order, it charts how a form of education, namely 'caring courses', was developed. These courses were produced to incite working-class women to do and take pleasure in domestic duty, enabling the regulation of themselves, the working-class family *and* also provide an available pool of cheap labour. Respectability was closely tied to the domestic ideal – a standard imposed from a very different social posi-tioning – which was promoted as a way of displaying difference from women who were positioned as pathological, polluting and poisonous. By charting the development of the caring courses in relation to wider discourses of respectability this chapter links into the next, Chapter 4, which explores how the women come to develop and monitor their own caring selves. It focuses on the technological practices encouraged on the 'caring courses' by explor-ing the caring performances that are made, some of which implicate the women in the construction of themselves as 'caring women'. It shows how working-class women do subjectivity differently to that often assumed in feminist and cultural theory.

The next chapter, Chapter 5, shifts focus into a more general analysis of how the women live class on a daily basis. It looks at how class is absolutely central to the women's trajectories through subject positions. Their subjec-tivities come to be produced through processes of disidentification and dissimulation, showing how the dialogic judgemental other is central to their productions and how class operates at an intimate and emotional level. It also maps out how class is reproduced through constraints on capital exchange and suggests it may be more useful to think of social class as being about access and exclusion, that is, what people do not have rather than what they have. Whilst the women did not want to be marked as working-class they were more ambivalent about femininity, as Chapter 6 shows which maps out how respectability is constructed against sexuality, exploring how the women make investments into femininity whilst not recognizing themselves as feminine. The use to which femininity as appearance is put to make performances, masquerade and mimic others is analysed.

Recognition becomes even more central to processes of identification when heterosexuality is investigated in Chapter 7. Through historical development the term lesbian has been associated with sexualized Black and White working-class women and sexuality is always mediated through respectability. By exploring another attempt by the women to generate distance from being classified as working class, this chapter explores how they live the category heterosexuality through institutionalization and material practice, yet refuse to recognize themselves as heterosexual. This chapter questions the value of the concept of heterosexuality. The final chapter explores the classed addresses of feminism, analysing the women's knowledge of feminism and the feminism that was available for interpretation at the time of the research. It looks at how investments in respectability and femininity block investments in feminism. It suggests ways feminist theorists may generate dialogue with working-class women (and in so doing produce more adequate theory).

Motivations and Parallels

The motivation behind this research was the development of the kind of theory whose function is, Lyotard (1984) argues, to contest, to overturn a reality, social relations, the relations of human beings to things and to others which are glaringly unbearable. It began as a naive motivation to instigate social change more generally. I now realize this may be more difficult to achieve, although it still remains as an ideal. I want the book to establish a challenge to the complacency of theories which make working-class women invisible or those which pathologize through ignorance and assumption and to challenge the ease by which lazy politicians can wheel out 'pathological working-class women' to gain credibility for reactionary political campaigning.

The motivation is also partly autobiographical and produced from my experiences of marginalization:

> I read a woman's book, meet such a woman at a party (a woman now, like me) and think quite deliberately as we talk: we are divided: a hundred years ago I'd have been cleaning your shoes. I know this and you don't. (Steedman, 1986: 2)

My mother's sister was a domestic servant when she was young. It was just over sixty years ago. My mother avoided the same fate because she was younger. This book has been very painful to write because I was/am so close to the subject matter. I write this as my mother unpacks the crystal glasses she has bought me to mark my respectability. I have never achieved the respectability that my parents spent their lives desiring and struggling for (I am not married with children, supported and protected by an economically secure male, sexually contained, and my house is rarely immaculately hygienic – although to others my independence and my job may appear as highly respectable). If my parents surround me with the appropriate symbols they hope I may be marked. Respectability is thus an amalgam of signs, economics and practices, assessed from different positions within and outside of respectability.

What I did not anticipate was how emotional the research process would be. The chapter on class was excruciating to write as I realized how I, too, had strongly invested in respectability when intimidated at university. I was forced to remember how I had lied about my mother's and father's occupations because I was scared to be recognized as inferior. I naively (over)'did' femininity, in a way I had never done before, in an attempt to generate distance from sexuality. My capacity to accrue educational and cultural capitals, however, has only increased my sense of marginalization. I am more aware of the 'right' standards and knowledge and also of the judgements made of those who do not fit. I understand the desire to belong, to be normalized, to go unnoticed, not to be judged, but I am also aware of its impossibility. Proximity to the 'right' knowledge and standards does not guarantee acceptance. They just generate more awareness of how 'wrong' your practices, appearance and knowledge actually are. Fortunately during the 1980s I had an alternative discourse that could make me feel more comfortable: Marxism. Marxism afforded protection against the degradations and judgements which are experienced by the dialogic recognitions that are made based on the valuing of others and historical legacies. Yet, as will be obvious from this book, Marxism was not enough.

The writing of this book was fuelled by passion and anger. I watched 'class' analysis disappear from feminism and cultural studies as it became increasingly more of an issue for the friends I had grown up with, the people I live(d) with and the women of this research. I felt caught in two worlds: one which theorized increased movement, access and playfulness and another which was regulated, circumscribed, denied and criminalized. As the differences between the two worlds widened (when fashions in postmodernism peaked) I used this book to try and make connections, to enable me to generate theory which can speak across the void, to make class matter.

The saddest part of writing this book has been the impossibility of adequately conveying the complexity, resilience, good humour and sharpness of the women of the research. They are so much more interesting and insightful than this book can convey in words; sadly the affectivity of the research has nearly disappeared through the academic analytical filtering process. They provided knowledge that my formal education had closed-off and they gave me lots of support and great times. I will always be grateful to them, not only for enabling my social mobility and securing greater respectability, but also for becoming my 'dialogic other' that helps me counteract the pretensions and judgements of others. They enable me to feel justified in my discomfort with some feminist and cultural theory and to investigate why. I only hope I have done them justice in my representations. They, I am sure, will be the judge, in the end.

Notes

1 Throughout the study 'White' is used with an initial capital to generate distance from normalization (see (charles), 1992).

2 Duneier (1992), for instance, has shown how for Black men in Chicago respectability is also a central concern.

3 Skeggs (1994c) shows how a group of young Black female rappers resist all attempts to contain their sexuality through discourses of respectability.

4 Council estates are the UK equivalent to US project housing.

5 This may be to do with national differences. Class was never as central to American feminists as those in Australia, Canada, Ireland and Britain.

6 This is a crucial issue at the moment with the restructuring of higher education in the UK. Only those at the privileged research universities will have time to publish. They will become representative of academic feminism (See Skeggs, 1995c).

7 Harvey (1993) notes that whilst the Republican and Thatcher governments were waging a no-holds barred, across the board class war against the least privileged sectors of the population (see for instance Segal (1991) on the feminization of poverty), very privileged theorists were saying that class did not matter.

8 Walkerdine and Lucey (1989) suggest that because the working class have failed to fulfil the revolutionary potential which was itself a projected fantasy of the middle classes they have been abandoned. More recently the middle class have become the focus of sociological inquiry (see Savage et al., 1992).

9 This should not be confused with the theories of Wright (1985, 1989) and Savage et al. (1992) who define assets as either property, skill and/or organizational. Savage (1992) argues that organizational assets are intrinsically vehicles of male power.

10 Moi (1991) argues that insofar as gender never appears in a 'pure' field of its own, there is no such thing as pure 'gender capital'. The capital at stake is always the symbolic capital relevant for the specific field under examination.

11 Moi (1991) provides an excellent example where she shows how the relationship of Simone de Beauvoir with Jean Paul Sartre enhanced de Beauvoir's total capitals.

12 Bourdieu (1986) suggests that ethnicity and gender have differing functions. Ethnicity, he argues, distributes its members into social classes according to its location in the hierarchy of ethnic group whereas gender acts as a distributing mechanism *within* the social group. Gender, by this formulation, is thus a secondary characteristic and capital remains neutral. However, McCall (1992) suggests an alternative reading of Bourdieu, which draws on his understanding of embodied cultural capitals to suggest that dispositions are gendered. Thus, gendered dispositions are themselves forms of capital, hence embodied feminine cultural capital. Gendered dispositions are constitutive rather than wholly derivative of the social structure (McCall, 1992).

13 A. Young (1990) argues that in the linguistic process called metaphor certain properties of one thing are carried over, passed onto and imposed on another object so that the latter becomes written or spoken as if it were the former. This process involves both substitution and displacement. It is never just a description.

14 See Skeggs (1991b) for a development of the account in Chapter 5 of how masculinity is used as an institutionalized strategy in the classroom and how femininity and sexuality are deployed as tactics to counteract powerlessness.

15 The state, Waquant (1993) argues, is the great reservoir of symbolic power, the central bank of symbolic credit.

16 See Smith and Katz (1993) for a critique of the use of spatial metaphors.

17 They may also be produced from textual and filmic structures.

2

Respectable Knowledge: Experience and Interpretation

This chapter attempts to make transparent the processes involved when doing feminist ethnography. It provides a partial account because it would be impossible to reduce into text and convey completely the research encounter: so much happened over such a long period of time. It is a feminist account of doing feminist research which engages with debates in feminist methodology and epistemology.[1] It is an account of power and legitimation, the focus of which is experience and interpretation. This chapter provides an underpinning for the rest of the book as methodology underpins all theory. To ignore questions of methodology is to assume that knowledge comes from nowhere allowing knowledge makers to abdicate responsibility for their productions and representations. To side-step methodology means that the mechanisms we utilize in producing knowledge are hidden, relations of privilege are masked and knowers are not seen to be located: therefore the likely abundance of cultural, social, educational and economic capitals is not recognized as central to the production of any knowledge.

Methodology is itself theory. It is a theory of methods which informs a range of issues from who to study, how to study, which institutional practices to adopt (such as interpretative practices), how to write and which knowledge to use. These decisions locate any knowledge product within disciplinary practices and enable and constrain engagement with other theoretical and political debates. This chapter unpacks the processes involved. It moves from the specific to the general and from the practical to the theoretical to make explicit how these links are made. I continually recognize how my locatedness informed methodological decisions and ultimately the final product. The chapter addresses questions of epistemic responsibility and authority.

Questions of epistemic responsibility are not, Code argues, uniform in type or in provenance:

> Some of them focus on the construction of knowledge, others on its deployment and dissemination, some more on process, others more on product. Some bear upon the credibility of inquirers, their interests in the inquiry, what they stand to lose or gain in power and prestige. Others bear upon the willingness of such inquirers to submit their most cherished conclusions and commitments to critical scrutiny: upon what they are prepared to let go or re-examine in the interests of truth and justice. Some epistemic responsibility questions are about how knowledge is put to use, and about its social-political-institutional effects. (1995: 21–2)

This chapter will investigate some of these issues through an analysis of the

research process. The occupation and recognition of social and cultural positions by the women is a central focus of the research; this chapter will
examine how the subject position of researcher was inhabited. Researchers
are located and positioned in many different ways: history, nation, gender,
sexuality, class, race, age, and so on. We are located in the economic, social
and cultural relations which we study. These positions inform our access to
institutional organizations such as education and employment. They also
inform access to discourses and positions of conceivability, what we can
envisage and what we perceive to be possible. Representations also circumscribe the subject positions which we occupy. For instance, through reading
numerous accounts (representations) of feminist research I have learnt what
it means to be a feminist researcher and position myself accordingly. This
positioning process is not without contradiction. Researchers are positioned
within institutions, by history, by disciplinary practices, by dominant para-
digms, in theoretical fashions, in genre style, by funding arrangements, and so
on. All these positionings impact upon what research we do, when and how
we do it. However, there is no straightforward correspondence between our
circumstances and how we think: we are positioned in but not determined by
our locations.

Objects/Subjects of Ethnography

Wherever and whoever we are we are always implicated in relations of knowing. These relations have historically produced positions of power for the
subjects and objects of knowledge to occupy which they may reproduce and
challenge. The traditional distinction made between object and subject highlights the role knowledge plays in the (re)production of power and legitimacy.
Certain knowledges are normalized, authorized and legitimated; only certain
groups are seen to be respectable, to be worthy objects or subjects of knowledge. Traditionally it was only bourgeois White men who were seen as
legitimate knowers, producers and subjects. Lloyd (1984) charts how reason,
because of the symbolism used, was conceptualized as transcendence, by
which practice came to mean transcendence of the feminine. Epistemology –
the theory of knowledge – was proclaimed as an abstract dislocated form of
theorizing which was not located, loaded with values and contextualized.
This meant those who produced it were not responsible for their output. In
this process all others were classified as 'others' through their deviation from
the 'norm' and were objectified in the process (Bourdieu, 1977). It was only
subjects who could know; objects were known.
    White bourgeois women were designated objects of knowledge through
the classification of respectable femininity and Black and White working-class
women through the classification of sexuality. It was through this designated
naming that they came to be known. In rare cases they were able to make the
transition into knowers. Game (1991) describes the process in knowledge
construction whereby designations of 'oppressed groups' are constituted as
objects of knowledge in order to effect a return to the self, the subject of

knowledge. The process of knowing and designating the other is always made through a reference to the self. The subject is produced through the object. As Cohen (1994) notes, one tradition in anthropology has been to deny to cultural 'others' the self consciousness so valued in the theorist. The attempt to objectify others, however, signals the instability of those who claim themselves as subjects, as Hart notes: 'creating the illusion that such objects exist is precisely the anxious effort of groups that depend on making these categories to shore up the fiction of their own impermeability' (1994: 91). During the research I was continually aware of the ease with which those researched can be constructed as objects of knowledge without agency and volition. My position within the academy and its disciplinary practices, based on rational knowing, implicated me with the potential to reinscribe the women as other, as outside of legitimate knowledge. Yet it was my experience of feeling as if I was a misrepresented object of sociological and feminist knowledge that motivated my working with a group of White working-class women in the first place. The pressures, seductions and ease by which rational knowledge can be applied had to be continually resisted.

Walkerdine (1987) notes how bourgeois discourses, such as caring and child development, became naturalized through the development of various forms of regulative practices, through concerns to regulate conflict and convert it into reason. The practices and knowledges by which we 'know' in the academy are generated from positions in historical and contemporary bourgeois relations. Just as Chapters 3 and 4 demonstrate how standards to be achieved in caring practice are predicated on a bourgeois model for care, it is possible to see knowledge practices in a similar way. Feminist theory is not exempt from this practice. A concept of the norm is produced which is read back onto those who do not have access to the forms of capital and knowledge of those designated as norm and are thus found wanting. The tacit and normalizing effect in knowledge operates by taking one group's experiences and assuming these to be paradigmatic of all. When only the middle class speak to the middle class the knowledge will be taken as legitimate and reproduced. It is when different audiences are introduced and respond that challenges over the legitimacy of knowledge are produced. Many theorists do not try to hear or see anything other than from where they are located. As Code notes:

> These groupings are generated more as a byproduct of systematically ignoring concrete experiences, of working with an idealized conception of experience 'in general' so to speak, than as a conscious intentional practice of reifying experiences that are specifically *theirs*. (1995: 32; emphasis added)

Those who have deconstructed the concept of experience, for instance, have replaced it with concepts generated from their own subjectivity, produced through their own experience, which then operate as normative. For instance, many postmodern theories and theories of performativity assume that people can traverse the boundaries in which they are located, and many feminists have assumed that all women have equal access to ways of being (be it feminist, gendered, sexed, etc.). This assumption is made from the practice and plausibility of the writer/knower. Theories always bear the marks of their makers.

Thus the practices of working-class women have usually tended to be read through normalized knowledge which has been produced from the situated bourgeois knower (female and male). Whilst feminist methodologists have mounted stringent critiques of male knowers, class relations have often been left intact.[2] As Spelman (1988) shows, White Western middle-class women have set the agenda for the analysis of women. They have the institutional power, through circuits of knowledge distribution, to set the agenda for what we come to know in the name of feminist theory. Feminist theory, paradoxically, has tended to reproduce traditional hierarchies of respectable knowledge whereby 'pure' theory untainted by the experiences of others is often the most highly regarded (and institutionally rewarded).

In drawing attention to classifications and positionings I am not arguing for a direct correspondence between being and knowing, rather, that to ignore the location within structures of privilege and power relations as a condition of knowledge production, which includes the designation of objects and the conversion of cultural into symbolic capital of certain groups, means that what we receive as knowledge is always partial and always in the interests of particular groups. We always need to know in whose interests it has been produced and whose interests are represented by it. This is not to ignore the more traditional concerns of epistemology, namely why do some kinds of knowledge work when others do not, which will be addressed later in this chapter.

Many of the concepts used in feminist theory, Scott (1992) argues, have been produced from partial experiential descriptions. Motherhood, for instance, is defined from the experience of it: it is assumed that being becomes knowing becomes being. We understand it from the categories and representations which have emerged from those who have access to representation and in many accounts of motherhood we are left with a universal category filled by different descriptions. Yet motherhood may be experienced differently from the existing categories and representations that are available (as this research found). In feminist theory the move to the understanding of difference is particularly problematic. Difference is usually theorized through historical descriptions, and read off from categories already constituted. It is rarely understood through the theoretical categories which analyse *processes* of differentiation. In this way theory becomes a description, the representation of the revealed and reality is but the realization of the concept (Crosby, 1992).

Woman and femininity are often used with a similar lack of interrogation: femininity is often theorized as that which is different from masculinity which assumes femininity as a given. Yet as Nead (1988), Lury (1993) and Chapter 6 show, it was a category produced from a struggle to impose a model of an ideal bourgeois femininity, a masculine fantasy to which women were expected to aspire and achieve (Walkerdine, 1989). This fantasy was only ever achievable if the economic and cultural conditions were right. The representation continued to have explanatory power because it did represent a small group of women who aspired to achieve an ideal which would bring with it cultural approval, moral superiority and distinctions from others. As they invested in femininity the representation gained experiential value. Using the concept of femininity to apply to all women is to misuse a historically specific representation. It was produced in power relations, in the interests of particular groups, invested in by other groups and it cannot therefore, as Chapter 6 argues, be applied to all women. This means that all theorizing is tied to historically specific definitions and descriptors.[3] The explanatory power of feminist theory develops from interrogating the production of categories, their applicability, the experiences of them and from assessing their explanatory adequacy for different groups of women in different relations of power at historically specific times and places. This is how knowledge becomes situated.

For categories, representations and explanations to work they have to contain explanatory power in relation to the subjects/objects that they were designed to represent. Representations are not completely arbitrary. They may reveal something about their producers (as in the case of femininity being a projected male fantasy) but they also have to represent something about the experiences to which they lay claim. This is why so many representations are inapplicable to White working-class women: they cannot explain the specificity of their lives.

However, Scheman (1993) warns against becoming obsessively concerned with accurate representations. She maintains that academics should be more concerned with the opening up of institutional spaces. Yet I don't see why the activities are necessarily distinct. The representational challenges to the pathologizing of working-class women (Black and White) in which their experiences are seen to make a contribution to, rather than detract from, feminist theory may ultimately enable their access to institutional spaces.

Subjects of the Research

Over the 11 year time span of the research I kept in contact with the women. I spent the first three years doing ethnography, that is, intensive participant observation with a combination of other methods. I also spent time working on details of the national and local economy, housing, poverty and education statistics. I used this information to map out the general economic and cultural framework in which the women were located, producing a geography of their positioning and possibilities. To understand their movement through this mapping I traced the trajectories of the women through the education system and asked them for biographical details constructing a case-study file of each of them. I also conducted formal and informal interviews and meetings with family members, friends, partners and college teachers (Skeggs, 1994b).

I began with a methodology of historical materialism, unaware at the time of this naming, but as I emerged from the discipline of Sociology in the 1980s into the newly emergent Cultural Studies I took it on by default. It was nothing like as clear cut as it is now described. Johnson describes the 'moments' of this methodology as:

1 'appropriate the material in detail': which we may call 'research';
2 'analyse its different forms of development': historical analysis;
3 'track down their inner connections': structural analysis;
4 'presenting the real movement': 'presentation';
5 'the life of the subject matter reflected back in ideas': validation. (1982: 157)

As this chapter will show it was all a lot more complex and tracking down inner connections became more a case of tracing contradictions. I lived in the same area – a small provincial industrial town in the North West of England – and saw the women every day and spent as much time as was humanly possible, and they would allow, with them. I still continue to see some of them.

The research motivation was generated the year before the research formally started through my contact with a group of women I was teaching (to supplement my grant) on a Community Care course in a Further Education college. It later expanded to 83 women on three different caring courses: Community Care, Pre-Health Care and Pre-Social Care.[4] I was so inspired by their attitudes and responses that I began to think about ways of basing research around them. My first research question was framed as 'why do women, who are clearly not just passive victims of some ideological conspiracy, consent to a system of class and gender oppression which appears to offer few rewards and little benefit?' This question was of its time and is similar to those posed by Willis (1977) and Griffin (1985). The research then entered into a theoretical debate with Althusser and Gramsci, who influenced the formation of cultural studies in the 1980s (and the form it now takes). Now in the 1990s it enters into different debates, formulated through developments in feminist theory and my knowledge of it. The questions we ask, the problems which challenge us and the answers we find are always historically contingent and located (Haraway, 1991; Bhavnani, 1994; Skeggs, 1995a). This historical location, Code argues, 'participates in challenging the self-presentation of theory as an articulation of timeless or placeless universality, relocates it as a reflexive, self-correcting interpretative practice' (1995: 2). The research spans the move in feminist theory from structuralism to post-structuralism. The substantive empirical 'data' stops me being entirely seduced by new and fashionable theory. I reassess new theories in relation to their applicability to the women of the study.

I knew little about methodology and began the research by just hanging around and talking to the women as much as possible.[5] I was doing ethnography by default. Rather than reproducing the colonial method of traditional anthropology for studying the other through the provision of detailed field-notes and description, I followed a particular angle which was developed at the Centre for Cultural Studies (CCCS) to enable links to be made between theory and practice, structure and culture. Chris Griffin (1980), at CCCS, provided guidance through discussions of her paper on feminist ethnography. Issues centred on power relations and how to avoid constructing the researched as object or other. Responsibility and accountability were central. The development of this form of ethnography enabled concerns of feminism and class to be grounded and links to be made between the theoretical and empirical.

This ethnography was politically motivated to provide a space for the articulations and experiences of the marginalized. Marcus (1986) scathingly describes this as 'ethnographer as midwife' – who delivers and articulates what is expressed as vernacular in working-class lives. Yet, for those marginalized, pathologized and othered in most mainstream research this provision of representational space was considered to be important. Code (1995) argues that rhetorical spaces limit the kinds of utterances that can be voiced with the expectation of being heard, understood and taken seriously. She maps out the disastrous consequences of not having any rhetorical space. Similarly, Williams (1991) notes the legal consequences when what is heard is not understood because the available rhetorical understandings cannot fit the knowledge into already established classification systems. It was precisely this intention – to enable the experiences of working-class women and men, Black and White, to be seen as legitimate and valued and hence taken seriously – that motivated cultural studies ethnographies. The main impetus for this came from academics who felt themselves to be marginalized and their histories and cultural capital to be delegitimated and downgraded in academia. Cultural studies ethnography therefore is not a method; rather it is a theory of the research process which combines particular methods in certain ways. It is a methodology which combines theoretical positions and political intent; it informs how the different methods are combined and the way the researcher approaches issues of power, responsibility and ethics.[6]

After the first year's immersion in contact with the women I began reading around, searching for theories which could develop those I already carried around in my head and had brought to bear on the multitude of responses I was experiencing. From the outset my most prominent dialogue was with feminist theory in its many variants. I was mostly attracted to Marxist feminism for its explanatory power and its vocabulary of anger and injustice: it addressed concerns in my life and the women's and as the research progressed I found other theories such as post-structuralism, Bourdieu and Black feminism enabled sense to be made of the micropolitics of power I was experiencing and documenting.

The theories we use arise from a variety of influences: disciplinary location; access; their ability to address concerns produced from our experiences and histories; their explanatory power and their practical adequacy. Why is it that some theories have the ability to encapsulate experiences whilst others make no sense? And why do we gravitate towards particular theories? The theories I used were based on their explanatory power to help me understand what was happening during the research. I was continually modifying theories in a dialectical relationship with the women.

I moved through many theories. Theories of the state were useful at the beginning of the research to understand how the state was involved in reconstructing the intimate relations of education to enable working-class people to hold responsibility for their own allocations into unemployment. The modifications I made to theories of identification enabled me to encapsulate the processes of dissimulation and disidentification which applied to class, femininity and feminism. In this sense knowledge becomes more than just a matter of power, normalization and legitimation because only some theories work. Legitimation becomes a matter of struggle over interpretation but it is impossible to impose (normalize, legitimate) ideas if they have no explanatory purchase. Many of the theories at our disposal do not work at the level of concrete experience (as I found to my cost), hence the need to develop theories which can account for that which has hitherto been unexplainable. And hence the need for arguing for the superiority of some theories over others. Theories are not relative: some have more practical adequacy in relation to their subjects/objects of study. Feminist theories are usually more adequate to understanding the lives of women than those which do not take women and power into account.

Contextualized Experience

Experience as a property of the individual developed as a concept and representation from the seventeenth century in England (Abercrombie et al. 1986) and became, as Macpherson (1962) argues, the cornerstone of seventeenth-century political theory. It was assumed that: 'every man is naturally the sole proprietor of his own personal capacities (the absolute proprietor in that he owes nothing to society for them)' (Macpherson, 1962: 270). The ownership of experience became part of what constituted the person and made them unique, hence, possessive individualism (see Lury, 1997). Yet it was only those with the requisite knowledge and access to discourse who could produce themselves as individuals. It was only the bourgeoisie (usually male) who were considered to have depth of experience; it was their experiences that were classified as 'real' (Watt, 1957). This particular angle on individual experiences has a specifically national (as well as raced, gendered and classed) inflection: not only did the English White bourgeois man have knowledge and was a subject but he also had real experiences; others had none worth knowing about or documenting unless they reaffirmed the selfhood of the 'real individual'. These political legacies inform contemporary analysis of experience and interpretation. The association of experience with individuality, Cohen argues, was reproduced in recent British Conservative dogma, which recognized individuality only as a class and race specific value, reserved for those who either by birth or by achievement had the right to be themselves (1994: 172).

When feminism tried in its earliest guises to reclaim, validate and provide space for women's experiences, it brought with it the baggage of individualism and immediately entered into an epistemological space for the battle over whose experiences count as knowledge. Experience, de Lauretis (1988) maintains, is the *basis* of feminism in the sense that feminism began the moment women started talking to each other about their experiences. And feminist theory developed as a way of understanding these articulations: it produced new and different explanations which could more adequately encapsulate the experiences of women. From this base began moments of shared ontological recognition such as 'it happened to you too' and from these recognitions interpretative frameworks were proffered which came to be known as feminist theory. For instance, women's experiences were interpreted to be a product of patriarchal power, capitalist power, global organization, and so on. Transformations occurred in the understanding of women's sexuality: writing about the myth of the vaginal orgasm (Koedt, 1973) generated a paradigm shift representing experience otherwise unnamed (Whelehan, 1995); it provided a discursive recognition. Code (1988) notes how discursive schemata engender action/inaction: the concept victim, she argues, carries with it a baggage of inaction. From the discussion of shared experiences women were able to formulate a new way of seeing; this could then be used to reinterpret prior experiences. It was this dialectical process that informed the development of feminist theory in which the relationship between experience and interpretation was inseparable; they informed each other. The theories then became more and more sophisticated at critiquing themselves. It was in an attempt to challenge descriptions and classifications and the universalist assumptions that were made from descriptors of male experience (disguised as objective knowledge) that the concept of experience itself gained validity for feminists.

A whole body of feminist theorizing was engendered which developed a dynamic of its own and fought for its own legitimation and institutional space so that feminists could speak to each other (rather than spending their energy challenging masculine knowledge). Sometimes the reasons for the interpretative frameworks became lost and the political intent disappeared (see Spivak, 1990) and sometimes the term experience became so loosely defined that its value was lost (see Lazreg, 1994). Attempts were made to link feminist theorizing directly to the experiences of women, usually by women who were marginalized from the institutional space generated for feminism in the academy. This attempt was named as feminist standpoint epistemologies.

As I have argued elsewhere (Skeggs, 1995b) feminist standpoint theory centres on the claim that all knowledge springs from experience and that women's experience carries with it special knowledge and that this knowledge is necessary to challenge oppression.[7] It is because women are placed in a position to struggle against the forces and powers that oppress that this experience provides them with different understandings and knowledges:

> Women's subordinate status means that, unlike men, women do not have a clear interest in mystifying reality and so are likely to develop a clearer and more trustworthy understanding of the world. A representation of reality from the standpoint of women is more objective and unbiased than the prevailing representations that reflect the standpoint of men. (Jagger, 1983: 384)

The key to standpoint theory is that the *experience* of oppression engenders particular knowledges (Hartsock, 1987; Hill-Collins, 1990). For some standpoint theorists these positions of oppression generate epistemic privilege:[8] only those who have the appropriate experience of oppression are able to speak about it. This reduces knowledge to a formula of being = knowing (ontology = epistemology), a formula which has dogged philosophers since Kant. In this case experience becomes part of the empiricist tradition in which experience is the source of knowledge. Paradoxically, as Lazreg (1994) notes, this means that the experiential feminist position aligns itself within the very tradition which it sought to critique: that of positivist science. Standpoint theory also grants an authority and hierarchy to certain groups and silences others (Bar On, 1993), leading to confrontations over identities in which differences are collapsed into a 'listen to me' 'hear my difference' power play (Probyn, 1990). Weed (1989) notes how the received feminist notion of experience has blocked ways of disrupting the subject/society opposition. This opposition, she notes, enables one term to stand in for another in which the political can be reduced to the merely personal.

Standpoint theory can be seen to be a product of its time, when women were claiming universal oppression to establish their place on an academic agenda. It was a response, Griffiths and Whitford (1988) argue, to the experience of trying to force one's perceptions into preconceived categories and the pain and distortion that this led to. However, standpoint still retains resonances within contemporary feminist theory leading, Haraway (1990) argues, to the building of explicit ontologies and epistemologies which police deviation from official women's experience. There comes to be a correct way of being a woman from which others are judged, leading to a form of identity politics based on the idea of 'authentic subjective experience' which restricts politics to the personal.[9] It also assumes that there has to be an identity before an identity politics can take place (Butler, 1993). And that structural positioning determines knowledge and usually that one structural position (such as gender or class or race or sexuality) provides particular knowledges, without analysis of the multiple positions which can be occupied in contradiction and ambivalence. From this experience is used as evidence to substantiate knowledge claims. Evidence, however, only counts as evidence when it is recognized as such in relation to a potential narrative or theoretical construction so that the narrative/construction can be said to determine the evidence as much as the evidence determines the narrative/construction (modified from Gossman quoted in Scott, 1992: 24). This is why experience is such a thorny issue. It marks a space where speaking and silencing are enacted.

However, what feminist standpoint theorists achieve is an ability to focus our attention on the subject at the centre of the production of knowledge. The subject is then not an abstract concept but a site of accountability (Code, 1995). It also needs to be noted that the critiques of standpoint may represent an attempt by those who had been displaced from the centre to the margins to regain their authority. Standpoint theory also made it very clear that there is no such thing as a disinterested knower and that the positions from which we speak (and how we speak) are a product of our positioning vis-à-vis forms of capital and that this informs what we decide is worthy of study.

So the use and the concept of experience has clearly been problematic to feminist theorizing. The different meanings it holds, the different forms it takes and the different uses to which it is put, mean that it is very difficult to know exactly how it is being used. Sometimes it refers to external events experienced, sometimes referring to the way those events are registered by people, and it is very common to slide between these meanings. Moreover, some experiences enable us to understand the world and others do not. Not all experiences are relative in terms of explanatory power.

However, it would be impossible to abandon the concept of experience completely because it is formative in generating feminist theory (anything that assumes there is a difference between women and men makes recourse to experience) and because it is a key way to make connections between the epistemological and the ontological. Experience is important as a practice of making sense, both symbolically and narratively as a struggle over material conditions and over meaning (Brah, 1992). Even if we wanted to abandon the concept of experience it would be unlikely that we could do so, for as Riley (1987) argues, feminism can never wholeheartedly dismantle women's experience because women are constantly experiencing it and constructing themselves through it.

So I want to hold on to experience as a way of understanding how women occupy the category 'women', a category which is classed and raced and produced through power relations and through struggle across different sites in space and time. I do not, however, want to argue for experience as a foundation for knowledge, a way of revealing or locating true and authentic 'woman'. Nor do I want to suggest that we have to have experiences before we can take up a standpoint. Experience informs our take-up and production of positions but it does not fix us either in time or place. Foucault (1974) argues that being is historically constituted as *experience*.

> Experience is the process by which, for all social beings, subjectivity is constructed. Through that process one places oneself or is placed in social reality, and so perceives and comprehends as subjective (referring to, even originating in, oneself) those relations – material, economic and interpersonal – which are in fact social and in a larger perspective, historical. (de Lauretis, 1984: 159)[10]

I begin from the premise that it is not individuals who have experience but subjects who are constituted through experience (de Lauretis, 1984; Scott, 1992). I want to suggest a place for experience in feminist theory which does not write off experience as inconsequential but which sees experience as central to the construction of subjectivity and theory:

> For each person, therefore, subjectivity is an ongoing construction, not a fixed point of departure or arrival from which one then interacts with the world. On the contrary, it is the effect of that interaction – which I call experience; and thus it is produced not by external ideas, values or material causes, but by one's personal, subjective engagement in the practices, discourses, and institutions that lend

significance (value, meaning, affect) to the events of the world. (de Lauretis, 1984: 159)

It is through the experience of subjective construction that we come to know and be known. This enables the shift to be made from experience as a foundation for knowledge to experience as productive of a knowing subject in which their identities are continually in production rather than being occupied as fixed. It also suggests that not all experience produces knowledge; this depends on the context and the experience. It also means that women can take standpoints (on particular issues such as feminism, for instance) rather than being seen to own them through the accident of birth. Stress is thus laid on the access to instances of take-up, movement, recognition and occupation of the positions available and it is assumed that these are neither fixed nor fixing. This recognizes that knowledge is situated, is produced from social subjects with varying amounts of cultural capital, located in a nexus of power relations. Also, that there is a relationship between the ontological and the epistemological but that this is not determined.

Interpretative Processes

All experience is processed through practice, discourse and interpretation. We do not have pure experiences. Representations are interpretations. Experience is at once always already an interpretation and is in need of interpretation (Scott, 1992). Experiences are always in the process of interpretation (even if not in the form of critical reflexivity), as are the interpretative frameworks which are brought to bear upon them which enable classificatory systems to be built around them so that some experiences are classified as authentic and others as theoretical.[11]

The interpretative process is often ignored in feminist accounts which seek to prioritize experience, or to set up experience in binary opposition to theory (in which, logically thinking becomes a non-experience). If all knowledge comes from experience then how do we deal with and know that which we have not experienced? We are constantly experiencing and interpreting. Experiences are different and some experiences are considered to be more valuable than others. We need categories to interpret our experiences. This is not just on a grand scale in which generalizations are made about men's experiences being more socially valued and legitimated than women's (which is of course problematic because of the universality applied to gender differences) but at the level at which some experiences are considered worth knowing about in the context of research.

So whilst subjectivity (theirs and mine) is always implicated, it was me who made decisions about what I thought was worth knowing about. I made interpretations and selections from their and my experiences within the research context which best illustrated the research inquiry, namely the production of subjectivity. Also, their accounts are just as partial as my selections. In the process of representing their experiences, encountered as they were lived, I reduce them to written utterances. Representation usually involves the translation into the literal. The multitude of expressions, nuances, feelings, of embodiment in the research were lost often because they were unrepresentable. They did, however, inform the understandings generated through the research rendering partiality and incompleteness inevitable. Partiality occurs in all research; it is because it is so obvious in ethnography that ethnographers have taken on board debates about partial productions. This process of continual selection and monitoring further contributes to the challenges to the belief that experience is an origin or foundation of knowledge that is more immediate and trustworthy than secondary knowledges (I. Young, 1990).

Recognition is one of the means by which experiences are interpreted. When experiences are recognized through naming and marking, positionality is understood and responded to. The same process applies to theoretical recognition when we recognize the explanatory power of particular theories. Recognitions, Visweswaran (1994) argues, are the discursive links to social positioning. Or as Bourdieu (1977) argues, private experiences undergo nothing less than a change of state when they recognize themselves in the public objectivity of an already constituted discourse.[12] Because we are constantly experiencing experience, moments of recognition may transform not just that which we recognize, but also that which has gone before and that which is to follow. The value (and the destabilizing quality) of feminist interpretative frameworks is that they engender reassessment of previous interpretative frameworks. They pull prior experiences back into the interpretative viewfinder for reassessment and in doing so they make us question who or what we are. It is these recognitions, McNay (1992) argues, which enable the links between personal experiences and political solutions (such as feminism) to be made.

Knowing is always mediated through the discourses available to us to interpret and understand our experiences. This is how I made sense of what happened when, after writing-up some of my interpretations and sharing them with the women, their interpretations were sometimes different. Why should I expect them to reach the same conclusions, produce the same analysis? They were not, after all, centred on exploring the construction of subjectivity as a process. They also had different interpretations from each other. This is not surprising for we are positioned differently in relation to discourses of knowing. I use an academic framework (which is now part of my cultural capital) to explain their experiences; they use the different discourses to which they have access (their cultural capital). Our cultural capitals have different values – both in terms of sites of legitimation and tradable value (see Chapter 1 for an explanation of how forms of capitals can be traded). The women's frameworks for understanding have been developed from their contextual position just as mine have. Their knowledge is after all situated, although it is also changing, forming and moving. It is produced through their experiences from their positionings and through the access they have to different ways of knowing and speaking. We all have differential access to frameworks for understanding and some of these are institutionalized and can enter circuits of representation. Our different takes on knowing were highlighted through the discussions we had of interpretations. Their knowledge enabled my knowledge. I was constantly learning from them. However, I would not argue that they were completely knowable or knowing. I only had access to parts of their lives and could make interpretations on that limited (although more than most) knowledge.

We cannot know ourselves so how can we expect to be the absolute knower of others, although we can be vigilant, responsible and critical. As the writer, I had the ultimate power of production but my interpretations were not produced without consultation and discussion. Rather than change my analysis to fit the analysis of the women of the research, which has been suggested by some feminist researchers, I want to make a claim for using the interpretations produced through dialogue, but over which I have ultimate responsibility and which are generated in relation to the research questions I investigated. I discussed my ideas and interpretations with them and they would challenge, contradict, confirm, etc. This would enable me to reassess my speculations and frameworks, sometimes leading to modification, abandonment, but also to reassertion. Questions of epistemic responsibility and the ethics of this interpretative process were most obvious in relation to social class. The women did not want their actions interpreted as class responses for this reproduced the position they wanted to disassociate from (see Chapter 5). However, their rejection of class did not lead me to abandon it. In fact, it did the opposite. It heightened my sensitivity to its ubiquity and made me construct theories to explain their responses.

My refusal to reject what they rejected made me question how I could be both accountable and responsible whilst wanting to retain my interpretations. Code (1988) argues that ways of knowing can be judged on the basis of the responsibility manifested by cognitive agents in making knowledge claims, and in acting upon assumptions that they know. This she argues eschews any idea that ethics and epistemology are separate areas of inquiry. They are intimately linked. Code (1987, 1988) argues against epistemic indolence and epistemic imperialism and for epistemic responsibility. She argues that responsible knowers look for the fullest possible explanations to understand the situation at hand; they recognize their implicatedness in the production of knowledge and claim responsibility for it (rather than claiming it magically produced). It involves understanding things, rather than adhering to received theoretical wisdom and fashions:

> To achieve the 'right' perceptions implied by such an approach requires honesty and humility, the courage not to pretend to know what one does not know, the wisdom not to ignore its relevance, and the humility not to yield to temptations to suppress facts damaging to a cherished theoretical stance. (Code, 1988: 191)

My theoretical constructs have been produced by searching for the fullest possible explanations, by refusing to adhere to received wisdom and by continually 'testing' my theories with the women over a period of 11 years. As a feminist researcher I was not concerned that my interpretations would 'taint' the research. Had I not offered views, values, assessments and ruminations as I spent three years full-time with the women they would have thought me strange. Ethnographies 'at home' are produced through dialogue. There was absolutely no way I could not respond from the position of who I was/am. To do otherwise would have invoked subterfuge and deceit and since a great deal of my research was based on trust I was as open and straightforward with them as I am with friends; this is, after all, what they became. To strategically muster a disingenuous research performance would be unsustainable over such a long period of time. However, I did become aware of the different types of interpretation in which I was engaged. It was a lot easier to offer interpretations of our shared problems than it was to explain some of the theoretical interpretations I had made, mainly because I had used the educational capital to which I had access and from which they had been excluded. Interpretations have different places, values, functions, appropriateness and purposes.

Coherence and Contradiction

My desire to make sense of the many disparate and contradictory experiences, Walkerdine (1988) would argue, is a result of my will to power and my desire for mastery through knowledge. This led me at times to map my frameworks directly onto their experiences without listening to or hearing what they were saying. And this was even when I knew about the micropolitical power relations of research. It was a product of my desperateness to understand the infinite number of things that were happening around me that led to this lapse in reflexivity.[13] Visweswaran (1994) argues that this is a problem that extends beyond the agency and culpability of the researcher into the very organization of knowledge and the structure of inquiry. I was a part of the disciplinary practices that engendered my desires for control through knowledge. It is an occupational hazard and I should have known better. The desire for control is a fantasy and cannot be enacted in the research process. This does not mean that we cannot be rigorous and systematic about what we do, rather, that there are gaps, lacks and spaces which we cannot know or control. In my thesis, which is very different from this book, I ascribed the women with a level of rational thought. I interpreted many of their actions as part of a cost–benefit approach to life. So that the choices they made were interpreted as a rational weighing-up of pros and cons. This is, in retrospect, more a result of my desire to impose order than of their dispositions.

This, and other issues of representation presented almost continuous ethical dilemmas. It was difficult to find the appropriate forms of expression which could adequately express the processes experienced by the women. My political intention was not to reproduce them as fixed occupiers of particular classifications. I wanted to generate a sense of their movements and the transmutability of boundaries. But as the study progressed constraint and containment, rather than movement, became apparent. They could not move from the structural locations of class, race and gender: they could occupy the categories very differently but they could not transcend them. I wanted to portray the complexities, nuances, contradictions and heterogeneity of their experiences. I was particularly concerned to avoid what Appadurai (1988) identifies as metonymic freezing – an imprisoning process of representational essentializing whereby parts of the lives of 'others' come to epitomize the whole.

There is a continual tension between theoretical generalization and the multitude of differences experienced in practice. A traditional approach when dealing with numerous in-depth transcripts, notes and tapes is to search for themes. I did this to begin with but felt that it was producing a greater homogeneity than I was experiencing. Noting contradictions and differences helped me to pursue not only the gaps between words and deeds but also to note how many contradictions are held together on a daily basis and how searching for coherence is an impossibility, an ideal and a fantasy.

One of the main values of ethnography is to be able to explore how contradictions are lived and the differences between discourse and practice. Time enables an analysis of which differences appear as significant and systematic. For instance, the women constructed distinctions between themselves and others on a continual basis. It was only time which enabled me to understand which ones they considered to be significant. Respectability emerged as a key concept late in the research process as a way of making sense of their continued identifications, dissimulations and resistances. Respectability also gained greater significance as they grew older. Whereas it initially hinged on sexuality, as the research progressed, it could be seen to be linked to family practices and wider discourses of caring. Once I was sensitized to this I started seeing issues of respectability everywhere: in my family, in myself, in approaches to the topics studied in academia, in everyday speech about sexuality. Respectability became a way to hold together class, gender, sexuality and race: they mediated each other.

Validity and Plausibility?

Traditionally validity means 'logically coherent'. I use it here to mean more than this, more than a structural judgement. I take valid to mean: convincing, credible and cogent in which the analysis made can be evaluated as rigorous and responsible and the account given substantial and satisfactory. A valid account provides the most plausible explanation for the phenomena studied. My prolonged contact, constant critical reflexivity, sense of responsibility and commitment to the women of the research means that I have produced what I consider (and hope you will evaluate) to be the most plausible explanation to understand the processes by which a particular group of White working-class women produce subjectivity.

Validity implies that a judgement is to be made; it thus depends on who is making the judgement. It also suggests that certain criteria have to be in place for judgement to take place and it has been the role of feminist theorists to question exactly what constitutes validity. Judgements of worth, Foucault (1974) argues, are based on standards that are imposed by and further entrench structures of power. Yet to pose knowledge as only about power and counter power means that we can only take sides, missing what Taylor (1994) identifies as the search for recognition and respect. It assumes that all knowledge is relative. I'd want to argue, especially after the care, pain, labour and ethical crisis that have so often been experienced in the production of this research, that some research is better than others. Research that listens to others rather than making assumptions about their existence is, I would argue, more plausible. Some forms of analysis have greater explanatory power, some can provide accounts which avoid non- and mis-recognition, some can acknowledge their responsibility, situatedness and place in the power relations of objectification and subjectification. Taylor (1994) developing the work of Gadamer suggests that real judgements of worth suppose a fused horizon of standards; they suppose that we have been transformed by the study of the other so that we are not simply judging by our original familiar standards. Some research just does not stand up to the test of plausible explanation or practical adequacy.

Traditional methodologies would cite objectivity and the use of methods of validation such as triangulation (whereby interpretations of responses are made from a variety of sources). However, there are two main uses of the term objectivity which are often collapsed into each other: first, in relation to the practical adequacy of accounts and second, in relation to our values about what we study (Sayer, 1995: 3). I brought values to my research; it would be impossible not to do so. But I also proceeded with the utmost care and critical attention in trying to produce the most valid account possible. I used rigorous and systematic procedures to generate my analysis and produce my account. The account of the production of the research in this chapter should provide a basis from which to evaluate the preceding analysis. Just because we value something does not mean that we cannot come up with an objective (in the first sense) account. Also, values may enable us to recognize things that others would prefer to overlook (gender, race, class, etc.).

My favourite commentary on objectivity is by Gouldner (1964) who argues that the myth of value freedom is supported because not to be objective is to be seen as unmanly or lacking in integrity. Objectivity, he argues, is a value judgement if it is concerned with accepting the status quo and leaving the issues of oppression and suffering unchallenged. Since the Marxist, Weberian and feminist critiques of objectivity in the 1980s, feminists such as Harding (1991) and Haraway (1991) have resurrected the term, making arguments for a 'strong objectivity' in which the processes of research production are made apparent and accountable in the production of research through the situating of knowledges.[14] Acknowledgement of the partiality of any research production is necessary before any claims for objectivity can be made. Objectivity, therefore, requires taking subjectivity into account. Objectivity becomes the means by which connections are made between different knowing subjects who are always located. It is in the connection between different forms of situated knowledge that this feminist research is produced. Thus validity is not just based on rigour, standards, responsibility and recognition of situatedness and partiality, but also on the connections that are made in the relationships established.

Connections: Difference and Similarity

Ortner (1991) notes how in anthropology extensive debates exist about how we produce 'others' but she asks who produces us? I brought histories, locations and identifications to the research. These informed the interpretations I made. These are continually undergoing the process of critical reflection. Reluctant as I was to become interested in myself, questions of who are 'they' informed who 'I' was. This was less a Hegelian notion of spirit in which we recognize ourselves through the being of the other, or discover oneself in the other (Callinicos, 1995);[15] rather, the power relations of the research meant that I could not ignore my own positioning *vis-à-vis* the women. My location as a feminist academic with sociological and cultural studies knowledge, coming from a similar historical and economic–social–cultural location informed the questions I asked and the understandings I made. This was a process of differentiation and recognition of similarities *always* informed by power and inequality. It was a process of connection and disconnection: of partial, full and non-connections. Yet I feel a reluctance to include the next section because just as the women did not want to be fixed by the position of class nor do I. I am aware that evaluations of knowledge are often made by fixing the writer/knower into a particular standpoint (and those who dismiss standpoint theory are just as likely to be seduced by the desire to know the knower). I do not want the complexities of the women's lives to be reduced to my history. I speak from many changed/changing positions. This research was produced through my shifting locations (class, sexuality, geography, age, disciplinary, femininity and feminism) as well as from the stability of others (race, nation and gender). It was traces from all of these that informed my interpretative frameworks which themselves shifted through my interactions with the women.

Although I began the research because I recognized a strong similarity between the women and the positions I previously occupied I did not assume that I could put myself in their place. It was a place I had left. I did have some similar experiences: I left school at 16 similarly unqualified. I signed up for a caring course. I was engaged at 18. I could not see the point in education and my life centred on hedonism, on going out or preparation for going out.

I was also only three or four years older than they were when I started the research. The similarities decreased as they took on more responsibilities. Some of my prior experiences connected to theirs. But my experience of higher education generated enough differences to make us dissimilar. This was particularly acute in terms of plausibility structures (Berger and Luckmann, 1971). I could envisage a future of independence, employment and material security. Their employment futures were far less secure and dependence through marriage offered a potential way of achieving material security in a local labour market where employment was scarce. In their different ways it was these envisionings that established significant differences between us. This became more acute as the research progressed and I moved universities, found a permanent job, bought a house, a car and my economic and cultural capital increased. However, because I was already living in the area in which the research took place and because I once had been very similar to the women of the study I felt less like a class tourist who voyeuristically explores the differences of the other.

It was far easier to make connections when we were all students (even if at different levels). The importance of structures, histories and forms of capital became increasingly obvious and stood out as a sign of difference, especially as their lives became harder and the constraints increased. With age they came under increasing cultural and economic pressure to be married; whereas my access to higher education provided more justifications not to be. I had entered an alternative value system which protected me from the pressures they experienced. This acute awareness of difference threw the power differentials between us into relief in a way which had been hidden in the past. Every time I walked away from a visit in the later stages of the research, I experienced a sense of physical and metaphorical escape: it could have been me. This generated an enormous burden of guilt which blocked my ability to handle the situation. The privileges which I embodied I experienced as flaunting. I tried different strategies to ignore or refuse my difference, but it was so obvious that it could not be denied.

I recount these affective responses not as confession but to show how the usual normalization of the research–researched relationship was difficult to achieve. I was not educated into a position of class normalization. I was not used to being positioned as a legitimate knower (I experience my position in academia as fraudulent which, according to Walkerdine (1990), is not uncommon). My experience of marginality and movement (across class boundaries) had enabled me to purchase distance on both where I came from and where I was. I did not have the comfort of feeling I belonged and was suspect of my investments. I was more like Deleuze's (1986) 'nomadic subject' who engaged with the women from a position of identity but was also subject to potential changes from that encounter. Marginality was probably the only constant. Marginality has been articulated as a position of epistemic privilege (as in standpoint theories) and as an enabler of self-discovery and provision of unique opportunities of new vision (Wolff, 1995). Mannheim (1936/1960) established a whole tradition of methodological prescriptions in sociology which valued the 'relatively autonomous' analyst who embodied double vision to see where they came from, where they were going and where they did not belong. Marginality does offer respite from normalization yet it also underpinned the research with anxiety, guilt and anger.

I experienced my position as privileged researcher, itself a visible acknowledgement of class transition, as deeply disturbing, generating an uncertainty

about positioning which in turn influenced the research production by inject-
ing tension, a result of my projected anxiety, into our relationships. The
research produced many affective responses: outrage, powerlessness, hurt,
pain, distress, shame, rage. I never really achieved the passionate detachment
advocated by Kuhn (1982); over time I learnt to establish more distance but
it was always difficult. Reflexivity is too loose a term to describe my varied
attempts to generate distance from overwhelming emotional engagement.
These moments did not just occur during the empirical part of the research
but also in the writing-up. Some of the chapters were exceedingly difficult to
write and many a tear was shed as I struggled with issues of representation:
anger as their accounts connected to my own experience and despair about
what really can be achieved by this writing. On cynical days I can say all it did
was to help me out of potentially dire circumstances; on other days I just feel
powerless to do, achieve or change anything. Hopeful days are rare. I reiter-
ate Gramsci's mantra 'pessimism of the intellect, optimism of the will'.

It was impossible to romanticize or heroize their experiences and responses
(even if I had wanted to) in the same way as has been done by White male
working-class academics working with White working-class men (see critiques by McRobbie and Garber, 1976; Griffin, 1985; Skeggs, 1992; Skeggs,
1994a). First, there are wider discourses that authorize the supposed authentic masculinity of working-class men (see Tolson, 1977) and make this
heroization possible. Second, there is very little that is heroic about caring and
femininity. Third, their responses were too complex and contradictory for
them to be narrativized through romance or heroism.

Knowledge Normalization/Legitimation

The explanations we proffer, I have argued, involve us taking responsibility
for our theoretical constructions. We decide which areas are worthy of study
and which are not. The abdication from the study of class in feminist theory
means that theorists are abdicating from responsibility for class-informed
knowledge. By not taking it on board, or by opting out by claiming conceptual ambiguity/irrelevance, it is assumed that it does not matter and that
others will take responsibility for it. One of the major failings of this research
is my lack of responsibility for studying the category of race and paying it the
·same attention as I did class.

Race is less developed in the research as a result of my normalization in the
production of knowledge during the initial intense stages of the research. It
felt disingenuous to introduce it into the follow-up studies, to somehow add
it on when it was not part of the initial research investigation. However, I
established another research project on race in 1987 and 1989 which involved
interviewing groups of young women (amongst others) on similar Further
Education courses.[16] This alerted me to the similarities in the pathologization
of Black and White working-class women. From this I was able to develop
concepts of respectability, positioning and investment which provide the focus
for this book. It was thus race which informed the theoretical analysis even

though it was not studied as a category in production. This work is now being developed further.[17] Black feminist writers such as Angela Davis (1981) and Audre Lorde (1984) provided inspiration and a legitimation for my sense of class-based alienation generated during the research.

If, as researchers, we are in a position to contribute to knowledge normalization does this mean we also have the power to legitimate? Kitzinger (1994) asks how feminist researchers validate the experiences of women. In response, we need to investigate which institutional positions and relations of power limit/enable our doing so. What circuits of value exchange are we part of in which some experiences are valued and others not?[18] For instance, where are working-class women (Black and White) within the institution, within relations of knowledge and where is their experience given value? Moreover, is feminism sufficiently established amongst the legitimators of knowledge to be an authorizing discourse? Its presence on the margins of a great deal of academia would suggest not. In the micropolitics of the research process power relations (generated through positions in institutional and disciplinary locations) are occupied, yet they may not be recognized or valued. But, if they are, if I have the power to authorize the accounts of these women, what does it mean to them? I do not have the power as a feminist researcher to convert their cultural capital into symbolic capital or to give it an economic valuation in order for social and economic change to occur. What I can do is challenge those who have the power to legitimate partial accounts as if representative of the whole of knowledge and to challenge the classificatory systems which position 'others' as fixed. These classificatory systems have real effects (as evidenced throughout the book) and operate in the rhetorical spaces that are opened and closed (Code, 1995). They work as symbolic spaces where the dialogue of identity between subjectivity and culture takes place (Hall, 1987).

The women did position me at times as a representative of legitimate knowledge which enabled them to be seen as worthy of study. This had a value to these women and to know that their experiences have impacted upon serious theoretical analysis and study does have a small significance for them. But in context, the research was negligible in their lives. It was enjoyed for what it was at that time and they approached it as they did most things – with irreverence. For some, I provided a safe space to discuss things of concern; a safe space to stay; discussions which stretched their plausibility structures and made them feel worthwhile. The political impact of the research often occurred in this space. I provided feminist understandings and interpretations for the things that were troubling, intriguing or exasperating. Providing explanations which linked the individual to structures not of their making helped dislodge feelings of personal inadequacy. They had already been classified as academic failures when I met them. Along with unemployment this was experienced at an immediate intimate level. They blamed themselves for the lack of jobs and their lack of interest in schooling. The ability to put this into a wider perspective blocked their tendency to victim-blame and take on responsibility for social structural problems.

They get on with their life as the battles over the legitimacy of knowledge

are played out in academia. The political consequences of epistemological
battles hopefully should mean that they may be pathologized less through
representation; that they may be taken more seriously. If this knowledge
impacts upon social policy or popular culture in a positive way or in a way
that blocks the continual representation of working-class women as a disturbing site of social order then I will have made a partial achievement. It is
a smaller ideal than the ones I had hoped for when I began the research, but
it is a start.

Conclusion

This chapter has shown how methodology is the archaeological foundation
from which theories are constructed. It has shown how theories are inseparable from issues of epistemology and method. It has explored how a
particular methodology, that of feminist cultural studies ethnography, proceeds to produce knowledge with a particular purpose in mind. That is, to
provide a rhetorical space where the experiences and knowledges of the marginalized can be given epistemic authority, be legitimated and taken seriously.
The intention is to undermine any attempts to construct normative positions
in feminist theory which do not acknowledge their production from positions
of power and privilege and which operate as if unaccountable to any group.
This challenges the dichotomy of subject/object which is frequently reproduced. This research was undertaken with a desire to effect social change and
this chapter has shown how this desire was enacted and constrained through
knowledge production. Emphasis was placed throughout on the concept of
experience to show how we are all produced as subjects with subjectivity,
through our experiences, through the interpretation of these experiences and
through time. The interpretations of our experiences, as researcher,
researched, known and knowing, are always historically located, a product of
the different positions available to us in discourse, in theory. This differential
positioning presents difficulties when producing representations.

This chapter highlights why experience as a concept cannot be abandoned
but must be analysed in its specificity. Experience is central to the production
of subjectivity, to the production of raced, classed, sexed and gendered
'woman'. It is also the means by which links can be generated between the
epistemological and the ontological. Responsibility and accountability are
dependent upon experience. And it was the study of a particular group's
experiences that led to the modification, generation and rejection of theory. It
is unlikely that I would have been able to establish these theoretical challenges
without them.

As this chapter shows, my desire for control of knowledge initially led me
to produce representations which were more consistent with this desire than
with the experiences of the women. Epistemic responsibility involves recognizing our desires, power and implicatedness in the different practices we
occupy. The validity of our accounts is based on this responsibility, on our
accountability and the connections we can make to others. This chapter

suggests that feminist theorists have a limited, but necessary, role to play in the legitimation of rhetorical spaces produced by those who do not have access to circuits of knowledge distribution. In writing this book I hope to provide a space for the legitimation of my interpretations of the women's experiences. I have produced these through the most rigorous and accountable ways I know and I hope the methodological debates in this chapter enable evaluations to be made in the spirit in which they were produced: systematic and rigorous, responsible and with care, with a continual critical awareness of the situatedness and partiality of our knowledge productions.

Notes

1 These debates are also explored in Skeggs (1994b, 1995b). A more general map of processes in the production of feminist cultural theory is provided in Skeggs (1995a).

2 Obversely, class relations have been deconstructed leaving gender intact (see Johnson, 1982).

3 These argument do not just apply to empirical research but to any research whose foundation is that women are different because of their experiences. Gynocentric textual analysis was developed on this basis (see Probyn, 1993a).

4 At the time of the research the courses were classified on the Houghton scale as Grade 5, the lowest grade of work. The courses occupied a low position in the sexual division of knowledge which operated in the college. This was also reflected in the poor standards of the buildings (see Skeggs, 1986).

5 It took some time to establish credibility and avoid suspicion (see Skeggs, 1994b).

6 There are numerous theoretically named ethnographies: naturalist; realist; modernist; social constructionist and postmodern, which are informed by their theoretical positions (see Skeggs, 1995b).

7 Those associated with this position are often called empiricist feminists (see Harding 1991).

8 The use of the term standpoint has become closely associated with ossified positions in feminism. Its use in labour history had a completely different meaning. It means taking a standpoint – anyone can do it – and making a connection. It is not tied in to experience but to political commitment (see Popular Memory Group, 1982).

9 See Chapter 7 in Fuss (1989), and Brunsdon (1991) for the implications of these arguments for feminist pedagogy.

10 de Lauretis (1984) articulates a long tradition in sociology in which experience of the social structure is produced as 'self-conception' which informs the interpretation of experience (see Abercrombie et al., 1986).

11 Gilroy (1990) notes the dangers of the term authenticity when applied to marginalized groups. It is usually used to signify closer links to nature and to legitimate distinctions and exploitation (Fryer, 1984).

12 Although Visweswaran (1994) notes how this fails to theorize the third term between the 'what goes without saying' and 'the what cannot be said'.

13 Code (1995) maintains that the totally responsible researcher is also an ideal, too much a product of the individualistic thinking of liberal humanism. It is impossible to be completely self-aware, to know one's background assumptions, unconscious motivations and to make simple decisions to bring about personal changes that would result in responsible epistemic conduct. There are, she argues, structural impediments to such voluntarism.

14 The original thesis contains a chapter on methodological justification which fully engages with the debates in social science on objectivity and value freedom. I particularly liked Weber's (1949) concept of 'value relevance', that is, if the study is considered to be important in the sense of being worthy of being known.

15 Winch (1958) developed what has been named as interpretative philosophy on the basis of one person's interpretation of another's selfhood is their own self.

16 The findings and recommendations were produced for Hereford and Worcester Education Committee in reports: *Multi-Ethnic Educational Needs in Hereford and Worcester. Part 1* (1988) and *Multi-Ethnic Educational Needs in Hereford and Worcester Part 2* (1989). I followed up the reports with staff development programmes in the Further Education Colleges on Racism Awareness Training.
17 My next research project will foreground race: *Black Symbols/White Distinctions* (London: Edward Arnold).
18 The question of validation emerges from MacKinnon (1983) who argues that the main premise of feminist research is to uncover and claim as valid the experience of women.

3
Historical Legacies: Respectability and Responsibility

When I first met the women they were doing 'caring courses' at a local further education college. These courses, as this chapter and the next show, framed their prior and future caring experiences, and by default their experiences of femininity, feminism, sexuality and class. By consolidating their caring through incitement to particular productions of their 'selves' the courses came to exert a long-term effect.

Being framed, constrained and produced are the themes that run throughout this chapter. The historical analysis of the framing of caring and respectability through wider discourses of national insecurity, sexuality and class show how assumptions and fears about the working class in general, and women in particular, became institutionalized in the organization and practice of caring education. This means that when the women entered the courses they were offered subject positions framed by historical concerns, translated into current cultural currency, about their class and gender deficiencies – and offered reformist potential. Respectability, domestic ideals and caring all establish constraints on women's lives, yet they can also be experienced positively. They also reproduce distinctions between women: those who have invested in these constraints can feel superior to those who have not. So, historical, cultural and economic locations and capitals circumscribe access and provide the framework whereby respectable caring subject positions are offered and occupied in the process of subjective construction.

This chapter provides the historical background to the caring courses in particular and the positioning of White working-class women in general.[1] It shows how White working-class women were positioned as both pathological and civilizing and maps the emergence of positions of respectability. It charts the type of provision and the reasons for the emergence of caring courses, hence providing the framework which the women come to occupy. It documents the many attempts to induce women to enjoy their domestic labour and responsibilities, which Foucault (1977a) identifies as a form of productive power whereby social regulation can be achieved willingly, even pleasurably, by the participants themselves. It provides the background to the rest of the book by setting out how particular legacies were formed which continue to inform the positioning of women through class, race, gender and sexuality.

Civilizing Women: 1800–1900

Caring courses are part of a discourse, translated into institutional organization, in which women are given the responsibility for civilizing the nation.
This also means that they can be blamed if things go wrong. The positioning
of women as a civilizing force was the means by which the national crisis over
fears of internal revolutionary threat, external invasion and internal destruction through the polluting effects of the working class, was displaced. This
framework was cemented by the crisis of empire during the mid-1800s.
Colonial expansion was validated by the moral values which would be generated from the mother country; morality and colonialism were closely
interwoven, not just in terms of justificatory strategies, but also as a prereq-
uisite for economic success. As Nead (1988) notes, the Christian unity of the
nation, and order and regulation at home were believed to be essential for
success and expansion abroad. Social stability was considered to be dependent upon moral purity; the moral condition of the nation was seen to derive
from the moral standards of woman; woman came to signify the success or
failure of the colonial project, on an internal and external basis:

> In our estimation, the great means of improving the human race must be sought in
> the improvement of the health of woman, for she is the matrix in which the human
> statue is cast. Improve her health of body, of mind, and of heart, and the human
> race would advance to perfection; deteriorate her, on the contrary, and in the same
> ration does it degenerate . . . In civilised nations matrons give the tone to society; for
> the rules of morality are placed under their safeguard. They can try delinquents at
> their own tribunal, expel the condemned from their circle, and thus maintain the
> virtue and the country of which it is the foundation; or they can, as in France in the
> eighteenth century, laugh down morality, throw incense to those who are the most
> deserving of infamy, and, by the total subversion of all public virtue, lead to sixty
> years of revolution. (Tilt, 1852: 13, 261)

All women are here given responsibility for the human race. Their task is
enormous and open to scrutiny. If they fail they are likely to induce revolution. The message is quite plain: if women refuse to take responsibility for
social order they can be blamed for its disruption. This is all done in the name
of virtue. Virtuous women protect the nation, non-virtuous women are sub-
versive. The abdication of responsibility by the male writer should be noted.
He will not perform the necessary virtuous duties but he will be the judge of
them. This commentary brings together the discourses of hygiene, sexuality
(through virtue) and morality, alongside responsibility for the maintenance of
social order. It also shows how women were viewed as potentially dangerous
if not regulated through their own civilizing self-regulation. In short, it provides the basis for the framework in which links were made between
degeneration, virtue, responsibility and social order. Debates about the education and control of working-class women are continually informed by this
discursive legacy.

The regulation of moral behaviour during the nineteenth century was part
of a wider formation of class identity, nation and empire. In 1904 the Report
of the Physical Deterioration Committee documented the increasing national

anxieties: the threat of a possible defeat in the Boer War (1899–1902) due to inadequate supplies of artillery men (Dyhouse, 1977); and the threat of a potential workers' revolution modelled on the French Experience (Stedman Jones, 1971).[2] One solution it suggested was the establishment of 'schools for mothers'. By 1910 the working class generally had become discursively consolidated by upper-class commentators and the State as a problem in two senses: first, as a potential revolutionary force; second, as social diluters of civilization and respectability. The State required fit and healthy soldiers and workers but feared that such people might orchestrate a working-class revolution. Early social policy provision was an attempt by the State to use and regulate the working class (Finn et al., 1977). The early schooling provision for the working classes was a means to compensate for a morally deficient family, to act as a stabilizing force and to impose upon children a middle-class view of family life, functions and responsibility. In general, it was hoped by the State that education would form a new generation of parents whose children would not be wild, but dependable and amenable (Johnson, 1979). The concerns about the potentially polluting and dangerous working class were seen to be resolvable if mothers were educated to civilize, that is, to control and discipline themselves and their husbands and sons who were likely to be the cause of anticipated problems. It is part of a process in which the mother acts as an invisible pedagogue (David, 1980).

Historical national anxieties were articulated through educational reform, welfare provision, Christian charity and evangelism, wider discourses and representations of sexuality, and also by the increasing prominence of 'rational/scientific' classificatory systems, developed from evolutionary theories, which, using a cultural logic of civilization, sought to codify most aspects of human life.[3] Using the language of eugenics, the working class were again coded as atavistic and potentially dangerous and polluting.

Furthermore, Weeks argues that the obsessive Victorian concern with sexuality served to provide the framework for considering the 'problem' of the working class as one of morality rather than class conflict, for example:

> From the end of the eighteenth century with the debate over population and the hyper breeding of the poor, sexuality pervades the social consciousness; from the widespread discussions of the birth-rate, death rate, life expectancy, fertility in the statistical forays of the century to the urgent controversies over public health, housing, birth control and prostitution. The reports of the great Parliamentary commission, which in the 1830's and 40's investigated working conditions in the factories and mines, were saturated with an obsessive concern with the sexuality of the working-class, the social order, displacing in the end an acute social crisis from the area of exploitation and class conflict where it could not be coped with, into the framework of a more amenable and discussible area of 'morality'. (1981: 19–20)

The debate over sexuality culminated in a series of social policies which shifted concerns from sexuality to the family, mapping out areas of family responsibility. By transferring the debate from one of revolutionary threat onto questions of familial and moral responsibility the structural and social relations of class conflict could conveniently be ignored and attention could be shifted onto specific aspects of working-class organization. The development of educational provision alongside labour market restructuring indirectly influenced family duties, commitment and responsibility, and also gave these responsibilities to the mother (David, 1980).

Yet it was assumed that not all mothers could be relied upon; legislation was put into effect to monitor and regulate specific mothering practices. Gittings (1985) has noted how the Poor Law Act (1899) undermined and penalized traditional working-class methods of childcare and supervision, especially the mutual responsibility for children amongst working-class women. The legislation, she argues, was both gender and class specific; for instance, the Maternity and Child Welfare Act (1918) was not aimed at helping mothers themselves but at monitoring them to ensure that they did their proper job of bearing and rearing healthy children 'correctly'. Such legislation developed in response to the assumption that mothers, although deficient, were potential moral regenerators and that the social ordering of the working class could be achieved through the family, but also in response to the assumption that the practices of working-class mothers were to blame for national ills, for example:

> The problem of infant mortality is not one of sanitation alone, or housing, or indeed poverty as such, it is mainly a question of motherhood. Expressed bluntly, it is the ignorance and carelessness of mothers that causes a large proportion of the infant mortality which sweeps away thousands every year. (Newman 1906: 221, 257)

Motherhood, coded within the discourse of the family – the site of colonial and internal representations of order and civilization – became the focus for educative reform. Whereas the home had been seen as a site of social stability, the family came to be more directly articulated and manipulated. In a study of France, spanning the eighteenth to the twentieth centuries, Donzelot (1979) documents how the State relied upon the family for direct support to effectively ensure public order, yet with increasing industrialization and urbanization which severed many family ties, the relationship between the State and the family became progressively inadequate as the eighteenth century wore on, culminating in various attempts by the State, through education and welfare provision, to regulate parenting, specifically mothering, and mould families into specific functions.[4]

These attempts to regulate mothering, through the family, alongside the increasing demand for domestic servants, provided the pre-conditions for the intervention of the State into the education of working-class women, initiating the legacy for the imposition of standards by others who could judge the working class as deficient.[5] The civilizing function of women documented throughout the 1800s now became formalized through state educational provision for working-class women. It was also institutionalized through other social policy such as the Child Welfare Act of 1918. Prompted by the Report of the Physical Deterioration Committee (1904) and a series of Special Reports on 'School Training for the Home Duties of Women' (1903) which recommended both 'raising the standards of domestic competence' among young working-class women and 'fostering the sense of domestic duties' in girls to 'overcome the extremely low standards of living and physical fitness apparent in the congested central districts of larger towns and cities', a Board of Education visiting party examined the provision of domestic education for working-class girls in Europe.[6]

This party, led by Alys Russell, was particularly impressed by work in Ghent, in which provision was organized around 'child culture' for girls aged 14 to 18. On return Alys Russell founded the first School for Mothers (1906), offering a range of services, including advice on infant feeding and a savings scheme. The foundation received a grant from the Board of Education in 1907 in support of classes held in infant care, cooking and the cutting of baby clothes. Further financial support was given by the National Association for the Promotion of Housewifery, who also initiated the idea of family placements. They advocated a system whereby school boards should place young working-class girls, aged 14 to 17, in middle-class homes in the local vicinity, to be consigned to a period of compulsory unpaid domestic service as an apprenticeship in housewifery. The model of bourgeois domestic standards as the ideal to which working-class women need to aspire was firmly established. The schools under the Russell Foundation received a grant from the Board of Education for organized class teaching until 1914 when the Local Government Board was made responsible for all grants in aid of maternity and infant welfare. By 1917 most provincial cities were endowed with schools for mothers. Although the schools were initially intended for young girls, Dyhouse (1977) has illustrated how by 1917 it became virtually impossible to draw any clear distinctions between the work of the schools and the 'Mother and Babies Welcomes' and Infant Welfare Centres.

By 1918 there were 1,278 voluntary and Local Authority Maternity and Child Welfare centres, all carrying out what was seen in the widest sense 'educational work' and whose main intention, Blunden (1983) argues, was not to enhance women's skills in the labour market, but rather to reinforce their position as unpaid domestic workers in the marital or parental home; or to provide unpaid care for the middle classes.[7] Evidence given to a Government inquiry (Great Britain Cd. 2175, 1904) established to investigate the low response to the national 'continuation classes' on mothering and domestic training, provided for those who were unable to attend college on a full-time basis, is indicative of such a concern, for example:

> At thirteen years of age the majority of these women would have begun work in a factory, to handle their own earning, to mix with a large number of people with all the excitement and gossip of factory life. They would in this case grow up entirely ignorant of everything pertaining to domesticity . . . Until as girls they have been taught to find *pleasure* in domestic work and until there is a great supply of healthy and suitable recreations and amusements in reach of all women, to counteract the prevailing squalor and gloom of these pottery towns, it is useless to expect them to relinquish factory life. (Great Britain Cd. 2175, 1904: para. 259; emphasis added)

This attempt to try to educate young working-class women to relinquish paid employment for unpaid domesticity by teaching them to enjoy such

tasks, not only illustrates the lack of knowledge about the economic conditions of working-class women but also shows how pleasure was used as a
form of productive power. By trying to teach working-class women to take
pleasure from bourgeois domesticity they could be induced to do it without
direct, obvious control. This is central to the rest of the study and to contemporary debates on domesticity; if pleasure can be gained from that which
is oppressive it is far easier not to notice the oppressive features of it. It also
means that the women could produce themselves as acquiescent, rather than
being produced by state regulation. The roles of the ideal woman were also
productive, as they gave to women particular *moral* significance and responsibility, which gave them status, self-worth and pleasure. Learning to enjoy
one's duties (as defined by others) was central to the earliest caring course
curriculum, for instance:

> The instruction should cover every branch of domestic hygiene including the prepa-
> ration of food, the practice of household cleanliness, the tendance and feeding of
> young children, the *proper* requirements of a family as to clothing, everything, in
> short, that would equip a young girl for the *duties* of a housewife. (Great Britain Cd.
> 2175, 1904: para. 230; emphasis added)

The education of working-class women in the 'domestic ideal', that is, domestic practices based on the structure and organization of the Victorian upper
and middle classes, in which moral precepts were incorporated such as 'clean-
liness is next to godliness', was seen to be the solution to national social
order. Particular feminine roles and functions, such as the feminine-domestic
ideal, were allocated a special status and importance and represented as a
desirable and unsurpassable goal to which all women would naturally aspire
and gain moral superiority from.

However, the domestic ideal carried its own baggage. It was part of a wider,
ongoing attempt to create a middle-class hegemony in which the practices of
the newly forming bourgeoisie were defined against the condemned excesses
and extravagances of the aristocracy (see Nead, 1988). Ideologies of domestic responsibility and respectability involved a negotiation and redefinition of
bourgeois beliefs and values (Gray, 1976). Thus distinctions could be constructed between all classes of women; but only those who achieved the
domestic ideal could articulate their superiority. Respectability became a
locus for a growing sense of class identity and social superiority amongst the
labour aristocracy, defining themselves against the 'rough' working class. It
was also defined in opposition to the imagined excess passion and sexual
deviancy of the women of the 'undeserving poor' (Hall, 1979).

The definition of female respectability became part of the wider formation
of domestic ideology and the propagation of home and family values. It
brought together domesticity and sexuality in opposition to each other.
Respectability was organized around a complex set of practices and representations which defined appropriate and acceptable modes of behaviour,
language and appearance; these operated as both social rules and moral
codes. They impacted upon women's use of public space whereby respectability only occurred inside the home and not in the public realm of the streets.

'Women of the streets' became a euphemism for prostitution. Upper and middle-class women could display their respectability and moral responsibility by trying to educate certain working-class women who were at danger from the immoral behaviour of the working class in general. This distinguished between the working class who could be saved and those who were irredeemable, enabling domestic classifications to be transposed onto sexual classifications which had already been established to differentiate between groups of women. The display of respectability became a signifier of *not* being working class. Nead (1988) identifies two different types of unrespectable women: the prostitute and the fallen woman – the fallen woman came from the respectable classes, she was victimized and had no connotations of power and independence, she retains her femininity because she is powerless and dependent. The representation of the prostitute was as immoral and seditious. The fear of the prostitute was also about the mixing of respectable and non-respectable classes and the breakdown of the carefully constructed boundaries between the pure and the fallen (Gilman, 1992).[8]

Dyhouse (1976) argues that the interest shown by the middle classes in domestic service was in part a response to the belief that young working-class women, too, could be moral regenerators of the nation. Domestic service offered a model for the wider relations between the working class and the middle class, that is, the working class economically and socially dependent, obedient, disciplined, clean and broken into the methods and routines of the middle-class family unit (Summers, 1979).

For some, domestic service was justified as a moral duty and service to save those from what could have been an immoral life. For instance in 'Lectures to Ladies on Practical Subjects' given by the Reverend Brewer:

> Remember ladies, it is not so with any other poor. Over the classes just above them you have a power, and you are entrusted with a mission . . . Unwittingly, you are exercising in your own families a vast social and political power; you are educating the poor under you, it may be without your consciousness for good or evil, and instructing them in the most powerful, because the most unpretending way, in all that you yourselves know and practice. The female servants in your household whose manners you have softened – who have learnt from you how to manage a household – who have caught up from you, insensibly, lessons of vast utility, lessons of order, lessons of cleanliness, lessons of management of children, of household, of comfort and tidiness; these women eventually become the wives of small tradesmen and respectable operatives. They carry into a lower and very extended circle the influence of your teaching and your training. (cited in Maurice, 1855: 55–6)

This moral duty became the basis for the development of social work practice at the turn of the century (see Hill, 1877). The giving of advice became the method used to communicate middle-class domestic standards. Donzelot (1979) argues that the transmission of advice by the State is the means by which control of the family, and ultimately control of the population as a whole, is won. It is not a repressive intervention but an invitation to authority. Advice, like pleasure, represents a form of 'positive power' whereby power is exercised through norms, disciplining, reward and manipulation of the conscience as opposed to power that operates through rules, prohibition and repression (Foucault, 1977a). Advice may also be of value for it can contain within it elements of practical usage. Advice can also be given as well as received: it may render the recipient as an authoritative giver. The concern with the standards of domestic servants, however, had dual functions. Whilst transmitting the dutiful requirements of bourgeois respectability, the middle-class women on home-visits could also recruit domestic workers of their own choosing. Prohashka (1974) has documented the concerns expressed by the middle classes at the shortage of 'suitable' servants, culminating in the establishment of a series of private training institutions, established by 1830, although their practice and recruitment is not well documented.

This historical background shows how general codifications which carry contemporary cultural currency, namely that caring courses represent just one attempt, in the light of many social policies, to regulate the practice of the working-class family, were put into effect. The caring courses are concerned with creating in working-class women the disposition to care and creating the affectual characteristics such as the acceptance of, and pleasure in, their place within the sexual division of labour and the family household structure. The historical legacies ensure that conflict between social classes is considered to be a problem of morality, rather than of structural inequality, in which the solution to the problem was seen to lie in familial regulation, primarily through the mother. Working-class women, especially (potential) mothers, are both the problem and the solution to national ills. They can be used and they can be blamed.

Resources of time, space and finance are displaced onto practices of respectability and wider discourses of sexuality inform the assumptions behind the education of working-class women. For as Foucault (1979) notes, the organization of education was predicated upon the assumption that sexuality existed, that it was precocious, active and ever-present. So the attempt to codify sexuality through the domestic-feminine ideal is a central feature of working-class women's education, as it is also a feature of their wider cultural/discursive locations.

By placing the focus on the enjoyment of caring education a form of productive power is instigated, which combined with the Victorian feminine-domestic ideal could offer working-class women routes to respectability, status, self-worth and the ability to construct distinctions against other women. This was institutionalized by the pedagogy in which middle-class women were used to transmit their practices (based on a wholly different economic, time-scale structure) to 'deficient' working-class women.

Such organizational and discursive legacies, as the study will proceed to illustrate, remain features of present caring course provision and the wider discourses to which working-class women have access. The next section will illustrate how similar concerns were expressed by the State during periods of economic and social uncertainty, in which young working-class women come increasingly to be defined, through education, as primarily domestic labourers. This allocating function is one of the means by which class divisions, through labour market divisions, are maintained through the gendering of the occupations available. Caring employment was not an empty labour market position waiting to be filled (as some class theorists would argue) but caring workers are specifically constructed as female. This occurs because of the conflation between caring for and caring about (Parker, 1980; see also Chapter 4) which equates feminine duty specifically with occupational role. Moreover, respectable caring is constructed through the absence of sexuality so that sexuality is involved in the gendered structuring process of the division of labour (Adkins, 1995).

Consolidation: 1900–70

After the initial concern with the provision of 'good advice' to mothers and prospective mothers, caring courses appear to have disappeared from the educational agenda. Blunden (1983) notes that the period 1910–30 in Further Education is characterized by responses to local labour markets. Yet they re-emerge in response to the economic and social crisis of the 1930s under the guise of the Juvenile Instruction and Unemployment Centres. These were introduced to alleviate the problems of the young unemployed with the remit to inculcate habits of discipline and self-respect (Bell, 1935). They offered a similarly gendered curriculum to that of the 'Schools for Mothers', for instance: 'the aim of every superintendent of a Girls centre is to have a cookery, laundry and housewifery centre' (Horne, 1983: 321). The low attendance at these domestic centres, similarly indicative of the previous lack of interest shown two decades earlier by young working-class women, was solved by making attendance compulsory up to the age of 18. It seems that working-class women had not yet learnt to take pleasure in the monitoring of their domesticity.

From the late 1930s to the early 1960s State attention was focused on mainstream education, introducing only parts of a caring curriculum. The wider discourse of caring became divided into domestic and feminine 'arts' on the basis of the class background of the women for whom it was designed and the further mapping of class-based divisions onto practical and academic education. The consolidation of the domestic with working-class women was achieved in most educational reports (Skeggs, 1986).

The maintenance of social order remains a central concern signified through the references to the 'destruction' and 'fragility' of family life:

> The durability of the family can no longer be taken for granted. If a secure home is to be achieved it has to be worked for. There will have to be a conscious effort to prepare the way for it through the education system on a much greater scale than had yet been envisaged. (Crowther Report, 1959: 37)

The family again came to stand in for the nation and family health became the measure of national health. But it was the working-class family, particularly the mother, who was put under scrutiny by the development of state agencies who could monitor her behaviour.

Ironically it was the development of these state agencies, designed to monitor the practices of the working class, which opened out (at the lower end, of course) occupational opportunities for working class women. During the 1960s caring courses in further education developed in specific response to occupational caring expansion, whilst general education still referred to working-class women's place within the home. The differences in development are indicative of a contradictory State concern with both the full-time regulation of the family, and the concern to supply enough labour for labour markets. The rationale for caring education was to change again in the 1980s. Rapidly increasing unemployment, especially amongst young people, regenerated concerns over social order. The pathological and civilizing working-class family came to stand as the site of all ills and solutions yet again. There were now already mechanisms in place whereby young working-class women could be given responsibility (and encouraged to take pleasure) in the maintenance of social order: caring courses. In this process they could also regulate themselves.

1970– : Paradoxical Caring and Containment

In the 1970s the occupational roles which enabled some working-class people to monitor other working-class people were shrinking, yet the courses were not. During the 1980s caring courses continued to expand whilst their corresponding occupational placements decreased. The corresponding division of labour, the personal social services, experienced a dramatic collapse in their growth and expenditure rate. Even government legislation on the development of Community Care (set in place by the Seebohm (1968)[9] and Bayley (1973, 1978) Reports and consolidated by the Department of Health report *Community Care in the Next Decade and Beyond*) has seen limited funding (Knapp et al., 1992). Real spending on Community Care has actually dropped (Baldwin, 1993). During the course of the research national cuts in capital expenditure have affected Community Care provision as local authorities have been prevented from borrowing the required amounts for the supply of services. Yet the courses expanded considerably as Table 3.1 shows. These figures suggest a notable increase at both national and local levels.[10] The development of Community Care as a legitimate form of social work practice (see Walker, 1982; Ungerson, 1982) suggests a merging between the once separated (through the wage structure) occupational and familial roles, in which young unemployed working-class women are perceived by the State as a means for absorbing decreases in formal – paid – welfare provision and providing wider familial regulation. The following statement illustrates the point more clearly:

> If the demand for such caring services greatly exceeds the supply, the existence of large numbers of long term unemployed may well come to be equated with the availability of a pool of carers: in particular it might be argued that it would be desirable for some people at least to be kept usefully occupied in caring for the frail and handicapped members of their own family. From this position it would be but a short step to the identification of certain groups of paid workers as meriting a transfer from 'employment' to 'occupation' so as to reduce competition for scarce employment. (*House of Lords Debates*, vol. 400, collection 973)

Table 3:1   *Student enrolment on college caring courses (1979/80–85/86)*

Year/ Course	1979/80	1980/81	1981/82	1982/83	1983/84	1984/85	1985/86	% increase
Pre-social care	17	28	36	42	66	75	73	329
Pre-health service	14	23	27	34	55	30	7*	114
Community care	11	32	48	74	107	73	82	646
Total	42	83	111	150	228	178	162	286

Source: College records
*PHS moved in 1984/85 into GCE department

The movement from paid 'employment' to unpaid 'occupation' suggests that women should no longer be paid for the caring work they perform. This ambiguity forms part of the contemporary conceptual definition of Community Care, for as Finch and Groves (1980) argue, the waged role of Community Care has never, in State legislation or rhetoric, been clarified. They argue that the original principle of care *in* the community (National Health Services Act, 1946) has since changed its meaning to care *by* the community, exemplified by the Wolfenden Committee (1978) and the Bayley Report (1978). Numerous studies have indicated that the attempts made by the State to introduce Community Care have resulted in more pressure and responsibility on the family, predominantly the female members (McIntosh, 1984; Ungerson, 1987; Glendinning, 1992).

The decline in welfare provision and the establishment of a formal framework for unpaid caring in the 1980s and 1990s has been accompanied by an increasing ideological concern by the legions of Tory governments about the family and declining moral standards, not dissimilar to the concerns expressed at the turn of the century. For instance, both Ferdinand Mount and Norman Tebbit (notable Tory politicians) have argued that the family is in 'crisis' and under threat of extinction. Peter Lilley, more recently in 1995, cited single mothers (always coded as working class) as vampiristic parasites on the health of the nation. Comments by Peregrine Worsthorne, a right wing commentator, make specific class assumptions: the 'family is best for us all' . . . 'but most the poor', the 'uneducated' and the 'humble' (*Sunday Telegraph*, 6 July 1980). Numerous right wing pressure groups have been established to 'protect' and promote the respectable family (see Durham, 1991). Alongside the increased expression of concerns over moral decline and national social order exists an ever increasing demand for domestic servants (although euphemistically labelled nannies, au pairs and cleaners) by the professional middle classes, as research by Root (1984) illustrates, in which both class and gender subordination is reproduced. A substantial number of caring courses students (16 per cent) who found employment after one year of leaving the course were employed in this category, which suggests that although the context for care, through the introduction of the Welfare State, has changed significantly, the class relations remain similar; the working class are perceived by the State to be both a potential service group and also a potential threat to the respectable social order. Their role as social regulators has become increasingly more complex, whereby, not only are they involved in the regulation of their own families, but are also involved in substituting the 'soft policing' role of the personal social services.

The courses are not, as their history suggests, just about regulating the women on them, but an attempt to regulate the familial organization of the working class generally. To some extent they keep working-class women in 'protective custody' (Lendhardt, 1975) and they do keep women off the streets whilst regulating the dole queue and enabling unemployment figures to look healthier than they might do otherwise. However, their major role involves enabling working-class women to know their place, winning consent for the social placement of them as unpaid domestic labourers, willing to sustain both their own families and provide Community Care if necessary. In this sense, the courses can be seen to provide specific subject positions which are part of a wider discourse of care in which the dispositions, attitudes and habits of the social relations of domestic labour appear as natural and rewarding; a dignified and respectable solution to unemployment in which they can gain social worth by taking up the moral responsibility for the familial maintenance of national social order. These dispositions also reproduce, not only class divisions, but also divisions between women themselves. Since the 1980s different discursive configurations and different institutional organization have constructed historically specific rationales for caring education. Whilst the relationship to the labour market has been tenuous, the relationship to the family has remained constant. What has also remained constant is that caring courses offer a means by which working-class women can gain some status and respectability by taking familial responsibility.

A substantial proportion of the women in the study did pursue caring occupations, although not all needed any prior training (see Table 3.2). From Table 3.2 the rates for caring work over the different years are 35 per cent, 57 per cent and 56 per cent respectively. For those that did not require any caring training the numbers decrease to 15 per cent, 39 per cent and 40 per cent. The majority of the jobs are in the secondary labour market and often temporary. Certain forms of caring work such as nannying decrease in participation with age. The unemployment rate decreased from 50 per cent when they left college to 8 per cent nine years later. The decrease was partly produced through involvement in part-time work (see Table 3.3).

Only 46 per cent were involved in full-time work, with 44 per cent in part-time work. Only 3 per cent defined themselves as full-time mothers (others defined themselves as unemployed whilst mothering full-time). The numbers with children increased to 49 per cent. These figures will hold more significance when the movement between occupational caring work and familial caring work are explored in more detail in the next chapter.

Table 3.2 *Occupational placement (1983, 1988, 1992)*

	1983 (%), n = 68 (aged 18/19)	1988 (%), n = 56 (aged 23/24)	1992 (%), n = 39 (aged 27/28)
Full-time mothers	3	5	3
EPH nurse	3	5	3
EPH care assistant/officer	3	11	3
Childcare assistant/officer	–	5	5
Nursery assistant	2	–	3
Child-minding	–	2	3
MH nurse	–	5	5
MH care assistant/officer	2	7	·5
Occupational therapist	–	2	–
General nursing	9	9	13
Auxiliary	–	5	5
Residential social work	–	–	8
Nanny	16	4	–
Dinner lady	–	2	3
Cleaning	–	11	10
Catering	–	2	2
Shop work	4	9	10
Factory	–	7	3
Sports centre	–	2	–
Higher education	6	2	–
Army	2	2	–
Bar work	–	–	3
Tupperware	–	–	3
Homework	–	–	3
Administration	–	–	3
Unemployed	50	5	8
Total	100	101*	101*

*Due to decimal points being rounded up

Table 3.3 *Full-time and part-time employment participation rates (1983, 1988, 1992)*

	1983 (%), n = 68 (aged 18/19)	1988 (%), n = 56 (aged 23/24)	1992 (%), n = 39 (aged 27/28)
Full-time paid	24	57	46
Part-time paid	23	34	44
Full-time mothers	3	5	3
Unemployed	50	5	8
Women with children	9	29	49

Conclusion

By drawing on the contradictory colonial and nationalistic discourse of
family as moral stability, woman as civilizing force and women as potential
sexual polluters and political threat, the original caring courses attempted to

educate working-class women to take pleasure from their responsibility as pedagogue to themselves and working-class men and thereby benefit the nation. Social policy legislation was put into effect to make sure that they did their job properly. The historical legacies which denote the working class as deficient, but with potential for future reform; which locate respectability with domesticity and which locate caring primarily as a woman's responsibility are institutionalized in the organization and practices of the contemporary courses. When the women enter the course they enter a long history of classifying practices as well as the organizational features of education built on the division of labour. The importance placed on moral responsibility by the historical and contemporary courses generates a form of productive power whereby working-class women can gain positions of respect and responsibility from being seen to care. Domestic service institutionalizes this economic and discursive organization even further. The brief expansion of the Personal Social Services in the 1970s enabled more formalized labour market positions in the caring services; the caring courses were then able to anticipate both the family and the labour market, conveniently switching to the former as legitimator when the latter was in crisis. The productive power of caring (by having responsibility for the moral welfare of others) was used by the national state and local colleges (responding to state policy) as a compensatory structure for unemployment in the 1980s, being most usefully deployed to mop-up welfare cuts (euphemistically called Community Care). Yet this framing of unpaid caring had another benefit for social order. If caring could offer positions of respectability and responsibility in opposition to powerlessness and designations of social worthlessness it could operate as a constructive holding mechanism for unemployed working-class women. They can invest in themselves as respectable whilst ameliorating any perceived threat to social order. They effectively prepare themselves for familial responsibility, unpaid caring (which was once the responsibility of the State) and can also fill low-paid caring jobs (if they are lucky). This framework of association between caring, respectability, regulation and investment provides the basis from which the women move through other positions of identification, such as sexuality and femininity, as the other chapters will show.

Notes

1 Black women were never identified as a civilizing force in the same way. Rather, they were part of the threat against which civilization was constructed (see Fryer, 1984).

2 The ideology of nationalism also influenced State intervention in familial organization. Dyhouse (1977) documents the tendency to regard international rivalries as a struggle in which only the 'fittest' and most 'efficient' nations could be expected to survive. The fears of 'national degeneracy' prompted by the rejection of the huge proportions of the population as unfit for Boer War service (in Manchester 8,000 out of 11,000) focused anxieties more closely on the standards of the working class.

3 See Heath (1982) for an exploration of Victorian sexual classificatory systems.

4 Hall (1979) and Donzelot (1979) maintain that the foundations for the assumptions made today about the natural and proper organization of family can be shown to have arisen at the

beginning of the nineteenth century. The representation of the home/household as a 'haven in a heartless world' was helped by veritable legal and ideological campaigns forged by the end of the nineteenth century (Rapp et al., 1979).

5 Although the middle classes had experienced instruction in the 'home arts' as early as the late 1700s in relation to their leisure time, it was not until 1904 that a specific interest was expressed by the State about a similar education for working-class girls.

6 *Report on the Inter-Departmental and Committee on Physical Deterioration*, vol. I Appendix and Index 1904, xxxII para. 293, para. 315.

7 Although the courses initially made no claim to enhance women's skills in the labour market, their development was in direct contrast to that suggested for working-class boys, in which education was seen as a means of equipping them with technically relevant occupational knowledge. A difference which highlights the different gender connotations inherent within the term 'vocational' (Marks, 1976).

8 It was the visible and public which had to be controlled. The tight boundaries and classifications were enabled by the interviews conducted with prostitutes which established a body of 'authentic' knowledge (see Nead, 1988: 151).

9 The Seebohm Report (1968) was introduced into Parliament by Richard Crossman who emphasized its cost-effectiveness in strengthening the family to care for its own members.

10 The differences between the national and local figures indicate the different responses to the local labour market. There now exists a Youth Training Scheme in caring which is seen as a potential source of nursing auxiliaries and care assistants (incidentally these are jobs that usually do not require any formal qualification). NVQs (National Vocational Qualifications) now also cover caring education.

4

Developing and Monitoring
a Caring Self

Belief systems concerning the self should not be construed as inhabiting a diffuse field of 'culture', but as embodied in institutional and technical practices – through which forms of individuality are specified and governed. The history of the self should be written at this 'technological' level, in terms of the techniques and evaluations for developing, evaluating, perfecting, managing the self, the ways it is rendered into words, made visible, inspected, judged and reformed. (Rose, 1989: 218)

This chapter charts what Foucault (1988) defines as technological practices by examining the processes by which the caring self is produced through the negotiation and performances of subject positions given by the organization of the caring courses and the caring curricula. These subject positions relate to wider discourses of caring and bring with them specific duties and responsibilities. The caring subject is constructed by the conflation of caring *for* with caring *about,* in which the practices of caring become inseparable from the personal dispositions. For those who had already experienced the negative allocative function of the education system by the age of 16, whose employment prospects are bleak and cultural capital limited, caring (whether paid or unpaid) offers the means to value, trade and invest in themselves, an opportunity to 'make something of themselves'. It enables them to be recognized as respectable, responsible and mature. This chapter explores how these 'selves' are produced, and how in this process the legacies and regulations outlined in the previous chapter are put into effect. It examines the investments and resistances the women make to produce themselves as carers through institutional and technical practices, showing how by making caring performances they come to recognize themselves as caring women. Their investments, performances and recognitions come to influence their future access and movement through subject positions within femininity and sexuality, as later chapters show.

To be a caring person involves having to display responsibility by taking on personality traits such as unselfishness. Responsibility as one of the key signifiers of respectability is demonstrated through self performances, such as conduct and manners, or through the care and obligations to others (e.g. familial, voluntary and occupational caring). The caring self is a dialogic production: a caring self cannot be produced without caring for others. Before a detailed examination is made of the technological processes of caring

I show how the women have already been positioned and position themselves in relation to caring. It is these positions which inform their responses to technologies of the self. Their 'selves' are constructed through concrete caring practices and through investments in these practices. The first section explores the women's motivations for becoming caring and respectable. This is followed by a detailed analysis of the caring techniques on offer in the college. The consequences of these techniques are explored in a final section which examines how the women have been able to perform and put their caring self to use.

The experiences documented in this chapter were all part of the earliest stages of the research. They show the beginnings of the women's investments in respectability and how and why they were made. This enables links to be made later in the book into other investments such as femininity and heterosexuality.

Local Positions and Opportunities

The women are not just positioned by the historical legacies (outlined in the previous chapter) but also by the range of opportunities available to them. Their own inheritance (and lack) of forms of capital means that their access to certain routes such as higher education and the primary labour market is already restricted. Their understanding of their possibilities is one of the motivations to pursue caring. To put it bluntly, there is very little else for them to do but go to college.

The college is situated in a North-Western industrial town which has a strong tradition of high female employment.[1] Labour market participation rates for females at the time of the research remained above the national rate of 50 per cent at 61 per cent. At the time of the initial stage of the research (1980–83) when most of the women were 16 and making the 'choices' about their futures, opportunities in the local labour market were drastically curtailed. From January 1976 to January 1982 under 18 female unemployment increased by 1010.3 per cent (Low Pay Unit, February 1982). According to the local Job Centre both factory and clerical work in the area had been reduced by 50 per cent. Out of a total of 2,500 school leavers in 1982 only 18 per cent were known to have found jobs (Job Centre, 11 January 1983). The opportunities for unqualified or poorly qualified 16-year-old women were small. The local paper ran a front page story on the 1,200 applications for just 14 jobs at the local coffee factory. In the light of these national and local unemployment trends most of the women who ended up on the caring courses held a realistic perception of their very limited future employment possibilities:

> It was either this or the dole, all me school mates are stuck on the dole, they're doing nothing so after the summer, I'd got bored so I thought I might as well give it a try, me Mum and Dad weren't too keen at first, like it costs them doesn't it, but like me Dad said it's better than being under his feet all day, he's on the dole you see. [Sally B, PHS O][2]

I didn't fancy being on the dole, me brother's been on it for two years now, and he's become a real miserable pig, always moping round and that . . . I thought I'd do something useful, well it looks better doesn't it, if you've been to college rather than sat at home and done bugger all, stands you in better stead really. [Fiona, PCSC O]

I couldn't get a job, it's as simple as that and this was the easiest course to get on without any qualifications the careers officer said, he gave me the form. It was something to do. [Diane, PCSC O]

I'm here 'cos I couldn't do anything else. Like I didn't fancy doing hair and I'm too thick for O levels, don't like that sort of thing anyway. It were this or cooking and I don't fancy cooking all the time . . . and you have to pay for them courses. [Julie, CC]

The college in theory allows for a place for every student who applies. The ever-increasing demand for caring courses, coupled with the informal policy of the caring section to interview every student who applies, ensures a full capacity. As Sarah, the Community Care Course tutor, notes:

All are given a chance, no-one is turned away, we try and fit their abilities, their aptitudes to the course, the only reason people are turned away is if they are physically unfit or have major personality problems which would make them unsuitable for caring, even those with appalling school records are given a chance.

The women are aware of this. Even though their previous experience of education has been relatively unsuccessful – only 4 per cent had three or more O levels, with 38 per cent with one or more O level and 49 per cent with only CSEs and two came from Special Schools as Table 4.1 indicates[3] – they had usually enjoyed school, seeing it as a place for meeting friends and having a laugh. This meant they were not adverse to continuing education. They also saw caring courses as a means to do something they knew they could already do. Most were predisposed towards caring, having been involved in caring previously, either paid (usually baby-sitting) or familial:

Like, in a way, you think you can do this course anyway, like it's nothing really new . . . we all know how to look after people and that so it's nice getting qualifications for something you know you are good at. [Julie S, CC][3]

I looked after our kids, they're all younger than me, they're not me real brothers and sisters, only half, me mum says I'm good with them, sometimes, like, they listen to me and not her, so really . . . our Darren [older brother] he said I'd be dead good at it, I look after our Michelle [brother's daughter] for him and Sandra, she told me it was dead easy to get on . . . it'll be a laugh anyway. [Julie, CC]

The decision to go on a caring course is not so much a positive decision, as an attempt to find something within constricting cultural and financial limits which they will be able to do and be good at. Caring is something at which they are unlikely to fail. It is a cultural resource to which they have (and had) access. It is a form of cultural capital. Connell et al. (1982), however, would see it as less of a positive move towards future development but rather a prevention of slipping downwards by putting a floor on their economic and cultural circumstances.

When the women arrive at the college they enter into the sexual divisions of knowledge instituted within the college organization. The educational hierarchy in the college is premised on the sexual division of labour which divides students on the basis of their previous gendered and classed educational capital. The caring courses are considered to be of the lowest status within the college hierarchy. Not only are the courses entered by default, they are entered with a clear awareness of distinctions. Eventually the women come to invert their differences by stressing the practical side of their courses over the uselessness of academic qualifications. This can be seen as the beginning of a process lived throughout their lives in which they attempt to gain some status and value for themselves through their cultural capital in the face of negation. They also enter a contradiction: they pursue caring courses because they have knowledge of caring, yet the courses train them for what they already know. The values and aspirations of the women are thus already located in different cultural fields to those who see education as only a matter of academic qualifications (cf. Boudon, 1974). Knowing their lack of qualifications, limited employment opportunities and restricted alternatives, the women make a realistic appraisal (as their mothers have) of what is available to them. A caring course seems like a good idea.

Celebrating the Practical

The organization of the curriculum of the caring courses provides the framework for the institutional responses that the women can make. The courses make their own divisions in knowledge; they divide subjects into academic, vocational and practical divisions. Students take O levels (11 per cent do A levels); occupational-related practical work (health-care, social-care practice, home-nursing and elementary nursing principles) and non-occupational practical work (needlework, domestic science, drama and creative studies, social and life skills). Most of the women find the academic side of the curriculum irrelevant and boring. They usually see the non-occupational practical side as a waste of time. The women invert the status values which are attached to the academic/practical divisions to generate some credibility:

> If we spent more time going out on placements and things we'd be a lot better off, and then at least we'd have something to show, like lots of experience, that's what jobs always want you know. [Lynn, CC]

This appraisal of the divisions of knowledge on offer involves an assessment of their own competence *and* assessment of the relevance that the knowledge itself has for their perceived future positioning. Mac an Ghaill's (1994) research shows that young working-class women have very clear ideas about the futility of caring courses. Here, the women can be seen to be positioning themselves by monitoring and conditioning their own aspirations by aligning themselves with the practical side of the course to the detriment of the academic side. A caring self is a practical, not academic self. Their rejection of the academic side of the curriculum is another attempt to find something at which they will not fail. It is a form of investment in themselves.

Their negotiations are representative of Gramsci's (1971) contention that institutional education can operate at the intimate level of subjectivity. For instance, Donald (1985) argues that the curriculum establishes hierarchical relations between different forms of knowledge (in this case between practical and academic). This organization also generates a network of subject positions in relation to these hierarchies – for example, it defines what it is to be cultivated and clever against what it is to be practical, useful and responsible. These subject positions provide character definitions. Together these definitions enable personalities to be defined. A caring personality is one which contains the characteristics outlined later in Table 4.2. Personalities thus come to be seen as the natural consequence of the aptitudes and practices of the people who occupy the subject positions available, these being defined through institutional organization based on divisions of labour and historical legacies. The women continually stress how practical and responsible they are, coming to see such behaviour as a feature of themselves, of their own personality, rather than part of a process of educational differentiation. This is how the curriculum is implicated in technologies of the self *and* the struggle to gain 'intimate and secure' social relations – intimate because it feeds into the ordering of subjectivity, secure because of the apparent naturalness of its categories (Donald, 1985). By occupying the caring subject positions provided by the organization of the curriculum, the women come to recognize themselves as caring subjects.

The technical practice of subject positioning is, however, not entirely straightforward. The practical side is not just valued for being practical but is assessed on the basis of its occupational relevance. Placements are considered to be totally worthwhile. They are the site where the developing caring subject becomes legitimated.

Placements can involve Elderly People's Homes (EPHs), hospitals, nurseries, primary schools, mentally and physically handicapped centres, children's homes and play groups. The placements are for one day per week plus a three week block placement every year.[4] Placements provide the women with knowledge and experience of occupational settings, indicating to them that they may be employable and useful; they also signal that they are capable, practical and responsible. This contributes further to their recognitions of themselves as caring subjects. Responsibility is one of the key signifiers and narratives of responsibility abound:

> There I was left on my own in this hospital ward, just me, everyone else had gone, for tea or something, and there were all the medicines to be given, They'd told me to give them out, by myself, measuring milligrams. I was ever so careful and I did it. I was scared at first though, now you just imagine if one of them had died I'd have to handle it all on my own, you know, by myself till someone came to help. [Theresa, PHS O]

> What they do is give you their jobs to do so they can nip off for a break. At first I wondered where they had all gone. But I didn't mind. I liked going round talking to the patients and sorting things out for them. The more I did the more I got to do though. When they realize you can do things they just pile them onto you. It's all

right though, lots of people think you're a real nurse and you can tell them what to do and they do it. [Sandy, PHS O]

For Theresa, the ability to handle this responsibility signifies more in self-esteem than academic competence ever could. Here she is dealing with matters of life and death over which she feels she has absolute control. For Sandy the amount of work given is set against the authority which accompanies it and being seen to be competent is highly valued. Competencies become related to personality characteristics. They give her a means to revalue herself. From this incident, one amongst many, it can be seen that placements allow a means for demonstrating their responsibility, maturity and capability:

> They're good, they make you stand up for yourself, you know, you've got to learn to survive, like on my first day when they told me to read the charts I didn't have a clue so you've got to learn who to ask so as not to look stupid, sometimes though they give you all the dirty work, like at Alsworth (EPH) I had to do it all, they must've thought here's a mug. [Andrea, CC]

> Left me alone on the first day on the ward . . . you think how can they do this to you, like never tell you how to read the charts and that. [Karen, PHS O]

> I'm surprised I didn't kill half of them, like it says on their bed ends about no liquid and that, they didn't tell us so I just gave them all a cuppa, they couldn't say anything mind, 'cos they didn't tell me. [Ann, PHS O]

Although aware of the potential for exploitation, this is overcome by feeling responsible in an occupational setting. They even become responsible through exploitation. Many have had prior familial responsibility but it has not been externally legitimated. Their caring performances are given a value; responsibility is a tradable competence in the caring occupational sector as well as being a valued personality characteristic. Whilst experiencing degrading work (such as cleaning toilets and bottoms),[5] some violence from some inmates on the placements and coping with harrowing emotional situations,[6] they dealt with this by constructing a form of dignity in their labour, which takes on a significance beyond itself, becoming rooted in the naturalness of their personality. Responsibility provides respectability. It is what Willis (1979) identifies as a 'quality of being' which contains essential subjectivities of self-esteem and dignity. The inclusion of occupationally related placements provides subject positions of responsibility which enable the women to define themselves as practical, caring, employable women. Their ability to perform *well* on a placement secures support for identification with a caring personality:

> I never thought of myself as a really caring person, it was only when I got into the second year I realized that I knew and behaved the way caring people are supposed to, you know, looking after my gran and the house when me mam's at work. I knew how to do all these caring things before, but it was when I was involved in them as part of this course I realized I must be good at it. [Sam, PCSC O]

> Placements for me were a revelation. I was really worried at first I thought I'd never be able to cope. I didn't tell anyone like, but I was shitting myself at first. But it really was easy. The warden she said I was made for it. She said I was a natural.

You know, she said that when I finish I should ring them, there might be a place for me there. That'd be good wouldn't it? [Kelly, CC]

The warden at Ayers said I shouldn't bother with the course. She said I could do it without all this stuff. She said it's a waste of time. I just listened to her and she said that I was good because she didn't keep having to tell me what to do. She said I was good because I knew what was needed without telling. I was made for the job, she said. [Jackie, CC]

By making a good caring performance they consolidate the recognition of themselves as caring. Sam, Kelly and Jackie have all reassessed their previous feelings of inadequacy. These placements have designated them as intuitive, natural carers. Their placement experiences institutionalize self-formation by the validation of practice. All these validations enable a location with respectability. In this case, the prior feminine cultural capital of the women has been fully capitalized upon; they gain a value from its use in a public setting. Their identification of themselves as carers is given further weight by the relationships they make with those in the occupational setting (e.g. elderly, mentally/physically handicapped, nursery children, problem children) in which the 'clients'' helplessness and dependency leads them to feel even more capable and responsible, as Karen suggests:

I've done two placements now and they've really opened my eyes. I didn't realize there were so many, you know, so many, well, like completely helpless old dears and that, like they can't do anything, you know they really need help and there's not enough, so like, you know, what you're doing is really useful. Like they need you to be there or they wouldn't get any help. God knows what happens when we leave. [Karen, CC]

If I'm being honest it does make you feel good. I know it's awful, I've thought about it, it's their helplessness that ends up making you feel good. But you just can't help feeling needed. I feel quite empty, you know at a loss, when we have to come back to the college 'cos we don't do much good here. You know it's not like doing A levels and that, that doesn't help anybody. [Rose, CC]

Such comments suggest that a caring identity is based not only on the fulfilment of the needs of others and selflessness but also on the fulfilment of their own desire to feel valuable. Their altruism makes them feel good. They are aware of their position in the social hierarchy of knowledge and to dissipate its effects they position themselves as morally superior caring subjects. In the process they become ethical beings, who define and regulate themselves according to a moral code which establishes precepts for conducting and judging their own lives. Placements which provide external validation provide evidence for the women and others that they are responsible, respectable and capable. Kuhn (1995) argues that caring is evidence of a responsible self, a sign of the desire to be respectable. It is their experience of being known as caring by others that consolidates their own investments.

The seduction of caring may be that it offers a means to feel good, even morally superior. This is a powerful incentive when set against the prospect of unemployment. Their experiences of being worthwhile and externally valued give them an authority from which to speak. Their self-esteem, their quality of being, becomes based upon the dependencies (and potential for negating the autonomy) of others. This desire to be valued, to be doing something worthwhile, is reinforced on the courses by the expectation that they will become involved in voluntary work. The women are asked to provide continual support (outside of classes) for a group of EETW (Extended Education Transition to Work Course) students who have experienced problems with education or have special needs. Their 'supervision' of these students provides constant reinforcement of their own responsibility. It also supports Cohen's (1982) contention that the powerless are being trained to supervise and control those with even less power. The practice is not experienced as a form of mutual aid but as a means of reinforcing distinctions between them. It also predisposes them towards voluntary care after the course has finished. For those who experienced immediate unemployment after college voluntary work, which they knew they could do, gave legitimation to their practices and enabled the continued validation of their caring identifications. It enabled them to prolong the recognition of themselves as caring. This meant they took on unpaid caring within and outside the home. Their placement occupational experience locks them into generating their sense of themselves through caring labour. They become part of what Rose identifies as a new worker subjectivity:

> The worker is an individual in search of meaning, responsibility, a sense of personal achievement, a maximized 'quality of life', and hence of work. Thus the individual is not to be emancipated *from* work, perceived as merely a task or a means to an end, but to be fulfilled *in* work, now construed as an activity through which we produce, discover and experience our selves. (1989:103)

Occupational caring becomes the means of finding meaning and dignity, assuming responsibility and respectability. The women find their own worth embedded, reflected and enhanced in the quality of their caring performance, be it undertaken as paid, voluntary or familial. Their caring subjectivity is produced across a range of sites. Whilst occupational caring generates legitimacy and validation, the courses promote the family as the ultimate and primary site for care.

Classifications of Caring Practice

Their identifications with a caring personality are given even more legitimation through the overt course definitions of caring practice. The courses perpetuate a 'culture of respectable familialism' whereby the curriculum outlines 'suitable' performances, personalities, standards and expectations associated with caring. The courses always present the family as the primary site of caring, even when emphasis is made of occupational potential. Parts of the curriculum are similar to the conduct and etiquette manuals of previous centuries, whereby minute detailing of caring practices enable clear definitions to be constructed between good and bad, right and wrong, normal and deviant. The continual classification of caring practice is the means by which forms of economic organization and personality type come to take on the status of the 'only way to do it'. This means that even though placements and entry to the course enable them to trade on their feminine cultural capital this is now put under scrutiny to see if it is the right sort of capital for caring personalities. Rather than the reaffirmation of previous feminine cultural capital, which the women thought they could use and from which they could benefit, the classificatory systems of caring practice which the courses employ can throw doubt on their own previous caring practice. It is this doubt which generates the anxieties and insecurities that enable caring to be promoted as a form of 'expertise', and which secures continual performances to 'prove' that they really are caring.

The women do a minimum of three projects on 'the family'. Such projects generally involve: the presentation of photographs of the student's own family, catalogue cut-outs of ideal families, pictures and historical detailing of extended and nuclear families and the classifications of 'problem families' which are represented through 'factual' case studies and suitably appropriate images. They study maternal deprivation, child development, and do creative skills which involve the construction of toys, children's garments and articles for the home. In some instances responsibility is constructed from specific consumption practices, in which students are given advice on the suitability of particular products. The Health Care component of the courses details pregnancy and child rearing: students are provided with programmes for potty training and schedules for when babies should walk, talk, teethe and so on. Children's bad habits are described and remedies advised.

A great deal of the detailing of family practice is generated by the giving of advice. The advice given on the courses is based on a model of full-time care, where the carer always has enough time to listen, to understand and to respond to the needs of others. It is never assumed that carers themselves may have needs, nor that they may have other responsibilities outside of caring, such as full-time paid employment.[7] This is the paradox of the caring self. Foucault argues: 'One must not have the care for others to precede the care for self. The care for self takes a moral precedence in the measure that the relationship to self takes ontological precedence' (1988: 7). Not so for the women of the study. The care of the self is a distant object. It is others who take moral precedence, even if the self is constructed through them. Yet the caring self, as it is lived and produced on a daily basis, is a gendered (classed and raced) self. The self is always a product of these processes. The caring self is produced through care for others. It is generated through both self production and self denial. The selflessness required to be a caring self is a gendered disposition. The ontological precedence, outlined by Foucault, in the care of the self, is evidence of a bourgeois individualist practice. It is the prerogative of someone who does not have to care for others to be seen as worthy of respect. The women of this study have to continually prove themselves as respectable through their caring performances for others.

Normality is produced on courses through the designation of good and appropriate caring practices. The courses are not so different from the social reform identified by Rose:

> Normality appears in three guises: as that which is natural and hence healthy; as that against which the actual is judged and found unhealthy; and as that which is to be produced by rationalized social programmes. These criteria of normality are simultaneously used to enable the identification of normality and to demonstrate appropriate conduct. If reality and normality fail to coincide then they should be able to identify abnormality and pursue external intervention. (1989:131)

The courses reproduce all three of these reformist guises. In particular the evaluation of practice implicates the women in judgements about others and themselves. The women are encouraged to develop and monitor responsibilities through their own assessment of good and bad caring practice. This Walkerdine (1984) identifies as a narrative strategy used frequently in girls' comics in which the characters in the story are able to bring about the desired family structure through their own actions. Passivity, she argues, is actively produced as a result of the struggle to overcome 'bad' characteristics:

> Selflessness, even though it brings pain and suffering, brings its own rewards (knowledge of good deeds and righteousness). If the heroines are displayed as passive victims of circumstance, all bad and difficult actions and emotions are invested in others . . . selflessness becomes a virtue and doing anything for oneself is by implication bad and selfish. (1984: 173–4)

The display of selflessness is crucial to their production of their caring selves. Their self is for others.

The women learn to be very specific about bad caring practice through the evaluation of the practices of 'non-caring' others: they are presented with a multitude of different case studies and videos from which they are expected to list and locate faults. Hygiene is a strong signifier of respectability *and* of good caring practice. Caring has to occur in the 'right' settings and these are always hygienic. Students are trained to identify non-hygienic and polluting environments. For instance, in Health Care they are given a picture of a disorganized room and are required to find 28 faults and detail how they can be rectified. This clearly establishes what the appropriate standards are. Routine everyday commentary also contributes to making the distinction between good and bad practice. In Basic Caring Principles, after studying photographs of non-accidental injury cases, students are required to give lists of possible causes. Highest marks were given for personalized faults, then social problems. Just like mainstream conservative discourse, unmarried mothers were judged to be more likely to be violent with their children.

This continual mapping out and evaluating of the caring practices of others enables the women to see just how difficult it is to care properly and how they therefore require 'expert' advice. It is not enough just to care and to display caring, they have to do this by the appropriate and designated methods. This suggests that a caring personality cares in very specific ways; ways which are continually open to the judgement and scrutiny of others. The final logic of this position is that the family is based on specific caring practices, where all problems are solvable as long as the right and correct methods are used, and the sexual division of labour is perceived as inevitable and natural.

Heath (1982) identifies this process as the constant narration of individuals in which the person learns their individuality through the ceaseless telling and retelling of personal failings and anxieties and dilemmas cast in the form of a series of never-ending narratives. When the women participate in finding the right solution or the correct practice they reproduce the genre of individuality, learning how to make sense of what are effectively collective problems. The 'right' practices enable them to recognize and produce themselves as subjects in alignment with the standards and judgements of others. These standards help to produce the measure of respectability. This means that the women's attempts to invert the academic/practical divisions of knowledge to generate some value for themselves from their prior knowledge can never be fully achieved. It also means that in the processing of good and bad practices, the women themselves become the objects of classification. They then read back into their own actions according to the classifications of others.

However, in this process of the detailing of family life and mapping responsibility, the women are not passive receptors. They recognize that they are being categorized as inadequate. They interpret what is being detailed through their prior familial knowledge, or just deride it for its infantilization, as the following comments suggest:

> Oh yea, I can just see me mam's face when I tell her she's been making beds wrong for the last umpteen years, she'd clatter me. She [reference to teacher] lives in cloud bloody cuckoo land . . . It's a waste of time all this stuff, they must think we're stupid. [Marie, PCSC O]

> You know what we've been doing this morning, eh? . . . we've been bathing dolls, yea, straight up, I bathed two dolls this morning, neither had any clothes on either. [Cindy, PHS O]

> Come on, it wasn't dolls really, it was getting us used to babies, that's the idea, you learnt to hold their head up and that didn't you. [Rachel, PHS O]

> Hold its fucking head up, what . . . it couldn't exactly fall down, it didn't bend you know wallybrain, I don't know what she takes us for, we're all standing there watching her bath a doll, I just thought to myself, 'what are we doing here?' like, you know, coming to college to bath dolls, says it all really doesn't it? . . . You don't come to college to bath dolls that's what I'm saying, playing with bloody dolls, I'm 17, I didn't even like dolls when I were 7. [Cindy, PHS O]

The detailing and scrutiny of family life establishes evaluative frameworks not only for domestic practice but also for the type of personality and personal characteristics that a carer should have. Some women come to reassess their own family care:

> I sometimes wonder if me mam had been different, you know if she cared more, went out less, looked after me dad more and that . . . I wonder if he'd have left still, you don't know do you . . . I expect you'll never be able to tell but it makes you think, when I'm married I'm going to make sure I'm really careful about what I say, you know not lose me temper all the time or moan about everything like our mam. [Yvonne, PHS O]

Maybe if I'd listened to our Darren he wouldn't have got into all that trouble, you know maybe it's like she said he just needed someone to talk to. I never really took any notice of him 'cos he was younger than me and he'd always been a pain in the arse, now sometimes I think well why was he such a little bugger, you know was it me ignoring him, could I have done anything to help him like, you know, you never know; me mam said it's daft to think like that because you can't do nothing about it, but sometimes you think maybe you could've made it better. [Fiona, PCSC O]

Through the processes of evaluation doubts and anxieties are created about their own previous caring experiences; this helps to devalue rather than reaffirm the cultural capital they brought with them to the course. It also makes it more difficult for them to resist the caring practices which are being presented, because the practices are so closely related to the aptitudes of the carer. The courses contribute to the development of an individualized caring conscience in which the women come to take responsibility for all the problems in their family, positioning them as not adequate carers who always have to prove that they can care in the correct way.

The women began the courses with a sense of inadequacy but tried to ameliorate this through the only thing they had which could be traded on an educational market; a significant part of the course regenerates this sense of inadequacy. This can, to some extent, be offset by their experience of responsibility which legitimates and proves their respectability. They have to work on themselves continually to live up to the criteria and practices established by the courses, which were framed by class relations that placed working class women in a relationship of continually proving themselves as adequate to the standards of others. This means that their production of subjectivity is always open to scrutiny by others.

The 'Right' Sort of Caring Woman

The course text book, *Working with People* (Summers, 1981), describes caring as a collection of specific attributes and attitudes, such as unselfishness, warmth and understanding. The subject position of caring involves far more than having the 'right' skills: it involves being a particular sort of person. And the attributes of the 'right' sort of person are closely interlinked with wider cultural discourses of femininity and motherhood. The link made between femininity, caring and motherhood contributes towards naturalizing and normalizing the social relations of caring. Their ability to make challenges to the caring curricula becomes even more restricted when they take on caring dispositions. Challenges would then involve them resisting themselves.

Not only is a caring personality defined by wider feminine and maternal discourse, but the definition of caring as a personality type is sustained through the conflation of two different meanings involved in any definition of caring, that is: caring *about* which involves social dispositions that operate at a personal level and assume a relationship between the carer and the cared for, and caring *for* which involves the actual practice of caring, involving specific tasks such as lifting, cleaning and cooking, and does not necessarily relate to caring about. This conflation of the actual skills involved in caring and the expected dispositions of carers is illustrated by the women's attempts to describe caring. They were asked to describe what they thought caring involved and could only answer by changing the question to what being a caring *person* involved. Table 4.2, generated from discussions with the women, lists the social dispositions that they relate to caring, ordered in rank of what they considered to be the most important caring attributes and the qualities they considered themselves to have. These practices enable the formation of a domain of recognitions which constitute themselves with specific knowledge of 'caring'.

Table 4.2   *Qualities of a caring person*

A caring person is . . .	Essential for caring (%)	Own qualities (%)
kind and loving	100	100
considerate about others	100	100
considerate	100	100
understanding	100	100
warm and friendly	100	100
reliable	100	98
sympathetic	100	98
tactful	100	80
never selfish	100	85
never cruel and nasty	100	81
never unkind	100	80
gentle	98	85
patient	95	83
affectionate	95	89
clean and tidy	95	82
never sharp-tempered	100	72
never unpleasant	100	79
never impolite	100	75
respectful	81	81

n = 83, all figures given as percentages
Source: adapted from Ungerson (1982)

Table 4.2 indicates that the women not only consider certain personality dispositions to be essential to caring, but in the majority of cases they feel that they actually have these dispositions. Such characteristics are indicative of feminine duty, such as always putting oneself last, always being there when needed, gentle, never selfish, and so on. They confirm the wider discourse of caring in which conflation occurs between doing and being: you cannot do caring without being caring. *To be* caring means that you have to embody the personal dispositions. Caring involves the assimilation of actual practices which cannot be divorced from personal feelings. The experience of the self and the knowledge of the self become organized in relation to the caring schema established by the course. The curriculum is organized in such a way that certain dispositions are invalidated and denied, others are valorized, advised and legitimated.

As Probyn (1993b) notes, the questions raised here are of a fundamental epistemological nature: how do the experiences and knowledges of the caring self, of one's self, and the knowledge that resides in the relationship between experience and knowledge come to be organized. I would argue that it is the institutionalization of predispositions to care, which themselves are a product of feminine cultural capital and wider discourses of how women should be, that come to be given legitimation through their association with a potential future which provides responsibility and evaluation. The 'caring self' is both a performance and a technique used to generate valuations of responsibility and respectability. Doing caring, that is their caring practices, are fundamental to their concept of the self. To be caring is an enunciative position in which social and self combine. To speak as a caring person produces an identity of value for the self, which also capitalizes on prior female experience. To speak from a caring subject position confers occupational/moral status and authority: to speak as a nurse, mother, warden, provides a valued morally responsible position of enunciation.

Intuition is the ultimate caring disposition. This is defined on the courses as both instinctive and a result of experience. Experience, the disposition which develops the predispositions, is the key factor in generating intuitions which are naturally established. Caring becomes a feeling, and the women are assessed on their ability to feel. It is their affectual responses which they and others monitor. In this sense they are stripped down to their most intimate levels and measured, monitored and classified on the basis of 'natural' dispositions. All structural divisions and inequality are reduced to the ability to feel the 'right' things. The women come to value that which has been defined as intuitive. After all, it cannot be taken from them. In this way the course content consolidates their earlier placement experiences:

> You can't be taught to be caring, that's why this course is no good if you haven't got it in you anyway. [Jill, PHS O]

> You can't turn off from caring, that's just it, you either care or you don't and if you can turn off to me I reckon that means you don't. [Linda, CC]

This emphasis on feelings and natural dispositions makes it difficult for the women to take up positions of resistance, for what comes to be at stake is their sense of self, their feelings:

> I think this course has taught me to recognize my feelings. In the past I'd just dismiss some of the things I'd felt as daft but now I'm learning to trust my intuitions. You know, if I feel a situation's not right, now I'll say something. [Kelly, CC]

> When I was at Brambles (EPH) there was this old lady who wasn't right, you know she just seemed like she was trying to tell you something, like something was wrong. Well, I said to them I said there's something wrong with her but they just ignored me and she stayed there all distressed. You eventually learn to trust your own feelings. Now I know I was right and I should have made more fuss. [Eileen, CC]

Total involvement, as Linda articulates, is seen as a central definer of what it means to be a caring person, which means that when the women have their own families they feel forever guilty about the care they provide. The ideal mother intuits, takes absolute responsibility and emotionally manages all those in her care, and others. It is an ideal that for just practical reasons alone, cannot help but fail. They are disposing their selfless selves to enormous amounts of guilt-inducing caring labour.

Not only do the women have to develop the appropriate personality dispositions if they want to be seen to be caring, they have to display these dispositions through performance. The PCSC Health Care examination illustrates the processes involved. One question asks students to choose between unexpectedly being asked to baby-sit for a friend or going to see a film with another friend. Ann's response is:

> My reply to the mother would be, yes, I would love to baby-sit for her. Although I would be a little disappointed about missing the film at first I would definitely say yes. The reason for doing this would be that I could phone my friend and arrange to go to the film another night. If she was a true friend she would understand. In dealing with this situation I would display self-discipline. I would be helping the mother who needs help by putting her before the luxury of seeing a film which I could most probably see at another time. [Ann, PCSC O]

By choosing to display self-discipline Ann was awarded 18 marks out of 20. This is a dutiful feminine answer – Ann has learnt to display ungrudgingly her love for baby-sitting. She has achieved that which centuries of rhetoric have suggested working-class women should do – she takes pleasure in self and other regulation. Her disappointment, which is only small, can be assuaged by the understanding of a truly caring friend; an other's needs come before her own luxury. Ann has learnt to submit herself. Interestingly, when I talked with her about her response a less dutiful rationalization occurs:

> She's [the Health Care tutor] always going on about self-discipline and putting yourself last. Like I know you should but you don't always, like if it were a really good film, *Flashdance* or something I really wanted to see, I'd probably go – well I'd find somebody to baby-sit, me mam or something . . . anyway it doesn't say why she needs a baby-sitter, maybe she wanted to see the same film, so then what'd you do, eh? [Ann, PCSC O]

So, Ann has learnt the right answer but does not absolutely adhere to it. She challenges the dutiful side expressed in the question but then checks herself by making provision for alternative arrangements, then realizing that this may not be good enough she queries the basis for the need for a baby-sitter in the first place. This sets into motion the process, well documented by feminist cultural theorists, that women always feel guilty for having any pleasure of their own outside of pleasing others (Modleski, 1984; Radway, 1987; Gray, 1992; Stacey, 1994). It also adds further weight to the guilty conscience that they are developing. Ann's final question suggests a few doubts about her own commitment. For Ann to admit that she would rather go and see the film would be a massive admission of failure to adhere to the standards established by the course and ultimately by herself. This suggests that some distance can be generated from caring performances and that caring dispositions and affects may not be absolute. However, although the women may be conscious of making caring performances this does not detract from the overall production of their caring subjectivities. The conscious performance is only one aspect in the process of the production of their caring subjectivities. The continual evaluation of themselves as caring may be a more powerful inducement which may ameliorate any distance that can be created.

Their ideals, expressed when on the course, lock them into situations of continuous evaluation of their own practice resulting in guilt-culture, and with enormous responsibility for domestic labour, for example:

> Of course I'll bring up my children by myself, you can't go shopping them out, you shouldn't have them if that's what you'll do . . . No, I'd never expect a man to help, they wouldn't know what to do, you know, have you ever seen a man with a baby? They look stupid, sort of awkward, you know they're just not made for it like we are. [Ann, PHS O]

> I think it's awful how rich women who should know better shop out their children, I just can't see the point in having them if you don't want to care for them, that's what it's all about, I think it's really awful, what are the kids going to grow up like knowing their mothers don't really care about them, it's like those who send their kids off to paying schools, they never see them. I don't reckon that sort should be allowed to have children. [Sally, PCSC O]

By claiming themselves to be 'real' carers they must prove their responsibility. In doing so they are able to invert class divisions and claim moral superiority to the middle-class women, who by 'farming out' their children are behaving in a way that is uncaring, unnatural and irresponsible. Sally insists that biological reproduction should not be allowed if full-time care is not provided.[8] These articulated class differences demonstrate how different cultural and emotional investments are made in caring. By considering themselves as practical, caring women, naturally predisposed to care, the women are able to develop for themselves some status, responsibility and moral authority, which ultimately involves them in colluding in the propagation of social and sexual divisions in which they are ultimately subordinate, forever monitoring and evaluating themselves and always guilty. It is this desire to prove themselves as respectable and responsible which, more so than any other element, enables them to produce themselves as caring subjects.

When interviewed again in 1988 and 1992 there was an almost total cynicism about the courses but what had remained was a firm subjective construction as carer. The exploitative and often humiliating conditions of occupational caring work had led them to believe that occupational caring was not that positive, but it was still the main means of external validation by which their caring selves came to be constructed. Awareness of the use and abuse of patients and the prioritizing of profit over care had come to most as a stark revelation. This challenged their ability to use caring as a means for establishing moral authority outside of the home but it was still consolidated through child-care. Guilt was a continual presence in their commentaries about families and the distance they were able to produce through caring performances was diminished in the displays of care with their own children. Caring had become a daily reiteration that was in no sense challenging through its performance, rather it was reproductive.

Conclusion

The caring self is constructed through many practices, processes and techniques. It is embodied in the institutional and technical practices of the caring courses. The women enter these practices with little educational capital to trade and with bleak outlooks. They try to make the best out of what they have and to stop matters becoming any worse. This involves them using their feminine cultural capital, which takes the form of caring experience, and which, through contact with institutional practices, becomes devalued as the courses map out the 'right' techniques to care. This generates enormous anxieties, doubt and guilt, which to some extent predisposes them for emotional responsibility and motherhood – another unachievable ideal by which notions of the self are developed through naturalness and normalization. To assuage this constant anxiety and devaluation of themselves and their prior background and experiences they invest in the responsibility and performance of caring for others. This is given the greatest legitimation when practised in an occupational setting. Placements enable caring to be displayed as a performance of moral superiority. Placements also enable them to recognize themselves as 'real' carers. This is consolidated by the responsible tasks they perform. But placements also generate a dependence upon dependent others for a sense of self worth. Their selves come to be constructed in relation to the powerlessness of others. Their investments in themselves can only work if they invest in others and others invest in them. The giving of caring can be seen as a form of gift exchange. A social relation is effected through the gift of part of oneself (Diprose, 1994) in which the receiver is expected to enter into a reciprocal relation, or a position of debt. They hope their caring practices will produce a return of respectability, but this is always under evaluation and never guaranteed. In trying to escape the negative classifications of dialogic others the women invest in caring and put themselves under greater scrutiny. They become visibly respectable but at a great cost to themselves.

The desire to be valued and to demonstrate respectability and responsibility predisposes the women to voluntary and unpaid caring. They can easily be exploited in the search for some positive valuing. The techniques of the self – for self-knowledge, self-reflection, self-examination – ultimately become a form of self-surveillance. The panoptical gaze of the good, moral carer enables disciplinary practices to be enacted upon themselves (Bartky, 1990). They become the objects of their own classifications, produced from their location in class relations which positions them as always inadequate, deficient and potentially pathological. Their investments and practices generate an individualistic, intuitive form of caring dependent upon external validation and continually subject to scrutiny in which they are consigned to forever proving themselves through the reiteration of reproductive caring performances.

Notes

1 The town is based on two major industries – manufacturing and services – which at the beginning of the research employed over one-third of the borough population and by the end only one-fifth (local census newsletters). The industrialization of the town centred on the development of the railway network, in part, a reflection of a national wave of urban growth between 1841 and 1901.
2 The situation would be very different now as 'training' has been made compulsory in Britain for 16–18 year olds.
3 GCSEs replaced O levels. CSEs were the Certificate of Secondary Education, designed to provide qualifications for those not considered suitable for O levels. The caring courses the women followed were: Preliminary Social Care (PCSC), Preliminary Health Service (PHS) and Community Care (CC). For the PCSC and PHS courses some students followed O or A levels. This is denoted by an O or A following the course name. PCSC was governed by the social work training board (CCETSW); the other courses were validated at the local level. The PCSC was seen by students as a route into basic-level forms of social care which did not require a degree, such as residential work. The PHS was seen as pre-training for nursing and the CC course was very general care training (see Skeggs, 1986, for further curricula details).

Table 4.1 *Qualifications on entry*

	PCSC	PHS	Community Care
3 plus O levels	3	1	0
2 plus O levels	8	4	0
1 O level	15	12	0
5 plus CSEs	7	3	7
3 plus CSEs	0	3	18
1 plus CSE	0	0	5
No qualifications	0	0	1
Total	29	23	31

*entry 1981–83

4 The allocation always creates complaints and most students just want the highly prized and severely restricted nursery placements. They quickly become aware of the status divisions within occupational caring.
5 See Banks et al. (1992). They describe the forms and types of exploitation endured by students on a YTS caring course.
6 I visited some of the women whilst they were on placements and was deeply disturbed by some of the distressing emotional situations which they were expected to handle.
7 The paradox is that these models of good caring practice are taught by those who are not full-time carers themselves.
8 The ability to have children is equated with the ability to care for them. The naturalizing of biology has a long history and a powerful, established set of cultural representations (Stanworth, 1987; Spallone, 1989; McNeil, 1991; Franklin, 1991).

5

(Dis)Identifications of Class: on Not Being Working Class

Class is a communist concept. It groups people as bundles and sets them against one another. (Margaret Thatcher, *Guardian*, 22 April 1992)

Why do they take their class position so personally? (Sennett and Cobb, 1977)

Class was central to the young women's subjectivities. It was not spoken of in the traditional sense of recognition – I am working class – but rather, was displayed in their multitudinous efforts *not to be* recognized as working class. They disidentified and they dissimulated. Theirs was a refusal of recognition rather than a claim for the right to be recognized. It was a denial of the representations of their positioning. This should not surprise us, for as Chapter 1 noted, the label working class when applied to women has been used to signify all that is dirty, dangerous and without value. In the women's claims for a caring/respectable/responsible personality class was rarely directly figured but was constantly present. It was the structuring absence. Yet whilst they made enormous efforts to distance themselves from the label of working class, their class position (alongside the other social positions of gender, race and sexuality), was the omnipresent underpinning which informed and circumscribed their ability *to be*. This is a chapter about that relationship between positioning and identity. It is about the experience of class. Class operated in a dialogic manner: in every judgement of themselves a measurement was made against others. In this process the designated 'other' (based on representations and imaginings of the respectable and judgemental middle class) was constructed as the standard to/from which they measured themselves. The classifying of themselves depended upon the classifying systems of others.

Class is experienced by the women as exclusion. Whereas working-class men can use class as a positive source of identity, a way of including themselves in a positively valorized social category (Willis, 1977), this does not apply for working-class women. Warde (1994) asks if class in general ought to be defined by exclusion and deprivation, rather than by trying to locate attributes such as occupation and education which are shared by all class members. It is deprivations that persist over time even when actual occupations change or household composition alters. The exclusions occur because the women do not have *access* to economic resources and cultural ways to be anything other than working class. Their structural positioning does not enable access to productive resources. As this chapter will demonstrate they do not have any of the requisite capitals (outlined in Chapter 1) to be middle class. The recent retreat from the study of class has been enacted by those who do have the requisite access and are claiming that their privilege is not an issue. However, access to knowledge is a central feature of class reproduction and it is very clear that those who want to dismiss class as a redundant concept want to abdicate responsibility from the relations of inequality in which they and the women of this study are very differently positioned. Class is absolutely central to how these women live their lives, exemplified in this chapter by their constant refusal to be fixed or measured by it.

The purpose of this chapter is to reinstate class back into feminist theory by showing how class informs the production of subjectivity. This is not just an analysis of subjective construction but an examination of how inequalities are consolidated, reproduced and lived as power relations. Class is primarily about inequality and exploitation. This chapter is divided into two sections. Drawing on the ethnography, the first section explores how the women articulate class, how it is informed by representation and how they are positioned by and position themselves in relation to class. The second section examines how the women lived class on a daily basis, analysing how they constructed their subjectivities through class-informed performances. It explores how attempts to escape class identifications through discourses of improvement and strategies of passing rarely succeed because of their lack of power to convert cultural capital into symbolic capital. Overall, it is a study of how social and cultural positioning generates denial, disidentification and dissimulation rather than adjustment. It is a study of doubt, insecurity and unease: the emotional politics of class.

Disidentifications

To me if you are working class it basically means that you are poor. That you have nothing. You know, nothing. [Sam, 1992]

The real working class are the ones you see hanging round the dole. They're dead scruffy and poor and they haven't a job but I guess they may be working if they are working class, they may be working. If they're working class they should be working so they work, I guess, in all the bad jobs. [Sheenah, 1992]

They're rough. You can always tell. Rough, you know, the women are common as muck you know, always have a fag in their mouths, the men are dead rough. You know. [Andrea, 1992]

Just poor, trying to get by on very little, it's not their fault there's no jobs anymore they're the ones who are struggling. [Michelle, 1992]

The ones who batter their kids. [Pam, 1992]

It used to be you were working class if you worked in the railways say and it didn't mean you had no money, but now it's changed. Now it means that you don't work, like it's not those with the good jobs now it's those without jobs, they're the real working-class. [Lisa, 1992]

No doubt Thatcherism has informed this slippage from working to under-class and has influenced the construction of distinctions within the working class. The real working class for these women is something from which they are desperately trying to escape. It is why they are doing college courses. They want to be seen as different. Their dissimulations are not unlike the historical and popular representations of the working class (especially working-class women). In their accounts the working class are poor, deprived, depriving, dangerous and degraded. They are well aware of the jokes about 'Sharons and Kevins', about 'tackiness', about white high heeled shoes. Other studies of class representation such as Hill (1986) suggest a normalization of the middle classes and a pathologizing of the working classes through representations. Historical studies such as Stedman Jones (1971), Kuhn (1988) and Nead (1988) chart a long history in Britain in which the working class have been (through representation) continually demonized, pathologized and held responsible for social problems. And as Lash and Urry (1994) note, representations are classifiers as well as a classified. The negativity associated with the working class is ubiquitous. Walkerdine (1990) charts the 'truths' generated from bourgeois fantasies by which 'The Working Class' is created as an object to be governed and regulated:

> And what of The Working-class? What are the fantasies proved time and time again in empiricist social science? . . . We are the salt of the earth, the bedrock of the revolution; *we* are working-class women with big hearts, big arms, big breasts; we are stupid, ignorant, deprived, depriving; we are repressed, authoritarian and above all, *we* voted Thatcher into her third term of office. We are revolting, anti-democratic. We suppress our children and do not allow them autonomy. How many more of these truths will there be? (1990: 206)

Moreover, the working class have not had access to the legal, aesthetic or moral authority which gives legitimacy to social positions (Lamont, 1992) which could generate positive valuing. The ubiquity of the pathologizing of the working class is shown in a recent case in Britain. Nick Leeson, the Barings bank dealer who lost an estimated £860 million on the futures market, had his working-class upbringing linked to his disastrous dealing: 'There is nothing wrong with where we came from' – responded his sister Sarah Leeson (*Guardian*, 3 March 1995: 3). In the light of limited and negative connotations it is not surprising that the women do not want to take on working-class identifications which have such long standing negative connotations.[1] As Chapter 4 demonstrated these pathological representations are continually reproduced on the courses; representations which the women learn to disassociate themselves from by the employment of the 'right' caring practices. Steedman (1986), Walkerdine and Lucey (1989) and Walkerdine (1990) chart how these pathologizing representations generate a longing for a different place.

This is why for the women directly speaking of class is rare. Frazer (1989) found a similar problem when she asked two different groups of working- and middle-class girls to discuss class and found startlingly different responses. The working-class girls displayed an unusual reluctance to speak. They found class ambiguous, vague and embarrassing. This contrasted with a group of public schoolgirls who were well practised in discussing class. In the United States, Press (1990) notes how the women she interviewed for her research were groping for the proper words with which to conceptualize class differences. Similarly, McRobbie found a complete absence of class discourse from the general talk of the young women she studied, arguing: '[b]eing working-class meant little or nothing to these girls – but being a *girl* over-determined their every moment' (1982: 48).

Talking about class, however, is somewhat different from living it. Class connotations may be ubiquitous but they are rarely directly spoken by those who do not want to be reminded of their social positioning in relation to it. Class identifications were rare in the course of the research. As Berger (1980) notes, the identification 'I am' is more than a statement of immediate fact: it is already biographical. 'I am not' is similarly loaded. The following comments begin to chart the processes by which (dis)identification occurs:

> Well I think I'm working class and I'll tell you why it's because my mum has always had to work for a living. She really struggles to keep us well fed and clothed. Now I work in a garage at nights and the weekend to pay my way. She said she'd support me through college but I think she's supported us enough. She's worked herself to death. We must be working class. [June, 1983]

and later:

> No, I don't think I'm working class at all now. Not after we bought the house and that . . . I expect I'm now middle class . . . but it's like when we go to Dave's business dos, but I don't really feel like some of them, you know the real bosses' wives with all their talk and that. I sometimes feel really frightened to speak in case I show him up. I expect they're really middle class so I'm not really like them, but I'm not like the rest of our family without two pennies to rub together. You know, I just don't think class is a very useful term. I think I'm probably classless. You know I'm not really one nor the other. I don't really fit. [June, 1989]

These two differently dated comments from June illustrate how she draws on her prior knowledge to make sense of class. The key to her first definition is work and struggle. She is primarily dependent upon her mother and so defines herself through her mother's labour. In the second comment there is a shift to ownership and labour is absent. As in the earlier comments poverty is *the* sign of working-classness and she is not poor. June is computing her class knowledge by the measurement of her difference from and similarity to others. She realizes that she is not like those who can speak in a different way. She is different from both and she has run out of defining features. Therefore for her the concept is redundant. Refusal and denial generate disidentification for Anita:

> I think it's just daft trying to fit people into pigeonholes. They say because you live on a council estate that you must be working class. I remember all the stuff we did at college. But loads of people own their own houses and just because they're on council estates it doesn't make any difference. They own them. They're theirs. My mum and dad own their house now and even though my dad's unemployed now it still doesn't make him working class. He's going to set up his own business anyway he says. So they can't be working class. It's just a load of rubbish. [Anita, 1989]

Anita, who still lives with her parents, has a clear image of what it means to be working class. For her it is defined by house ownership and employment.[2] The knowledge she draws upon comes from academic representations, from lessons at college. Anita is adamant to resist the classifications she knows; she does not want to position herself where she can be measured in relation to others. Her comments show a clear awareness of the negative values associated with the working class. They also show that she knows that certain features of her family background would allocate her to the working class. She believes that ownership has superseded locality as the measure of class. (It should be remembered that this comment was made after 10 years of Thatcherism in Britain in which the government sold council houses with a long and strong ideological campaign to eradicate class as a social category but not as a social division.) Anita's vehement denial stands in opposition to the rare embrace of a class identity by Nicky:

> Yes. I'm working class and I'm proud of it. All the girls at work are. You'd have to be at our place the money we get paid. I can't bear those snobs who think they're better than you just 'cos they've got new windows and that. It looks stupid. They just don't want to own up to it. They're the same as us. They're bloody traitors, they're just snobs, that's what they are. [Nicky, 1989]

Nicky's local culture enables her to define herself with her workmates. She also uses economic criteria. She works as a care assistant at an EPH. As with the others she defines herself against an imaginary other – one signified here through windows (new windows were frequently put in place by those who had bought their council houses and wanted to signal that they were owners, hence different) – who make obvious attempts to construct their difference against people like Nicky.[3] Nicky's class politics are part of a larger historical internal working-class critique about those who appear to be buying out of their class (foreman rather than windows used to be the signifier). It is employment experience and economic criteria which have changed Angela's mind on her class position. Her first comment is made while she is still at college, without responsibility:

> Well my dad, he's got his own window cleaning business with his brother and he's always got plenty of money, not just for himself but for us as well. My mum earns good money as well. If I see something I just go and tap him. He's as soft as shite. He'd give us owt. So, we've got plenty of money and that so we're middle class. [Angela, 1983]

Her second comment made six years later illustrates her changed position. She now has two children to support on her own. Her father's business collapsed and her mother lost her job at the local chemical plant:

> I never wanted to think I was working class, but there was this programme on recently and it made me think about it. Look I've got £77 coming in a week and £79 goes out. I can't pay off the poll tax, water and rent arrears. It can't go out if it doesn't come in. I had to see a solicitor for the debts that I run up when I had Jenna. The bailiffs were over last week. I had to buy things for the baby. I had nothing. So they took me to court and gave me seven days to pay. It was for about £500 but with the interest it flayed up to £1500. Well how could I pay so they sent them

round. I haven't got nothing worth £1,000. Everything is second hand. So I said to him I've got no carpets in the kids' bedrooms and no wallpaper on the wall. The next door neighbour phoned the police. I don't have a phone no more. I know my rights. So, really what all this is about, why I'm telling you this, is it's stupid to think I'm not working class. I can't be anything else no matter how much hoity toity I put on. [Angela, 1989]

It is a television programme that instigates Angela's re-analysis of her economic situation. It speaks to her about her life. She evaluates herself in relation to the conditions in which she now finds herself. For her the cultural level of displaying class – being hoity toity – is minimal in relation to the economic conditions she endures on a daily basis. She cannot escape the fit between the representation and her life. June, Anita, Nicky and Angela all assessed themselves on the basis of their current position and all understood their background and economic circumstances through cultural discourses of classification. Charles (1990) found a similar diversity of factors for understanding and experiencing class by the women she researched. These understandings were not straightforward, they drew on fragmented understandings of popular representations of class.

Classificatory Positions

Academic understandings of class also work to mis/represent the working class. The heroic males of Willis's (1977) study were not unlike the Angry Young Men of 1950s popular representations (Skeggs, 1994a). The categories of proletariat and bourgeoisie came to have popular use and the defining of class through the division of labour remains as one of the central popular and academic means of classification (see Sayer and Walker, 1992). In popular and academic understandings status frequently comes to stand in for class.[4] Academic methods which describe inequality (and try to measure it) by using scales such as the Registrar General's reproduce classifications of inequality by distributing negative and positive values to the various positions they describe.[5,6] When I began the research I used every empirical measure possible to try and identify the class backgrounds of the young women. I collected data on their parents' occupations, family situation, housing, education, employment aspirations, plausibility structures, welfare use, consumer patterns and leisure pursuits.[7] It was very difficult to keep track of all the changes in class indicators. Parental employment was particularly transitory, family structures did not always remain intact and these factors impacted upon other indicators such as housing, consumption and leisure. When the research began the young women were 16 and mostly lived with families upon whom they were economically dependent. By the end of the study in 1992 many had their own families and their circumstances had changed drastically (see Tables 5.1, 5.2 and 5.3).

What we can ascertain from these tables is that a large proportion of the women's mothers were full-time housewives (21 per cent),[8] only 6 per cent of whom were involved in local factory work, hence not providing much access to the informal recruitment system used by the factories. Of fathers: 5 per cent

Table 5.1   *Community Care course (29 students), 1983*

Mother's occupation	no.	Father's occupation	no.
Domestic/school dinners	9	Traditional WC (RG IIIb – V)**	17
Housewife	6	Unemployed	2
Sales assistant	4	Clerk (RG IIIa)**	4
EPH matron/warden	3	Self-employed	3
Secretary/clerk	2	Absent	2
Factory	2		
Self-employed	2		
Total	28*	Total	28*

*One student without parents
**The Registrar General's classification IIIa denotes non-manual clerical and minor supervisory work; IIIb is skilled manual work; IV is semi-skilled manual work and V is unskilled manual work. The working class is usually classified by IIIb–V, although there is dispute over IIIa, see Goldthorpe, 1983.
Note: Total number of students for Tables 5.1, 5.2 and 5.3 = 83

Table 5.2   *Pre-Health Service Course (23 students), 1983*

Mother's occupation	no.	Father's occupation	no.
Domestic/school dinners	5	Traditional WC (RG IIIb–V)*	11
Housewife	4	Unemployed	4
Sales assistant	2	Clerk (RG IIIa)*	4
Nurse/auxiliary	8	Self-employed	3
Secretary/clerk	1	Absent	1
Factory	3		
Total	23	Total	23

*The Registrar General's classification IIIa denotes non-manual clerical and minor supervisory work; IIIb is skilled manual work; IV is semi-skilled manual work and V is unskilled manual work. The working class is usually classified by IIIb–V, although there is dispute over IIIa, see Goldthorpe, 1983.

had disappeared; 15 per cent were transitory (they are listed here for capital purposes); 8 per cent were unemployed and 49 per cent were involved in traditional working-class occupations. A large group, 22 per cent, were self-employed and this varied in scale from odd job man, window cleaner, mechanic, contract labourer and working the informal economy to one who owned an engineering company. For the majority if they had worked for employers other than themselves they would have been semi-skilled or skilled working class. Of the 5 per cent of the women's mothers who were self-employed their work ranged from a registered child-minder to an owner of a dress-design agency (with an unemployed husband). Just from these limited figures we can see that it would be impossible to subsume the social class of these women's mothers into that of their husbands, as has continually been stressed as necessary by Goldthorpe (1983) and critiqued by Stanworth (1984), because the women's mothers' labour participation rates are high

Table 5.3 *Preliminary Certificate in Social Care (31 students), 1983*

Mother's occupation	no.	Father's occupation	no.
Domestic/school dinners	8	Traditional WC (RG IIIb–V)**	13
Housewife	8	Unemployed	1
Sales assistant	2	Clerk (RG IIIa)**	3
Nurse/auxiliary/warden	5	Self-employed	12
Secretary/clerk	5	Absent	1
Factory	0		
Self-employed	2		
Total	31	Total	30*

*One student with no live father
**The Registrar General's classification IIIa denotes non-manual clerical and minor supervisory work; IIIb is skilled manual work; IV is semi-skilled manual work and V is unskilled manual work. The working class is usually classified by IIIb–V, although there is dispute over IIIa, see Goldthorpe, 1983.

and mothers contributed significantly to the family income, especially in the case of absent, transient or unemployed fathers. Nor do shakily self-employed and/or transient fathers easily fit into the Registrar General's classifications, especially when the mother is by far the main breadwinner. Such class heterogeneous families now comprise 39 per cent of British families (Wright, 1989).[9] It was all far more complicated than any straightforward scale would allow.

It was a lot easier to identify the young women by what they were not. They were not middle class as defined culturally and economically (see Savage et al., 1992). They were unlikely to pursue higher education;[10] their access to primary labour market jobs was severely limited;[11] their cultural knowledge and preferences were distinctly not high culture. Their leisure activities and consumption practices do not compare to Savage et al.'s (1992) descriptions of the middle classes. They were never in a position to disregard money, which Lamont (1992) and Bourdieu (1986) define as a major feature of the upper middle classes. They were never in a position to construct distance from necessity, which Bourdieu (1986) defines as a means of constructing distinctions. This difficulty of an accurate definition parallels with their difficulty in describing themselves as working class.

Class positions and class identity, however, are not the same. The young women had a clear knowledge about their 'place' but they were always trying to leave it. Bourdieu (1987) argues that the dispositions acquired as a result of social positioning in social space means that the occupant of a position makes adjustments to it: the sense of one's place must always be a sense of the place of others (Goffman, 1959). But what Bourdieu does not account for is the processes by which the adjustment is either made *or* resisted. Adjustment may not happen. There may not be a fit between positions and dispositions (McCall, 1992). When there is no legitimacy for a position – such as the White working-class sexualized women – therefore no symbolic capital – there may be no adjustment. They cannot adjust themselves to being in that category. This became apparent when exploring how the women constantly emphasized their movement from the category of working class through improvement.

Improving and Passing

The first time I had heard such emphasis being put on improving was when I interviewed the mothers, many of whom were concerned that their daughters should improve upon their lives. Improvement is a means by which cultural capital comes to take on greater value outside of the local. It is when it can be traded in a wider context. Education was the means by which they could convert their caring capital into an economic resource in the labour market; the use of femininity was the means by which they could try and secure future resources through the marriage market. Improving narratives came to take on a greater significance through the course of the research. They related to many aspects of their lives and were always based on generating, accruing and/or displaying cultural capital. They wanted to and/or were involved in improving their appearance; their bodies; their mind; their flats/houses; their relationships; their future. Class was configured through the improvement discourse because in order to improve they had to differentiate themselves from those who did not or could not improve. They were continually making comparisons between themselves and others, creating distances and establishing distinctions and tastes in the process. As Bourdieu (1986) argues, distinctions constantly proliferate. The women had a strong sense of what they did not want to be, but were less sure of what they wanted to be. The knowledge available to them to enable them to resist being classified as working class was based on media and educational representations and limited contact with middle-class people. The middle-class people they met were usually in positions of authority (such as teachers, doctors and social workers). As Press (1991) notes from her research, the working-class women she interviewed learnt about middle-class lifestyles predominantly from television. Their desires not to be seen as working class are lived through their bodies, clothes and (if not living with parents) their homes.

The body and bodily dispositions carry the markers of social class. As Bourdieu (1986) notes the body is the most indisputable materialization of class tastes. Bodies are the physical sites where the relations of class, gender, race, sexuality and age come together and are em-bodied and practised. A respectable body is White, desexualized, hetero-feminine and usually middle class. Class is always coded through bodily dispositions: the body is the most ubiquitous signifier of class. The demands of femininity are such that ideal femininity requires a radical bodily transformation at which virtually every woman is bound to fail, adding shame to her deficiency (Bartky, 1990). When compounded with class, sexuality and race an enormous amount of regulation is faced. This is apparent in the women's comments about the fears presented to them through the bodies of the others that they don't want to be.

Relinquishing regulation and responsibility for bodies (they call it 'letting go') was a dominant theme in their distancing tactics:

> You know you see them walking round town, dead fat, greasy hair, smelly clothes, dirty kids, you know the type, crimplene trousers and all, they just don't care no more, I'd never be like that. [Therese, 1983]

This is not dissimilar to dominant representations of working-class women documented by Rowe (1995) and cited in Chapters 6 and 7. Therese wants to display her distance from them, as does Marie:

> A woman down our way looks just like that, we call her Hilda[12] 'cos of the way she goes on, well her hubby left her and she was dead upset and surprised tell you surprised, I wasn't surprised, I wasn't surprised, I wouldn't be at all surprised if I looked like her and he walked out on me. [Marie, 1983]

The duty and obligation to take care of appearances for heterosexual relationships, as documented by Holland et al. (1991) takes on specific class and – by their absence – race manifestations:

> I like to keep fit. I think it's important to look after yourself. If you walk around looking all fat and scruffy people will think that you just don't care about anything, about yourself or about others. I mean how can you care about anything if you're prepared to let your body go to waste. [Wendy, 1989]

For Wendy the body is the carrier of class signals, of how she sees herself and wants to be seen. It is the external signal that tells others that she cares. Her labour and investments in her body are similar to the labour described by Steedman (1986); they function as descriptors of self. Wendy's body is a marked body, marked by class (and youth; these comments were made from the confidence of youthful bodies, when they were 16):

> We all go down to [X: the local sports centre] and do aerobics. It's a real laugh. We spend all night there. There's some women there though you wouldn't believe. They're huge. It takes them all their time to move from one position to the other. [Julie, 1983]

> Yea, they're always out of time, it's dead funny. They go bright red. Not just red; I mean bright red and by the end and they're all huffing and puffing. [Darren, 1983]

> It's dead sad really like if they'd have gone to aerobics in the first place it would be easy and they'd have never have ended up in that state. Your body's the only thing you've got that's really yours. They can even take the clothes off your back but your body it's there all the time. It's yours and you have to take care of it. [Julie, 1983]

These comments suggest that these women do see and invest in their bodies as a form of cultural capital. It is the means by which they can tell others who they are. Julie pertinently points to the possessive relationship she has to her body; it is seen to be owned and invested in by the person who inhabits it. They regulate their bodies to make sure that they cannot be seen to be one who does not or cannot care. Fat signifies immovability; social mobility, they maintain, is less likely in a fat body. Douglas (1988) notes how the body is the central metaphor of political and social order. The working-class body which is signalled through fat is the one that has given up the hope of ever 'improving', of becoming middle class. It is the body which is recognized for what it is: a working-class body that is beyond the regulation and discipline required to be part of social and cultural exchanges. Historically, Bourke (1994) notes, the white working-class body did actually look significantly different from the middle-class body because it was shorter and less healthy. It still is less healthy and less likely to live as long; whilst the obvious differences have decreased, bodies still send off signals about class (see the Black Report 1982, Benzevale et al., 1995; Joseph Rowntree Foundation, 1995). Bourdieu (1986) argues that bodily dimensions (volume, height, weight); bodily shapes (round or square, stiff or supple, straight or curved) and bodily forms (expressed through treating it, caring for it, feeding it, and maintaining it) reveal the deepest dispositions of class, gender and race. The texts of class, femininity, sexuality and race combine to produce a respectable body. It is one that is taken care of. It is the care of the self for the self and for others, a technology of individual domination of how an individual acts upon themselves in the technology of the self (Foucault, 1988). But also of how one deflects classification and deters the flow of cultural capital from the body.

The surface of their bodies is the site upon which distinctions can be drawn. Skills and labour such as dressing-up and making-up are used to display the desire to pass as not working class. Armstrong and Tennenhouse (1987) note how bourgeois women's desire was historically always coded (through dress, literature and visual arts) with respectability. Class is signified through elegance and sophistication which demonstrate a dissimulation from the working class but a simulation of the middle class. The fantasy of the 'other' (the middle-class, elegant sophisticate) becomes part of the construction of one's self. For instance, Mary makes clear distinctions between herself and other women and directly claims to be respectable. These are the ways in which class is spoken:

> *Mary*: I do get dressed up, I get dressed up, I call it getting tarted up but I'm not tarty. Karen will ring up and say 'are you getting tarted up tonight?' I'm aware that I can't wear certain things that are too tarty say mini-skirts, they're tarty. I just can't wear them, they don't do anything for me, they don't suit me. They're not me, they're not my character, they're not me, they're . . . I wear classy clothes. I don't want to sound snobby but I like classical dresses, things that don't go out of fashion. I expect them to last five years. People comment on it all the time. John actually commented on it at my party. I had a long red skirt and a blouse and he said 'you look exquisitely elegant, you look totally different'. There was a girl here in a mini-skirt and a tight top and all the men were eyeing her and I said I should have worn my mini and boob tube to him and he says no, you're elegant . . . I like to look good, I like to have things no one else round here will ever have. I spend less money now that I've got the house, now I buy a dress for £70 or so every six months. It's better than £20 on a mini-skirt every month.

> *Bev*: What's the image?

> *Mary*: I don't know I've always wanted to be different. You see them round here with all the same clothes. My clothing says I'm different. I think my clothing says I'm respectable. I probably do it without thinking. I'm not aware of it, half the time if I throw on a pair of trousers and a blouse it works . . . Then I saw a girl I hadn't seen for ages and she said you look really elegant. (1991)

Mary clearly constructs herself as different, as respectable. This is validated through the responses given by others (and in this case not imaginary middle-class others) who help to validate Mary's difference. (I specifically don't use the term legitimate as her friends do not possess the symbolic power to legitimate her cultural capital; the validation is local.) Clothing is used by Mary as a vocabulary which conveys moral quality. Hollander (1988) notes how objects of clothing do become invested with intangible and abstract elements that pertain to the moral and social order. Fashion – usually a form of working-class cultural capital (see Chapter 6) – is sacrificed for the sake of signalling middle-class respectability. Clothes are a means by which Mary pictures herself, pictures her difference and her respectability. Clothing enables an identification of the other and an identification with the other. Clothes are one element which display Mary's knowing (about representations and skills of how to put representations to work) taste:

> Taste is the practical operator of the transmution of things into distinct and distinctive signs, of continuous distributions into discontinuous oppositions; it raises the differences inscribed in the physical order of bodies to the symbolic order of significant distinctions. (Bourdieu, 1986: 175)

Classy clothes, exquisitely elegant and anti-fashion vocabulary combine to present a picture of non-working-classness, a picture that is reproduced daily through women's magazines without directly signifying class. Mary is quick to make distance from the tarty: the sign of the working-class woman. When Mary 'puts on' her image it is one which combines gender, race and class. She wants to position herself, to gain the value and legitimacy, of a respectable White middle-class woman. Yet elegance is a term which enables glamour to remain.[13] To be elegant is not to be completely desexualized; rather she does it with class (middle-classness). Mary's comments also suggest that just as the 'cared for' body came to stand for a 'self', clothes do the same. Mary does not wear mini-skirts because they are not her character, they are not her. Elias (1982) would argue that this is part of a long trend from the sixteenth century where the perspective developed that outward physical appearances were representative of inner character. This has led some writers such as Finkelstein (1991) to argue that a sense of self is the embodiment of the representational fiction of a self. It is a stylized self which enables the women to display how different they are from others. They use imaginary others dialogically to create distance from known others. Signifying difference and investing in herself has become a preoccupation for Jane C:

> I've just bought my gran's present, it's Monet jewellery. Good stuff. I've started buying for Christmas. I've bought this velvet coat, it's Pamplemousse. It's only from a catalogue – the extra bit with Freemans – it was only £50, not lined or anything. I just went mad. I went to Hobbs in Manchester and bought two pairs of shoes and got a couple of things from Next and hats and an Adidas track suit: it's not shell, it's good quality. I used to be a real impulsive spender but now I don't like that, now I shop go home and think about it. Sometimes I felt like I wasn't my own person and I'd come home with all these stupid things that I'd never wear. It was like I didn't own myself. [Jane C, 1991]

For Jane C having the right labels becomes a construction of 'rights' (as opposed to 'wrongs'). She knows, for instance, that Freeman's is wrong but excuses it because it is cheap. Every item comes with a label which signifies her knowledge and her difference. It is part of a knowing process. Jane C will not be shamed as she now knows what to do with her money although she claims she once did not. Jane C's desire to own the right objects includes herself. She knows the clothing signifiers of working-classness such as shell suits and she is careful to mark her distance from them. Clothing and objects are experienced intimately: they signify the worth of the person. This is not just about difference but also about deflecting associations of negative value. They are ways of protecting and distancing oneself from the pathological and worthless. These label name checks may seem trivial but as Steedman remarks of her own mother's desire for objects:

> There is no language of desire that can present what my mother wanted as anything but supremely trivial; indeed, there is no language that does not let the literal accents of class show. (1986: 113)

Steedman describes her mother's desires as the material stepping stones of escape. For Jane C this extends to more than clothing. She wants to mark her distinction and pass as *not* working class, not just through consumer goods and practice, but through activities that bear the mark of the middle class: opera:

> I've changed so much. I go to operas now [embarrassed laughter]. Don't laugh [*I wasn't*]. It's true. I saw *Carmen* two weeks ago. I went to Birmingham with my mum and nan. We're going to *Porgy and Bess* but it's meant to be very heavy. I just like the music, I don't understand what's going on in the foreign language ones but the music is so moving, and then we're going to Disney on Ice. I am a really different person. I like classical music. I listen to it on the radio when I'm at home. [Jane C, 1992]

I note the embarrassed laughter because Jane C did not feel entirely comfortable telling me this.[14] She wanted me to know, especially because I had asked about class, but she was not sure of my response. The problem with passing is that someone may catch you out. Jane C is aware that there are hierarchies within opera, indicated when she refers to *Porgy and Bess* as being 'heavy' and when she references her immediate pleasure (the way the music moves her) over the usual (middle-class) distanced analytical understanding of opera. She feels she has to defend her pleasure. She is dialogically aware that her taste may not engender approval, even though it is mentioned to signify her difference from others. Trying to pass as middle class, to be accepted into another group, to know how to be accepted, generates considerable anxieties for those who hope to pass. And passing may not get any support from others because it is an implicit critique of those from whom distance is being drawn and who do not want to engage in passing. Because the women draw upon representations to know what it means to be middle class they become locked into thinking that representing themselves in the same way will produce similar results. But representations are not dispositions. They are symbolic appearances produced as a result of struggles over cultural capital. They are part of a far wider symbolic nexus and can only gain value when they are converted into symbolic capital. For the conversion into symbolic capital they must have access to power networks; they have to be legitimated by those with power. They can never get it 'right' because they do not have access to the requisite amounts of knowledge and history which would enable them to know what getting it right really means.[15] One of the difficulties encountered in trying to take on cultural objects, attitudes and values which are not directly accessible from a working-class position is that it also involves taking on the middle-class pretensions which have been a source of ridicule. Bourdieu (1986) defines the practices perceived as pretensions as a result of the manifest discrepancy between ambition and possibility. To try to pass is to display ambition and the dis-ease at making it possible.

Their passing does not involve ironic mimicry (as has been suggested in Black passing attempts: see Bhabha, 1994) because it wants to be taken seriously; because it speaks from a position of powerlessness and insecurity. In this sense their attempts to pass are not a form of insubordination; rather they are dissimulations, performances of a desire not to be, a desire not to be shamed but a desire to be legitimated. They do not displace the middle class as normalized in a way that gay and lesbian passing may displace heterosexuality. Nor can they gain any pleasure from the passing as they could with sexual masquerade and gendered masquerade. Non-ironic passing engenders anxiety and insecurity.

Yet not all women can spare the time, energy or money to concentrate on their representational constructions, but still disidentifications with pathologized signs of working-classness are made:

> Don't worry much about my appearance now, like when I was 16. It seems light years ago. When I was single I would put make-up on and make my hair just so, now I don't bother. I've never been one for much make-up because I don't need to wear much. Plus we never go out to wear it. I don't know I've always seemed so worn out. We all go to me mum's for the hairdresser, Shirley she goes round there and we all meet up. I never spend on myself. I get things for birthdays and Christmas but if I walked out and came home and said to Pete I've seen a gorgeous jumper – now it's very rare I say anything like that – he'd say turn round and say go and get it. But it's rare that I bother. With clothes you have to put others before yourself. *I've got good **clean** clothes and that's the main thing. They're clean. I keep clean.* I'm quite happy to walk around in jeans and jogging pants and I do that most days. I want to be comfy. But mind I do get the urge to go out and blow it all, when the family allowance comes on Monday I go into town but I work out first what I can buy for those two [children] £69.80 for two – that doesn't even buy their shoes. When they go to school I go to Clarks.[16] [Linda, 1992; emphasis added]

Linda's concerns do not lie in showing she is visually different from others but in claiming a respectable disposition. She doesn't have the requisite capitals (economic, cultural, social and symbolic) to invest in such distinctions but she does have the educational capital of 'caring' which enables her to legitimate her distinction. For Linda having her hair done is a medium for sociability rather than a means to represent herself as different. But still she is concerned to show some difference and that she is respectable. Linda's lack of investment in herself may be a result of her occupying public space far less frequently than Mary or Jane C; she is less under external scrutiny. But also, her investments have changed. They have transferred to her children, who will now carry them for her. She gives them all the cultural capital that she can transmit. Her major concern is that she is doing right for her children. The concern shifts from displays of self-distinctiveness to displays of doing the right thing. The 'right' thing as you may remember from Chapter 4 means fitting into different class standards which are based on different financial and moral economies. Here it is down to buying the right things. Linda's own appearance is less of an issue than achieving the right standards for her children. This is even more of an issue for Jane M who is under public scrutiny and who enters the social spaces of the middle class by sending her son to a private nursery in a wealthy suburb of Manchester:

> *Jane M*: I'm always last clothes wise. I wear the same things day in and day out and they [the children] have a different outfit every day and lots of toys and their bedrooms have been done. So we want the best for them, if it's for them he won't worry about the cost. I never have the time for make-up, people have to take me as they find me. With the mums at school I couldn't compete clothes wise with all their designer labels and that, I don't even recognize. I do make some effort because I want to be accepted so I do get changed when I go to pick him up. I wouldn't go in my slobby jogging suit that I live in. I do want to make an effort.

> *Bev*: Is this about social class?

> *Jane M*: I don't want them to look at you and say they're the poor ones and it'll reflect on the kids and they won't be invited round to play so it'll be bad for them. You want to be accepted. (1992)

Jane M is more concerned to fit into the middle classes than display her difference from the working class. The emphasis is changed. Appearance seems to be purely functional for Jane M but she has to change it for potential external vetting so as not to bring shame on her son. The shame she feels about social positioning is not dissimilar to the shame induced through displays of sexuality (as shown in Chapter 7). She is very conscious that she is in a very different social class. This is not induced by an imaginary other, the product of representations, but from her experiences of middle-class women. She knows they have the power to judge and inflict shame on her family. And shame, as Scheff (1994) notes, is the most social and reflexive of all emotions: Jane M is conscious that the family money and cultural investments are for her children not for herself. Her children have the best to make sure that they are not recognized as poor, as working class (as she once recognized herself). She does not want to jeopardize her children's ability to capitalize on the nursery education – the educational capital – which they are struggling to provide.

Displays of distinction and sites of investment are not just produced through bodies, appearance, children and leisure. Every site becomes a marker. The home is a central site for creatively producing a sense of themselves (and sometimes their family) through the use and organization of consumer goods (see Carter, 1990). The home is an important site for displaying cultural investments. Homes also become the site for guilt as they cost so much more to put together. When the women showed me round their houses, wardrobes, kitchens, record collections, and so on, there was an almost constant apology for the things I was being shown:

> We would really like to have real antiques but they cost so much money and they're not as solid as this furniture. So this'll have to do until we can afford better. Personally, I prefer this to something that's probably full of insects. [Janet, 1986]

Here is expressed a knowledge that antiques should be preferred and are the 'real' thing, alongside an ambivalence about the age, stability and hygiene of old furniture. Janet is caught between two different discourses, that of hygiene and antique authenticity. The former is used to discount the latter. Janet knows what she prefers, but also knows what she should prefer:

> I know you're meant to have real paintings on your wall, but I love these prints [Athena's ballet dancers]. I just think the price for real paintings is ridiculous and frankly we've got other uses for our money. [Janet, 1986]

> When we moved in the kitchen was all white melamine, straight from MFI so we ripped it out straightaway. I put my foot down, I said we're not having that cheap stuff in here. The kitchen cost a fortune but I love it and I love spending time in here. But I'm afraid that to get it right in here means we've not been able to afford to do anything else, so I'm sorry the rest of the house dulls by comparison. I think I'd spend all my time in here if I could. It's my room. We would have done the rest but what with all the redundancies at ICI now you've just got to be careful. [Darren, 1992]

> A lot of the stuff in here is just rubbish that our family gave me. It's like I'd never be seen dead with that sofa. We had a real row about it at first. I said I'm not going to have it in here, in my house. Me mam, she said, who did I think I was, she said I should sit on bare floorboards. She said I couldn't have it after I didn't want it. But I had to have something to sit on, didn't I. So she agreed in the end. It's like the drawers upstairs, they're horrible, did you notice them? They shouldn't have house room really but I had nowhere to put things. [Janice, 1989]

> We wanted to buy all new when we moved in but what with the cost of the wedding we just couldn't. I was dead upset at first, I was ashamed to have people round with everybody else's castouts, but we're replacing it bit by bit. It looks odd though, don't you think? [Sharon, 1986]

The comments included here are expressed as questions in need of approval or as statements which dare to be challenged. All display a knowledge that there is another more highly valued way of doing things which they have yet to achieve.[17] The pleasure they get from their homes and the time they spend on them is always disrupted by their knowledge of a judgemental external other who positions them as surveillant of themselves, what Bakhtin (1984) identifies as a hidden polemic – the 'policing' of the superior other. This is not dissimilar to the women of Ann Gray's (1992) study whose responses to television viewing were always mediated through the discourse of populism. They were aware of what was considered to be in either good or bad taste and monitored their responses accordingly.

This surveillance covers not just what the women consume but also the way their labour is used to convert these consumer goods into an aesthetic disposition. It is their buying and creative practices which they evaluate on the basis of the imagined judgements of others. They are positioned by their furniture and paint. When a visitor enters the house they see their most intimate environments through the eyes of the other and they apologize. They continually doubt their own judgements. This is the emotional politics of class. They can never have the certainty that they are doing it right which is one of the main signifiers of middle-class dispositions (Bourdieu, 1986). This lack of certainty means that they cannot make use of social space in the same way; they close off their access through their doubt and scrutiny of themselves. They care about how they are seen in the eyes of the other. They feel they have to prove themselves through every object, every aesthetic display, every appearance. Their taste in furniture and aesthetic organization becomes along with their clothes, body, caring practices and every other aspect of their lives a site of doubt. A site where they are never sure if they are getting it right. They assume that certainty exists elsewhere; that others have it. There is no counter-cultural valuation of their homes.[18] The working class are never free from the judgements of imaginary and real others that position them, not just as different, but as inferior, as inadequate. Homes and bodies are where respectability is displayed but where class is lived out as the most omnipresent form, engendering surveillance and constant assessment of themselves. It is these areas where taste operates to commit symbolic violence, as Bourdieu notes:

> if there is any terrorism it is in the peremptory verdicts which, in the name of taste, condemn to ridicule, indignity, shame, silence . . . men and women who simply fall short, in the eyes of their judges, of the right way of being and doing. (1986: 511)

What they don't have is access to the cultural capital, to the right kind of knowledge. It is knowledge that is difficult to access and use when one is not accustomed to it, when it is not part of the background and dispositions which are used to define oneself. As Bourdieu (1986) notes, it takes a considerable amount of schooling and extracurricular work to impart the 'right' cultural capital. It is these very personal dispositions, their affections, which generate evaluations and regulations of themselves. As Kuhn notes:

> Class is not just about the way you talk, or dress, or furnish your home; it is not just about the job you do or how much money you make doing it; nor is it merely about whether or not you have A levels or went to university, nor which university you went to. Class is something beneath your clothes, under your skin, in your reflexes, in your psyche, at the very core of your being. In the all-encompassing English class system, if you know that you are in the 'wrong' class, you know that therefore you are a valueless person. (1995: 98)

Class becomes internalized as an intimate form of subjectivity, experienced as knowledge of always not being 'right'. Restrictions on access to the 'right' knowledge, the 'right' cultural capital, which can be traded means that there are limits to their passing as middle class.[19] Whilst many of the anxieties over bodies, homes, children and clothes may be experienced by middle-class women too, it is the particular manifestation that they take that gives them the classed character. The anxieties of working-class women are always made through reference to something to which they do not have access, be it money, knowledge or space. They know that nearly everything they do will be recognized as classed. This is very different to feeling inadequate but being normalized at the same time where the anxiety is not of a class based character. This is why gender and class are inseparable. The women never see themselves as just women; it is always read through class. This is evidenced clearly through their desires to pass.

The problem with the desire to pass as middle class is that it represents absolutely no challenge to the class system and reproduces the hierarchies and evaluations which regulate, devalue and delegitimate the working class. Passing also assumes a fit between the reality of one group and the naturalizing of its definition. The middle class do not need to pass. A lack of concern with class means that one does not have to try to pass to gain cultural (and other) capitals. The capitals already exist. They can, of course, be disavowed on an interpersonal level but this does not have any negative consequences for their cultural and social valuing. In fact there are many institutionalized ways and fashions which enable the denial of middle-classness: grunge fashion and music being the most obvious. The (young) middle class do try to pass, as the following comments demonstrate and they too are clearly taken as what they are trying to pass from:

> What I've come to notice which I think is really odd and it's because we go to the Kings Head sometimes, is that some of the really, really posh ones are dead scruffy. Like they make no effort at all. It's like you spend all your life and money trying to look good and then those who have loads just don't bother. It kind of reverses it. In the Kings it's a reversal the really rich are dead scruffy and the less well off are dead smart. It's stupid don't you think. [Sue, 1992]

> Yea, I've seen that in Alderly Edge with the younger ones. I guess it's because they're students and they are trying to show how clever and bohemian they are. But it is really clever because like if you were poor or at least not very well off you wouldn't dare look that scruffy because everybody would know just how little money you had so it's really only the very rich who can get away with it. What I mean is it's just like another way of maintaining differences between groups. You have to be really rich to be really scruffy or else you'd feel really bad and be dead ashamed of yourself but they're not, they get away with it. [Julie, 1992]

The consciously constructed non-respectable appearance of the middle classes does not work because there are many signifiers, of which appearance is only one. In this case bodies, use of space through movement and confidence send strong class signals. Moreover, playing at not being middle class does not jeopardize their ability to use and capitalize upon their cultural capital, nor is it likely to generate shame and humiliation when it does not work. In fact whole subcultures are established which play at not being seen to be middle class (Hulme in Manchester, for instance).[20] The other central difference is that the middle class have far more alternatives to how they *can be*. It is easier for them to play at passing simply because the ones who can judge their failure to pass have little impact and little social power. Their judgements do not restrict the conversion of cultural into symbolic capital. The working class have historically been unable to establish institutions to legitimate their knowledge and impose 'right' standards on others. The comments of Sue and Julie indicate a clear consciousness of what it means to have certainty about the right displays. They realize that it is only those who are wealthy who can play at being poor. They know that they do not have that option. They also know that this is how differences are maintained and that they are positioned through it. They know that there are certain ways of being and doing to which they do not have access. This generates resentment. There was not a clear split between those who wanted to pass and those who resented. These two affects were held together. The desires to pass, or not to be recognized as working class are generated from experiences of being positioned by others:

> We'd all gone up to Manchester the other Saturday, you know for a day out, the three of us. It was alright, in fact we had a right laugh . . . but we were in Kendals during the day, you know where the really posh food is, and we were laughing about all the chocolates and how many we could eat – if we could afford them – and this woman she just looked at us. If looks could kill. Like we were only standing there. We weren't doing anything wrong. We weren't scruffy or anything. She just looked. It was like it was her place and we didn't belong there. And you know what we just all walked away. We should have punched her in the face. We didn't say anything until about half an hour later. Can you imagine? Well and truly put in our place . . . It's things like that that put you off going. You feel better staying around here. [Wendy, 1986]

> That's like when you're walking through the perfume bit of Owen and Owen and they're spraying perfume all over the posh ones and you know you're not going to get any. Me and Jane we used to stand there till she sprayed us. [Morag, 1986]

> When I first went to work as a nanny I couldn't stand it. They really think they're something else. They treat you like shit. What I've noticed is they never look at you. Well they do at first they look you all over and make you feel like a door rag, but then they just tell you what to do. One of them once asked me if I had any other clothes. Some of them want you to know you're shit in comparison to them. I jacked it in shit money, being made to feel like shit. Even the kids. They learn really early that you're not worth the ground they walk on. They're bastards. [Cynthia, 1992]

> They always assume they have a right to anything and everything. It's like whatever they are doing that's their right. They just think the world is made for them. [Angela, 1989]

> When we were at school we used to beat them all up. We'd wait for them coming down our way going home from school. They frighten dead easy. But it's like now they're the ones getting their own back. They have money and cars and we're still hanging around here. [Therese, 1989]

These comments, selected from many, show the fear, the desire, the resentment, hatred and humiliation. Class relations are felt as they are lived, and these feelings generate strong emotions, sometimes violence, degradation *and* resistance. Space and place are consistent themes in their narratives. The women know they are being positioned as contagious, not-belonging or dirty: that is their situated knowledge. They know they occupy space in different ways. This is articulated as rights-to. They do not believe they have the same entitlements, the access to the same rights, which is made especially apparent in Angela's commentary. It is also shown in Wendy's account where she, at first, holds herself and friends responsible for the look they engender, 'we weren't scruffy or anything' she insists, as if being scruffy would warrant such a look. They are made to feel invisible, as Mary notes with anger and as Cynthia feels. It is this double movement of being made to feel invisible and under scrutiny which generates resentment. They are either designated wrong or they feel they do not exist. Cynthia also notes how even young middle-class children learn to position themselves in a social hierarchy. The middle-class gaze takes on a life of its own. It doesn't need to be enacted to be felt. However, knowing the very lucid criticisms made of the monolithic male gaze, which is said to similarly position women within its sights we need to be circumspect about how this works.[21] The gaze may be a product of their pro-jected fear of the other. Their indignance generates judgemental responses about those they feel are judging them. They do not feel this judgement as a 'right' but as justified responses to the indignity they have to endure. Those who are put in their place do respond. But the fighting outside school and the linguistic indignation are not enough to generate a coherent oppositional politics. It is also worth noting that class hatred is not just one-way as Frazer's (1992) research with upper-class girls suggests.

The women may make disidentifications from being positioned as working class but this does not mean to say that they want to take on the whole pack-age of being middle class. Whilst the imaginary middle class may represent elegance and sophistication, the real middle-class may behave in ways the women do not want to be associated with, as the following comments suggest:

It's the way they think they know about things all the time. Sue's [her sister] brother-in-law is a scream. He sits there pontificating. Talking absolute shite about everything. I just think he's a dickhead. We all do. Everyone takes the piss out of him. [Cindy, 1989]

They come into the restaurant ordering things in a hoity toity manner. They're really ignorant. It's fucking pizzas for Christ sakes. We'd put snot on their pizzas – you can never tell, and they're usually dead stingy with the tips. You can always tell the rich ones, they keep hold of their money. [Rachel, 1986]

What gets me about these people with loads of money is they look crap. They haven't a clue about style, about what to wear, about how to put things together. If I had that much money I'd look fucking brilliant. [Cynthia, 1992]

In this way they are involved in what Bourdieu (1986) would define as class politics. They are exposing the arbitrariness of taken for granted cat-egories; a political battle at which feminism has been so adept. They cannot pass as completely middle class because they do not want to. They respect (and resent) the power of the middle classes but despise them for the power they effect. The middle class is imaged as heterogeneous in their accounts of middle-class behaviour. It is not homogeneous, but an 'other' which has some desirable dispositions and powers. There are many ways of being, known from representations and their experiences of the middle class, which they do not want to be. The middle classes are often a source of ridicule and contempt. What the women desire is to be valued, not pathologized.

Conclusion

By insisting on the centrality of class to the lives of the women I am trying to claim and legitimate one important aspect of their experience which they consciously try to disclaim. Even though they dissimulate from class, their dissimulations are produced through it. In so doing I want to suggest that class is not just a representation, nor a subject position which can be taken off a discursive shelf and worn at will or a social position which can be occupied voluntarily. Rather, I want to suggest that class is structural. It involves the institutionalization of capitals. It informs access to and how subject positions such as respectability and caring can be taken up. There is not a free fall or 'choice' over subject positions as Alcoff (1988) would suggest, but rather circumscribed access and movement between subject positions. At birth we are allocated into these spaces with their concomitant institutional organization such as the institutions of heterosexuality, the family and the racial and sexual division of labour. They pre-exist our agency but we contribute to their reproduction and reformulation; they frame our responses. Identities are not then reflections of objective social positions which is how class is often theorized (if at all). This, as Calhoun (1994) points out, would be to see identities always retrospectively. Nor are the social positions essential categories. Identities are continually in the process of being re-produced as responses to social positions, through access to representational systems and in the conversion of forms of capital.

This chapter has shown how social positions and cultural representations are entered into. These bring with them and enable access to differential amounts of capital. For White working-class women this capital is limited:[22] it is difficult to trade with it on a market in which symbolic delegitimation has occurred. Their experiences were dominated by exclusion from areas to trade their inherited capitals. They find it very difficult to trade on being working class and even more difficult to find anything positive associated with their working-class positioning. As the historical and contemporary analysis of class representations suggests, we should not be surprised that the women do not want to be recognized as such. However, the definitions of working-class-ness were by no means straightforward. When they did attempt to identify themselves they first had difficulties finding a discourse of class and, second, had problems with the methods of classification used to define it. This was paralleled in the academic accounts of class where no clear meaning is agreed upon and where classifications systems are strongly contested. The women tried to make sense of their class positioning through employment, background, housing and money. They had a strong sense that their social and cultural positioning was unjust. They did not adjust to their social positioning (as Bourdieu 1986) would suggest. Rather they made strenuous efforts to deny, disidentify and dissimulate. These were affective responses; class was lived as a structure of feeling. Class is still a hidden injury (Sennett and Cobb, 1977). They attempted to display their distinction from being classified as working-class through a variety of methods. To do so they made investments in their bodies, clothes, consumption practices, leisure pursuits and homes. These investments indicated a strong desire to pass as middle class. But it was only an imaginary middle class that they wanted to be. They did not want to take on the whole package of dispositions. Their responses to classification were informed by fear, desire, resentment and humiliation. They were individualistic responses produced through their own bodies and influencing their movement through social space. In this sense they become implicated in a similar mechanism to that which enabled the construction of the caring self. Their class subjectivity monitors itself dialogically through the real and imaginary experiences, perceptions and judgements of others.

It thus seems unlikely that the actions of these women are likely to lead to class politics, to class organization or even to class consciousness of a directly articulated form. These women are highly sensitive to issues of class and difference but they have no discourses available for them to articulate it as a positive identity.[23] Their class struggle is waged on a daily basis to overcome the denigration and delegitimizing associated with their class positioning. This is why representations are a key site in this class struggle; they are where symbolic violence occurs.[24]

Who would want to be seen as working class? (Possibly only academics are left.)[25] Within the field of cultural criticism working-class people have come to be seen as bearing the elemental simplicity of class consciousness and little more. They have always been the site for the projected longings of the rebellious middle classes who put their investment in change in others rather than themselves. But these projections are here being refused. The women's consciousness of their classifications, their devaluing, their inability to get it right and their inability *to be* without shame, humiliation and judgement is part of the reason why they turn to respectability and responsibility as a means of establishing a valued and legitimate way of being and way of being seen.[26]

The next chapter will explore how the experience of the category 'woman' is negotiated through femininity. Femininity is always defined through class and as a result of this the women respond to it in a similar way: it is not taken on willingly and it rarely fits.

Notes

1 Black representations have similar historical negative connotations (Fryer, 1984) but the symbolic value of Blackness has been produced as a result of cultural struggles and marketing.
2 Thirty-nine per cent of the women are still single and 18 per cent still live at home. This is due to the lack of affordable housing, although two women own their own homes. Ownership is more likely if the women are married (31 per cent). Only a small number cohabit.
3 One of Britain's most popular soaps *Coronation Street* recently satirized the conversion of terraced houses by painting the outside of the house of the most working-class couple, the Duckworths, blue and yellow. The use of such a joke suggests the symbolic annihilation of those with aspirations within the working class to display their differences.

4 Status is frequently articulated *as class* whereas I would argue that status distinctions are social manifestations of class relationships. Status is a social mechanism produced within and through class divisions.

5 See, for instance, the debates in the journal *Sociology* which focus on the initial work of Goldthorpe (1983) to discuss how to accurately measure (hence represent) class. Feminists such as Stanworth (1984) have pointed to how these representations function to exclude women. Occupation, as Charles (1990) notes, is not the same as class.

6 I still remember some of the women's distress when having been given information on the RG scale they realized their father's occupation positioned them at the bottom.

7 This is not, however, a multivariate pluralist analysis of class which suggests that class is becoming redundant as a measure of social positioning. I do not see class decomposition as a generalized phenomenon (see Holton and Turner, 1989). In fact my empirical work drew me to see class as even more substantive in the construction of opportunities, aspirations, physical movement and ideals, than I thought at the beginning of the project.

8 All the mothers involved in housework had previously been in the labour market. The heightened labour market participation rates of middle-aged women indicate that many of this category will become re-employed.

9 Although again it depends how the figures are used. Graetz (1991) argues that the numbers are likely to be smaller because of the inflexibility of previous studies.

10 Initially none had any aspirations to pursue education after they finished at the further education college. As a result of lots of discussions and a trip to a university three did go on to higher education to do Sociology.

11 Through nursing and in-service courses one now works as a medical systems trainer. Two who pursued higher education work as qualified social workers.

12 Hilda comes from the character Hilda Ogden who was a caricature of pathological working class on the soap *Coronation Street*.

13 This is also age related. At a younger age Mary's concern (as for many of the others) was to be trendy. Trendiness is associated with youth. Wearing clothes which were seen to be associated with far younger women was seen to be nearly as bad as being tarty.

14 Nor do I telling you. Your responses will depend upon your positionings. But Jane C's comment exemplifies the problems representing those who are not middle class. They can be measured from a position of different knowledge and found wanting.

15 This is a pertinent methodological problem for the researcher who does not have the middle-class history and cultural understanding to know what 'getting it right' really means. The researcher, however, has greater access to those who do 'get it right' all their lives, and can therefore use her 'new' knowledge to make assessments of how others measure-up.

16 Clarks is the trade name of an expensive shoe manufacturer, which carries a reputation for sensible strong shoes.

17 One of the hidden injuries of class may be that a sign of being middle class is an indifference to such material signifiers through the normalization of their 'taste'.

18 This may be why Ikea and Habitat are so successful. They market 'taste' and modernity (in Ikea's case through national identifications) and provide the security of knowing it is possible to 'get it right'.

19 I am using the term passing to refer to trying to be something that one is not. This does assume that one is something and in this case the something is the occupation of a class position. It can also be a race or gender position that is being passed from/into/over. I am not using the term in the ethnomethodological sense implied by Garfinkel (1967) who argues that everyone is continually passing, i.e. doing something in order to be taken as she intends because I believe there are class-based limitations on what one can represent oneself as.

20 This playing at not being middle class is now being institutionalized through the *Homes for Change* scheme whereby the middle-class squatters take up permanent residences built from private and council funds, to form their own community. The working-class residents of Hulme were desperate to leave when the area became disrespectable as it was taken over by (middle-class) students and squatters.

21 See Stacey (1994) for an overview of the arguments.

22 This formula of capitals can be applied to all social configurations. It cannot, however, tell us how these configurations will be experienced. That is the job of the researcher.

23 For Black working-class women access to an alternative positive identity (being Black) may be available.

24 Feminism has been (relatively) successful at challenging the negative valuing of women whereas Marxism, as the only coherent oppositional position on class, has been unable to generate such a popular struggle and is now itself under enormous discrediting attempts.

25 Lynne Pearce notes in personal communication that only once one has been given middle-class citizenship can one take pride in one's roots and not be ashamed because 'what I was is not what I now am'.

26 Alex Callinicos notes in personal communication in response to this chapter that resistance to the term working class should not be seen to detract from the increase in trade-union consciousness that is occurring in 1990s Britain. He points out that there are still 9 million trade unionists in Britain and he identifies a trend whereby workers who previously saw themselves as professional (such as teachers, bank-workers and nurses) are adopting trade-union methods of collective action.

6

Ambivalent Femininities

Recognition is a significant moment in the construction of subjectivity. This chapter asks how do the women recognize themselves as feminine subjects. It explores the historical emergence of the category femininity and explores how the legacies of this historical production remain. Femininity is examined in its contemporary manifestations through the processes by which the women mediate textually produced femininity. It investigates how the women take up, try on and discard positions of femininity in order to make investments in the circuits of exchange in which they are located. The use to which femininity as appearance is put to make performances and to masquerade is analysed. Issues of glamour and desirability are explored as the means by which the material and semiotic are translated into the affective and experienced as a structure of feeling (Williams, 1961, 1977). There are close links between this chapter and Chapter 7 on heterosexuality, which together show how the category 'woman' is occupied, resisted, experienced and produced through processes of differentiation.

Femininity is the process through which women are gendered and become specific sorts of women. The process of becoming feminine, Smith (1988) argues, occurs in the spaces of textually mediated discourse, in the *dialectic* between the active creating subject and the organization of her activity in and by texts, produced in the interests of a wider global market.[1] The ability to engage in this dialectic is a matter of social positioning and access to texts. Being, becoming, practising and doing femininity are very different things for women of different classes, races, ages and nations. If subjectivity is produced through experience (as suggested earlier by de Lauretis, 1984 and Scott, 1992) we can see how becoming respectable proceeds through the experience of textually mediated femininity.

This chapter is organized into three sections. The first provides a brief historical framework to show how the sign of femininity is always classed. This establishes the framework for the analysis. The second section explores the assumed relationship between femininity and appearance, arguing that appearance is far more complex than it at first may appear. The third section shows how femininity is lived through glamour, desirability and marriage. The different feminine performances that the women make have different implications for their subjective constructions; some are meaningful, others are not. This should also have an impact on how we theorize experience.

Classed Femininities

Poovey (1984) charts how the emergence of femininity as an ideal was produced through textuality in the eighteenth century. The femininity produced
had an affinity with the habitus of the upper classes, of ease, restraint, calm
and luxurious decoration. It was produced as a sign of difference from other
women. Conduct books and magazines encapsulated this habitus with the
concept of the 'lady' which equated conduct with appearance. This ideal of
the lady continued to be reproduced into the nineteenth century where both
textual and visual technologies operated as a strong marker for the development of gendered notions of sexual propriety (Nead, 1988; Pollock, 1989;
Lury, 1993). Through the development of the textually mediated feminine
ideal the visual became the site where values were allocated to groups of
women and the construction of appearance as a sign of value became established. White middle-class femininity was defined as the ideal (see Chapter 3),
but also as the most passive and dependent of femininities. It was always
coded as respectable.

By the end of the nineteenth century femininity had become established as
a (middle-) classed sign, a sign of a particular form of womanhood. It was,
Walkerdine (1989) argues, a projection of male fantasy. Femininity was seen
to be the *property* of middle-class women who could *prove* themselves to be
respectable through their appearance and conduct. Because femininity developed as a classed sign it became imbued with different amounts of power, as
Ware (1992) has shown. White middle-class women could use their proximity
to the sign of femininity to construct distinctions between themselves and
others. Investments in the ideal of femininity enabled them to gain access to
limited status and moral superiority. It was their desire for value that led
them to evaluate others. Their take-up of their positioning and their display
of it through appearance enabled them to judge those who were lacking in
femininity, hence respectability. This generated struggles over respectable
appearance and conduct. Hall (1979) shows how middle- and upper-class
women, in the name of evangelicalism, would visit the houses of the poor in
an attempt to redeem them from themselves, that is from themselves as a sign
of dangerous, disruptive sexual women.

Working-class women were coded as inherently healthy, hardy and robust
(whilst, also paradoxically as a source of infection and disease) against the
physical frailty of middle-class women. They were also involved in forms of
labour that prevented femininity from ever being a possibility. For working-
class women femininity was never a given (as was sexuality); they were not
automatically positioned by it in the same way as middle- and upper-class
White women. Femininity was always something which did not designate
them precisely. Working-class women – both Black and White – were coded
as the sexual and deviant other against which femininity was defined
(Gilman, 1992). Ware (1992) shows how the categories of White middle-class
womanhood were constructed against those of potentially dangerous Black
women. And Davis (1995) notes how African-American women have, as a

result of these different significations, historically forged models of womanhood that continually and dramatically challenge prevailing notions of femininity.

The distance that is drawn between the sexual and the feminine was drawn onto the bodies of working-class women.

> This dynamic of representation is not 'woman' as a sign but femininity as (dis)simulation, a mask of non-identity, a bodily submission to 'ideas about herself'. (Lury, 1993: 204)

It is more difficult for working-class women to make a bodily submission to ideas about herself, for herself and her body is of a different class, within a different cultural and material economy. This is why when they do try on femininity they often feel it is the wrong size. It was designed for someone with a different bodily shape.[2] This is not just metaphoric play: White working-class bodies are generally smaller, less healthy and live shorter lives (The Black Report, 1982; Bourke, 1994). Moreover, the White female working-class body is often represented as out of control, in excess, such as that of *Roseanne*. Rowe (1995) argues that working-class women have often been associated with the lower unruly order of bodily functions such as that of expulsion and leakage (and reproduction) which signified lack of discipline and vulgarity. And, as Bourdieu (1986) shows, working-class women are considered to be distanced from having 'taste'. Rowe refers to a representation of working-class women by Alan King as:

> The hopeless underclass of the female sex. The polyester-class, overweight occupants of the slow track. Fast food waitresses, factory workers, housewives – members of the invisible pink-collar army. The despised, the jilted, the underpaid. (in Rowe, 1995: 57)

Femininity requires the display of classed dispositions, of forms of conduct and behaviour, different forms of cultural capital, which are not part of their cultural baggage: they are unlikely to display 'divine composure', which include the components of femininity as silent, static, invisible and composed (Cixous, 1980). Working-class women's relationship to femininity has always been produced through recourse to vulgarity. It is in the desire to avoid being positioned by the vulgar, pathological, tasteless and sexual, in order to prove their respectability, that the women of the study make investments in femininity. Even though they are positioned at a distance from femininity, investments in the forms of femininity to which they have access enable a movement away from the sexual; they offer routes into respectability, but not without incurring costs and implicating women in circuits of exchange. To do femininity they have to both appear and *be* feminine.

The division between the sexual and the feminine was most carefully coded at the level of conduct where appearance became the signifier of conduct; to look was *to be*. Appearance and conduct became markers of respectability, although these had to be coded in the correct way: too much concentration on appearance was seen to be a sign of female deviancy, as Lury (1993) notes: no good girl can afford to appear bad.[3] This legacy remains. Throughout this research value judgements were made on the basis of appearance. Appearance became the means by which the women felt they could know and place others. The hierarchy of placement was based on respectability. Ortner (1991) notes, for instance, how a group of middle-class college women interpreted the hair-styles of a group of working-class women as a sign of lack of sexual restraint. It is against this constant marking and positioning that the women make investments.

Investments in Femininities

The positioning, codifications and valuing of women as 'different' establishes limits on the amounts and forms of capital that are available and can be generated from a particular position. (This is a symbolic process with material results.) The women have already attempted to reposition themselves by means of class through disidentification and dissimulation (see Chapter 5). So far, in this study, from their locations they have tried to convert their limited forms of capital into something more valuable: the cultural capital they accrued through caring, for instance, was converted into educational qualifications, with the hope of further conversion into economic capital. Bourdieu would see this as a rational calculation of exchange:

> The interest the different classes have in self-presentation, the attention they devote to it, their awareness of the profit it gives and the investment of time, effort, sacrifice and care which they actually put into it are proportionate to the chances of material or symbolic profit they can reasonably expect to see from it. (1986: 202)

However, investments in femininity are more than trading in which gains can be calculated. In the process of making oneself tradable as a woman enormous costs can be incurred. As Radner notes:

> Feminine culture emphasizes a process of investment and return, of negotiation, in which the value of a given articulation of pleasure is always measured against its costs, the inevitable price of an invitation that is never extended freely, never absolutely, the terms of which change from day to day, from place to place. (1995:178)

The conversion rate for femininity is established through the historical circulation of signs, the institutionalization of the practice of these signs and their interpretation and conversion at the local level. In the struggle to survive, the women have to know which strategies of investment and which practices yield the highest profit. This always, as Butler notes, incurs some form of loss:

> This 'being a man' and this 'being a woman' are internally unstable affairs. They are always beset by ambivalence precisely because there is a cost in every identification, the loss of some other set of identifications, the forcible approximation of a norm one never chooses, a norm that chooses us, but which we occupy, reverse, resignify to the extent that the norm fails to determine us completely. (1993: 126–7)

They may make investments but they may not be captured by the category in which investments are made. Yet the process is always material. They also have few alternatives to femininity. When you have restricted access to small amounts of capitals, the use of femininity may be better than nothing at all. Investments in femininity may be able to accrue relatively high profit in some arenas (the institutions of marriage and heterosexuality) whilst being simultaneously devalued by others (the labour market, the education system). Femininity is as powerfully an economic imperative as a cultural one. Their cultural investments are anchored by this materiality.

Whilst it is obviously not so rational or calculated, I argue that forms of femininity (which itself has very restricted value) are taken on in an attempt to halt any losses. It is another instance of what Connell et al. (1982) describe as putting a floor on their economic circumstances. Investments are constrained by the capital one has in the first place. The conversion of feminine duty into occupational caring did not (as Chapter 3 showed) yield a high investment but it did offer potentially greater rewards than unemployment. With femininity the women operate from a position of default just as they do with class and caring. Most of the investments into themselves are based on stopping things becoming worse. Femininity is deployed to halt losses, as a way of trying to generate some value. Just because they buy into femininity as a way of flooring their circumstances does not mean that they *are* feminine. To be completely feminine for most women would be almost impossible: it would be *to be* without agency, to be a sign of powerlessness. Femininity is uninhabitable as a complete and coherent category.

Femininity is usually discussed in relation to appearance yet physical appearance may be less of a sign of femininity than wider practices such as caring. Investments in caring practice may be more productive of what it is to be feminine than investments in feminine appearance. Both, however, are necessary to the construction of the respectable woman. To become respectable means displaying femininity through appearance *and* conduct. Appearing to be is different from appearing as; there is a fine line between embodying and displaying dispositions. I will now investigate how physical appearance operates as a measure of femininity.

Judging by Appearances

The body, as a social product is, Bourdieu (1986) argues, the only tangible manifestation of the person. The sign-bearing, sign-wearing body is also a producer of signs which are physically marked by the relationship to the body (differences in bearing, posture, movement and use of space).[4] Just as we are born with access to different amounts of economic, social, cultural and symbolic capital we are also born with a physical body which may or may not fit into the sign systems which define what it is to be attractive. Physical attractiveness may work as a form of capital (corporeal capital) but as Bourdieu notes, this is often a class privilege: in France physical advantages are disproportionately allocated to the upper middle-classes through selective breeding and healthy diet.[5] Some people will be born with physical advantages (while others may feel they have to spend time, money and emotion trying to appear as attractive). Unattractiveness has little tradable value in the marriage and labour markets. Concern with appearance was a preoccupation for most of the women when they were younger but, as Chapter 5 shows, became less central when they had children and made greater investments elsewhere.

When they were young, the women were dependent upon their mothers and/or fathers for clothing. This dependence many saw to be the ultimate sign of immaturity and so took part-time jobs to buy clothes and make-up. As well as desiring to be seen to be attractive they also wanted to be independent and be able to construct their appearance for themselves:

> I hate going out with our mam. She wants me to wear the most ridiculous things you've ever seen. You know like flowery dresses and court shoes. She's obsessed, she's obsessed with pink. She'd have me looking like a fucking fairy if she had her way. I mean can you imagine me in flowery dresses, really old fashioned. I tell you. I said to her, I said last week, I said I've had enough. I said, I don't want nothing. It's not like you could trade it in or anything. It's ridiculous, who does she think I am? She's seen me in my clothes, she lives with me for Christ's sakes. She's just stupid. [Yvonne, 1982]

Here appearance, and more importantly, the autonomy to construct one's appearance is a site of contestation between the projections of mother and daughter over who they think 'she' is. The acrimony between mothers and daughters was often fought out through clothes. A substantial number of mothers wanted to influence their daughters' appearance. They did so when they controlled the finance (but usually not without battles) and the first sign of independence was often made through clothes. (This was financially a lot easier than leaving home.) Mothers wanted their daughters to appear to be respectable[6] and this meant displaying the right amount and type of femininity.[7] For Yvonne, however, her mother's desire for feminine clothing signals a refusal to recognize her as an independent women with her own tastes and attitudes. For Yvonne constructing her physical appearance is displaying independence and constructing a sense of who she thinks she is. Yvonne does not know herself as feminine and accordingly rejects all feminine signs of appearance.

To construct a sense of autonomy through clothing a particular form of consumer knowledge is required. The women had to know what to buy, where from, how to wear it, what to wear it with and on what occasions to wear it. The legacies of knowing one's place through clothing informed their 'choice'. The women had learnt the distinctions between style and fashion, between looking good and looking tarty, between looking feminine and looking sexy. The women's knowledge of femininity was not just absorbed directly from the traditional textual sources of femininity (such as magazines, advertising, etc.), rather, it was an amalgam of this and local knowledge. Textually mediated femininity was put into practice and effect through local interpretation. Looking good involved a substantial amount of labour but also collective discussion.[8] Clothes were nearly always bought with friends and preparing for the purchase by trying on hundreds of clothes was a regular recreational pursuit and a site of pleasure and often hilarity. The Saturday shopping expedition was looked forward to as much as the Friday and Saturday night trying-on sessions. Clothes were highly valued; they were invested in as a source of cultural capital, one of the few alternatives they had.[9]

Female competence, however, was required to make the 'right' decisions. Looking good involved dedication, commitment, labour, knowledge, friendship and being in an all female group. It is validated and made a site of anxiety through the multitude of women's magazines and adverts which play on the fear of not looking good. This is where the local became an important site for challenging the representations which were produced at national/global levels. There was a clear awareness that certain clothes were not for them. However, local interpretation could also invoke hierarchies of corporeal and cultural capital, as the following conversation demonstrates between Rose and Jean (1986):

> *Rose*: Now look at Sandra she's clueless. I wouldn't be seen dead out with her. I think her mum must buy all her clothes from a catalogue.
>
> *Jean*: And it must be a 1975 catalogue.
>
> *Rose*: No, not 1975, that'd make her trendy.
>
> *Jean*: Did you see her in that track suit last week. It was pink for goodness sake and she looked like a sack of potatoes. Well she's a disgrace to the female race. I mean just look at it.

These distinctions drawn by Rose and Jean at a local level are not a form of systematizing difference, rather, they are representative of the multitude of distinctions drawn daily. Even for those who draw the distinctions, who are skilled at doing femininity through fashion, their cultural capital can only be increased at a local level. It is unlikely that they can convert their competencies into a form of authority, into symbolic capital. Yet this does mean that they do not position middle-class women as the surveillant other (as they did with caring). Style is not seen to be something that middle-class women are seen to know anything about. It is seen to be a working-class competence. The practice of looking good should not be dismissed as a trivial activity. It was central to the women's sense of self: their interpretations, labour, display and performance.[10] It is a site of pleasure and fear; it is a 'structure of feeling' (Williams, 1961, 1977) which makes them feel good and bad about themselves. It enables them to share interests and intimacy with friends, generate admiration and signal desirability, but it also induces the fear of getting behind or not having the right knowledge, of getting it wrong. The act of construction was as significant as the final appearance. They operated with a long list of textually mediated cannots which were based around respectability and fashion, such as 'you can't wear jeans and high heels' and 'you can't wear white stiletto shoes and mini-skirts'. It is indicative that these cannots are frequently invoked as 'cans' in representations of working-class women.

The women distinguish between being looked at in 'admiration' and looked as a 'sexual object'. There is a complex interplay between being made to recognize oneself as a certain type of person (sexual clothing signifies those

who have no respectability) and being given external validation for not looking bad. These distinctions inform the ambivalences about themselves and
their relationship to femininity. Feeling good, through looking good, offers
momentary respite, provides valuing and offsets any potential positionings by
degradation. Putting oneself together to make a feminine performance is
where aesthetic creation, skill and pleasure combine together. This is often
done on a collective basis:

> We all get dressed up for a Friday night on the town, it takes hours, we all go
> round to Maureen's house, her mam's dead good and that, and we bring all our
> stuff, and then we try each other's things on and have a laugh. Like I always like to
> try Anna's stuff 'cos she's a bit outlandish, I'd never wear stuff like that. We help to
> put each other's make up on, apart from Anna who does her own and we just mess
> around. We have music playing all the time, Anna's brother gets all the new records
> so she steals them from him and we have a dance, then about four hours later we're
> ready to go. It makes you feel good, being all dressed up, it doesn't matter what hap-
> pens, you just feel good, feel special, instead of the same old boring you that you are
> at college. [Kate, 1983]

They learn to 'pass' as feminine together. The final product from these Friday
or Saturday night sessions, which were a regular occurrence, may look like
femininity but, in the production of it, raucousness, rudeness, outrageousness
and challenge to femininity occur. They may have the physical appearance of
femininity but their performance, their conduct is definitely not feminine. In
becoming physically feminine their look contradicts their performance. When
they spill into the pub and the club a lasting pleasure can ensue, based on
secret jokes and camaraderie.[11] They have constructed themselves collectively
and display their localized competencies. For many men it seemed there was
nothing more intimidating than this loud, laughing, together group of
women. They *appear* as terrifying. They were claiming their right to their
pleasure and social space. Their appearance made it even more disturbing, for
they looked the part of the traditional feminine young woman, yet all their
behaviour suggested otherwise.[12] Their feminine performance proves that
they are precisely that which they are not.

Doane (1982) argues that 'masquerade' enables women to manufacture a
distance from the image of femininity. I argue that working-class women
have never needed to manufacture any distance; they have always been positioned at a distance. Tyler suggests caution with the concept of mimicry,
arguing that:

> Theories of mimicry reinscribe white, middle-class femininity as the real thing, the
> (quint)essence of femininity . . . Miming the feminine means impersonating a white
> middle-class impersonation of an 'other' ideal of femininity . . . Feminist theorists
> of mimicry distinguish themselves from 'other' women even as they assimilate the
> latter by romanticizing them, assuming the 'other' has a critical knowledge about
> femininity because of her difference from what counts as natural femininity: white,
> Anglo, bourgeois style. It is only from a middle-class point of view that Dolly
> Parton looks like a female impersonator. (1991: 57)

Not only is the ideal of femininity a bourgeois sign but the attempts to sub-
vert femininity are locked within the same range of projections. The women

of the research are able to mimic femininity but their mimicry is often not recognized as such; it is often read as a display of femininity.[13] Or, even worse,
their fabrication is seen as a display of the authentically sexual and thus
pathologized. Even when they are not making feminine performances they
may be identified by others as doing so. They do take on, at times, the appearance of femininity, but they also take it off and they rarely identify as
feminine. They do not have a possessive relation to femininity. This generates
a temporality to the sign of femininity. The sign cannot guarantee a take-up.
It will not be and cannot be constantly occupied. For as Riley (1987) notes,
women have to recognize themselves as the term: they may not. Whereas
they felt positioned by class they do not feel similarly positioned as feminine.
They do not see it as something which is part of them. It is not fundamental
to their subjective constructions. However, it can be used tactically to have a
good time.

Going out gave them a reason for dressing up, it gave them something to
plan for and look forward to. They rarely dressed up when they did not have
to; femininity was often done as part of an 'occasion'. The planning that
went into preparation for parties was enormous and took over as the main
topic of conversation for weeks in advance. Going out was a hedonistic highlight. Femininity was performed in preparation but it had many more
meanings beyond the traditional. As Anne notes:

> You know what I really miss about having children is that I never go out with the
> girls anymore. We've all got kids and it would involve lots of organizing and really
> that would lose it. We're too old now but I used to love it, it was really wild. I can't
> really explain why it was so good, but we were all together and we all just wanted
> to have a good time. We used to drink when we got older but at first it was just pure
> adrenalin. It really was that exciting. We'd all look forward to it every week and
> we'd take piles of clothes to try on. It was all about experimenting and seeing what
> you could get away with [laugh]. We were really close. I used to feel it was a bit of
> a let down sometimes when we went out. Mind you it was a laugh taking the piss
> out of all the jerks who'd make comments and that . . . No, no it wasn't about men
> at all, they were irrelevant. Some would try and schmoose their way in but they were
> soon out. No, it was different from pulling nights. It was about us. You know, I
> really do regret it, it has such good memories. In fact it was the best part of my life.
> Now it's all worries. Then we thought we were free. We just enjoyed ourselves.
> [Anne, 1992]

Anne's lament at her lost youth suggests that the dressing up, the signifying of
heterosexuality, are more about friendships, hedonism, irresponsibility and
intimate solidarity. The putting on of femininity is experienced as a form of
camaraderie in which she is made to feel good about herself. This collective
putting on is about women being close, safe and self-indulgent. It is for themselves. It is a way of belonging and of feeling secure.

> If you know you look good you can do anything, well you think you can. You think
> I'm the most gorgeous, clever, wonderful person in this room. If you look bad, you
> know, you just want to hide. [Pam, 1988]

Appearance here is fundamental to how Pam feels about her ability to use
social space. She does not want to be seen, because being seen not to look

good is to be seen without confidence. The investment in not wanting to look bad has a powerful effect on presence. Pam feels her presence is eradicated if she does not look good. This shows how crucial femininity may be for making some women feel at all worthwhile. Tina is aware of the pressure she is under to put in an appropriate appearance:

> I thought I've had it up to here with these magazines. All you do is fork out to feel bad about yourself. I was sick of looking at these 14-year-olds with barely developed bodies who I was meant to look like. It used to really piss me off. I like the articles and that but I thought why fork out for something that just makes you feel inadequate. So I stopped and I binned all the old ones. I cleared them out of my life. But the odd thing was I still had a yearning for them. I felt I was missing out, that it was all going on elsewhere. It was as if I'd lost track on what was going on and there may have been important stuff I needed to know about. I mean they are quite good on health and that sort of thing. So I bought one just last week, over there, and you know it was stupid. There was nothing in it. [Tina, 1992]

Tina is no longer part of a group which confirms her belonging. But she still feels a desire to belong. She does not want to feel that she has lost knowledge and competency. She feels as if there is a secret knowledge which is shared from which she has been excluded. Her response illustrates the processes by which femininity is textually mediated. Tina displays an ambivalence towards the representations of femininity offered by magazines. She feels caught up but also able to resist.

Appearance is simultaneously and across time a site for pleasure and strength but also a site of anxiety, regulation and surveillance. The feeling of looking good can also be lost if it is not continually externally validated, as Janet suggests:

> During the holidays I get dead fed up, you know, we live miles from nowhere so I hardly see anybody unless I can get a lift back somehow and what I hate most is that I just doss around, sometimes I don't even bother to get dressed and you know if you do that for a week when you don't see nobody you start to wonder who you are and then it's really unnerving when you come back to college because you wonder if you still exist and you don't know what to wear and you feel as if everybody has been doing things and you've been on another planet. [Janet, 1983]

In this sense, femininity is very much a public performance dependent upon validation by others. Appearances, as Kate, Pam and Janet suggest, are more than just surfaces. They are intimately linked to valuations of oneself, to knowing oneself and to being an accepted part of a group. They do not recognize themselves by the category of femininity but their appearance (amongst other practices) is central to how they know themselves. This suggests that women are not feminine by default but that femininity is a carefully constructed appearance and/or form of conduct that can be displayed. It is a knowing construction, publicly performed.

The women can accrue capital through caring over time whilst they can only lose it through feminine appearance. Appearance depreciates at a rapid rate, for as Stacey notes: 'Feminine ideals are youthful ones, and thus successful femininity contains loss even in the rare sense of its attainment' (1994: 67). Time spent on appearance was more usually social than self-centred and, as noted earlier, appearance became less collectivized as they grew older, their responsibilities changed and they lost touch with large groups of single women in similar situations. The space and time to act out femininity became more limited and trivialized in relation to their family responsibilities and economic worries and could rarely be justified. Appearance was often a preoccupation of those who did not have their value legitimated elsewhere.

Temporary halts on depreciation could be made by single women with less financial and familial responsibility who had learnt (from advertising discourse) to pamper themselves. Feminine accoutrements, such as make-up and bodily lotions, were seen to be a 'treat'.[14] Even in the depreciation dynamic femininity could be experienced as positive and powerful, as feeling good about oneself. This is after all the most marketable fragment of feminism: the 'feel-good' about your life, body, your self is offered as a form of confidence. Consuming femininity becomes an incitement to individuality: different forms of femininity are offered to different magazine audiences (Winship, 1983). Women are addressed as 'free' to construct themselves through consumption.

Feminine constructions had appropriate times and places. Spending obvious amounts of time with make-up just to go to work or college was seen to be embarrassing and inappropriate, but spending the same amount of time preparing to go out is expected. One woman who was always perfectly put together whilst at college came in for a lot of verbal abuse:

> Have you seen all that make-up, it's like inches thick, and the heels, you'd think she were at a night club or something, it's ridiculous, it must take her ages to get ready on a morning and she totters around looking like a fucking Barbie doll. Just no shame. I think it's really sad, like there's no one here to impress, why bother, it's just stupid. She looks a real idiot. [Therese, 1983]

Connie's problem is defined through inappropriateness. She also wears clothes that signify sexuality (such as short skirts and stretch jeans which emphasize her body) without any coding through fashion. Therese thinks she should feel ashamed to appear as she does. Basically, Connie just doesn't have the right feminine cultural knowledge to code herself carefully rather than to display herself explicitly. Connie would be the perfect visual example of femininity; she looks very similar to a Barbie doll. She may be an accurate imitation but she is not admired or even thought desirable. She is seen to be only appearance, lacking in substance. Femininity is not an aspiration, but something which is struggled with to gain some value and to ameliorate invalidation. It is a performance not considered to be necessary all the time. Those who appear and behave as feminine across all contexts have very little value: their performance is considered unnecessary. Connie got the place and time wrong; she also made apparent the amount of labour involved in the construction of the performance. Making too much effort was seen to be a problem (not dissimilar to nineteenth-century judgements) but so were women who did not invest in themselves and were seen not to be making any effort at all.

To not invest at all in femininity is seen to jeopardize others' investments. It is also seen as a lack of collusion with the feminine. Those who do not bother make the others self-conscious of their investments. They are resented but also represent a state of being that some of the women desire:

> You know in a way it'd be good not to have to worry about the way you looked. You know, not care if your skirt's tucked into your knickers and that, no really it'd be a bit more relaxing. I said to my mum the other day, why do we bother with all this. It was having my bikini line waxed that did it. It was unbelievable. Pain. God. I thought I was going to die. I felt sick for ages afterwards and I said to her when she asked me why I wasn't eating, I said why do we do it? It'd be freedom not to care. [Cindy, 1984]

Cindy evokes a sense of being caught up in something which is beyond her control. She knows that she is part of something that produces submission, even pain, but she cannot see a way out, the risks may be too great: cultural stigmatization in her local situation; a challenge to all her friends who collude in femininity; a sign of difference; the loss of potential future emotional and economic security. To challenge femininity can invoke costs, but that does not mean challenges cannot be made:

> I used to shave my legs all the time, so much so that they nearly grew a beard. I was really paranoid and then I remember reading this article and I thought why am I so concerned, you know in the winter they're not exactly on public display and nobody sees them. Well my mum teases me about them and that can be a bit cruel at times, but she's hairy too, that's where I get it from. So I got to thinking about it and it's daft. We start to worry about our hairy legs like it matters. I do them in the summer now but that's all. They keep me warm in the winter. But sometimes I look at them and think ugh – ugly or what and then I think I like hairy legs on men so why is it so ingrained. To be honest I do think my legs look terrible, look, don't laugh . . . [*I didn't*] I just can't seem to convince myself otherwise. I wish I could. [Karen, 1988]

Karen has begun the long process of change but feels her rebellion as an aesthetic challenge. She has learnt from long contact with the texts of femininity that things should look a particular way. Bartky (1990) argues that the disciplinary practices on the body are part of the processes by which the ideal body of femininity – and hence the feminine body subject – is constructed; in doing this they produce a 'practiced and subjected' body, that is, a body in which an inferior status has been inscribed. But, as Cindy's and Karen's comments suggest, there is a reflexivity about the regimes of the body. Femininity is not desired; rather, it is seen as a structuring inconvenience, something which is difficult for them to avoid completely. Distance can be drawn from disciplinary practices. They were able to be far more critical of the incitements for feminine appearance than they were of incitements to be a caring person, although similar systems of self-monitoring and surveillance are established. Caring worked at an intimate level of subjectivity, as quality of being, whereas femininity was less immediate, intimate or important. They were implicated in it but it was not seen to produce the same rewards, although the sanctions may be worse. Femininity was necessary to displays of respectability but caring defined what it meant to be respectable. The nearest femininity came to being a form of subjectivity was through glamour.

Glamour, Desirability and Confirmation of Value

As suggested in the introduction to this chapter, for working-class women the sexual has to be disavowed. Glamour, however, is a way of holding together sexuality and respectability, but it is difficult to achieve. Pearce (1995) argues that glamour is always read as 'degrading' unless 'protected' and defended by other marks of middle-class respectability (such as education or wealth).[15] The women have to negotiate being glamorous and desirable – to which they all aspire – whilst not being marked as rough and common. Whilst the women were keen not to be associated with the sexual, they also knew that carefully coded displays of sexuality could generate value (such as their use of flirting in Chapter 7). They knew that their sexuality had a value that could be traded in their local circuits of exchange. This value was based on a conglomeration of variables, including: physically corresponding to dominant ideals of femininity, wearing locally designated appropriate clothing; limiting their sexual activity to avoid a reputation; not being aggressive, vulgar or domineering. These could all be negotiated through glamour. The women had to carefully code, display and conduct themselves to generate value. Glamour is the mechanism by which the marks of middle-class respectability are transposed onto the sexual body, a way in which recognition of value is achieved.

Stacey (1994) charts the historical association of glamour with Americanness. She argues that glamour was defined against British respectability in the 1950s in which it was understood to signify confidence, sophistication and self-assurance, but that by the 1980s it had been tempered by British middle-class restraint and respectability. Sherratt (1983) notes how by the 1970s glamour had moved into the British mainstream becoming a centralized concern for young women. She argues:

> Glamour was being conceptualized as a style of life, defined on the one hand as essentially the obverse of their own 'boring' present existence, whatever that may be; and on the other hand in terms of qualities of being. (1983: 54)

Glamour offers the ability to appear as something different from the mundane. It is an escape route. When discussing glamour, the following responses were evoked:

> Well when I said she looked really glam what I meant was that she looked gorgeous, you know quite stunning, like you'd really notice her, not because she was displaying herself, which is the main way to get attention, but because she looked really good. She looked, well, glamorous, well fanciable without turning it on too much. [Diane, 1988]

> You know it when you see it, sort of well put together and looking sexy but not tarty or obvious. There's nothing vulgar about being glamorous. It's good when it works, if it doesn't you just look stupid. I think it's also about attitude and the way you do it. I think you have to feel good to look glamorous. It's also then about how confident you feel. You can always tell glamorous women they're dead confident about themselves. [Fiona, 1988]

Glamour involves attitude as well as appearance, it is a 'structure of feeling' (Williams, 1961, 1977), albeit within the discourse of textually-mediated femininity. Whereas other forms of femininity are not experienced as subjectivity, the recognition of oneself as glamorous serves to engender an identification, enabling femininity to operate as a disposition *and* a form of cultural capital, even if only momentarily and always tied to performance. It is the attitude that makes the difference. It gives agency, strength and worth back to women and is not restricted to youth. They do glamour with style. Glamour is about a performance of femininity *with* strength:

> Yea I get glammed up, we all do. You have to be up for it though. There's no point if you're not in the mood or feeling down. You've got to feel you're invincible. Whistles, comments, chat-ups the lot, you've just got to look down your nose at them. I know when I look good. I make sure others do too. [Angela, 1992]

Glamour is a way of transcending the banalities of femininity which render women as passive objects, as signs of appearance without agency, as something which has to be done. This shows how femininity is fragmented in which some facets can be re-enacted with vision, pleasure and attitude in a way more appropriate to those for whom it was not designed. Femininity may be textually mediated, an artifice, a masquerade, a performance but through glamour it is also experienced as a temporary 'way of being'. To be feminine, as Butler (1990) argues, is a mode of enacting and re-enacting of received gender norms which surface as so many styles of the flesh. Glamour is one of the areas, one of the styles of the flesh, in which pleasure can be gained. Glamour enables the projection of desirability.

All of the women were concerned to be seen as desirable. To be fancied was a validation of themselves.[16] To be desirable operated in many ways. Alongside the regulatory heterosexual aspects of desirability – whose standards, who monitors and who does the desiring – it was a way in which their feminine cultural capital was confirmed as worth having. Desirability was a legitimation of the value of performing femininity. Being desirable gave confidence but, more importantly, it enabled one not to be seen as inadequate, undesirable and not belonging. It was a means of putting a further floor on losses generated through investments in femininity. The women needed legitimation to confirm their desirability:

> I don't know how to explain it. I don't really want a man at the moment. They're usually more trouble than they're worth and I want to get on with my career and I have all my mates. But I have to say it'd be nice if I knew that there was someone out there who was rooting for me. I want to know I'm really wanted by someone, anyone [laughs], anyone would do. I don't want them, I just want to know. [Clare, 1988]

> It's not about getting a man it's about knowing you can if you want to. If you haven't been involved for a long time (like me), you wonder if there's anybody out there for you. You wonder if you'll ever meet anybody. You start thinking that there's something wrong with me. I always get fat when I'm not in a relationship because I always eat to compensate. I want comfort and then I'm stuck because the more I eat, the more comfort I get, the less chance I have of being fancied. It's a vicious circle. I don't really want a boyfriend, I'm still recovering from the last one, but I'd like to know I could have one if I changed my mind. I'd like to know I'm still human. [Michelle, 1988]

Here men are necessary for the confirmation of desirability. For Michelle male confirmation of desirability is essential for her sense of being, her subjectivity. Note that real men are not wanted but rather the knowledge that one is heterosexually desirable is considered necessary for emotional security. Their sense of themselves as desirable is surveilled through images of (heterosexual) desirability – Michelle believes only thinness is desirable. Michelle and Clare believe that male approval is cultural approval. Yet, although not articulated here, it is only certain males who are designated as worthy of giving approval. Underpinning desirability is an implicit sexual market where exchanges are governed by estimations of relative value. The 'right' men have to do the desiring. They believe that male approval will give them cultural validation. This desire for male legitimation can be taken to extremes in which other women are rendered invisible. Even the friends who can make them feel good cannot confirm their desirability, as Diane notes with regret:

> Yea, I was thinking about Rose and she's really lovely and all that but she's also very stupid. She'll sleep with anyone just to be able to say 'look at me I'm really fanciable'. It's pathetic. Really, I mean, I think sleeping with any old oik makes her look less fanciable, like she looks sad and desperate, like she'll have anything. It's really embarrassing. I've said to her 'why do you do it?' and she's come over all superior, like as if shagging jerks somehow makes her more fanciable than the rest of us. Has she no self-respect? She's admitted that she doesn't even enjoy it much. I mean how many one-night stands are up to much . . . Why some idiot saying shag me makes her feel better than me saying she looks great is beyond me. I mean it makes dickheads seem more valuable than me, her best mate, than all of us. [Diane, 1988]

Diane is obviously angry (and to some extent jealous) that she has become redundant in this part of her friend's life. Diane cannot understand why Rose, who is very good looking, would want to have sex with men who Diane does not rate or believe hold equal value. Diane values herself and Rose far more highly than the men they come into contact with. She interprets Rose's lack of valuing herself as desperateness. Rose sees it differently:

> It's about having a laugh. And you do have a laugh. It's no big deal. It's just not serious. It makes me feel good. Even if the sex isn't always brilliant it's still fun . . . No, no, I'm not desperate to get laid . . . I don't know what it's about . . . It's not deep and meaningful. It's just some men are a real good laugh and they can make you feel good. You know, they can make you feel that all the effort was worthwhile. [Rose, 1988]

Rose wants some payback for her investments in femininity and these manifest themselves through desirability. To be physically confirmed as desirable is the confirmation that the performance of femininity has worked, that it was worthwhile. Here femininity becomes the ultimate legitimator of masculinity (even though pleasure and fun were gained in the performance); it offers to masculinity the power to impose standards, make evaluations and confirm validity. This is also a high risk strategy. Paradoxically, only those who conform to textually mediated masculine ideals of desirability, may have the confidence to expose themselves to judgement. Femininity does not have the discursive power to operate as an authorizing narrative. It is masculinity which provides the authorization.

Some women feel capable of finding male approval when they feel they require it:

> I feel more confident now with the kids, I don't need anybody. They're just trouble. I'm more of a flirt now, I like a laugh. I like playing and walking away that's what I like. My looks are my best asset. I go out, pull a fella, he'll say I'll ring tomorrow and you can say no and walk away. They're just not worth the bother. I wouldn't trust anybody with my children. The children having somebody is most important. If someone was really good with the kids and I didn't really like him, well I'd make a go of it. If I fancied someone and he wasn't interested in children, he'd go. [Angela, 1992]

For Angela, aware of the trading value of physical attractiveness, confirmation of desirability is set against the needs of her children. She also feels confident in her physical appearance and powerful enough to attract and use men for her purposes. This confidence is a product of a long hard struggle against the bad behaviour of her ex-husband. Angela has had male validation and knows from her experience that it is not worth much.

Lynne is still married and feels that external cultural validation may not be enough:

> I'd always felt very secure in the way I looked. And also we'd been going out together since school and so it was never a big issue. He always said I looked nice when we were going out. But really I don't think he noticed and then with the kids all our energy went into them. But now, now they're grown up a bit, I just feel he's not interested anymore. He still buys me the odd bar of chocolate, but, you know, er, well, it seems, well, it seems he's just not interested. He can't have someone else 'cos he doesn't have the time. It's just like after the kids he just went off. It was as if he'd done his bit [laughs]. And now, now I've got more time and the kids aren't here all the time, well now I think has he gone off me. I know I've put on weight but I was never that thin. I've asked him if he still fancies me and he just says yes shut up and then turns over or walks away. He's not interested in talking about those sorts of things. He says 'we're happy aren't we. We've got a good family. What more do you want?' And he's right I'm better off than a lot of them round here. But you know I'm beginning to wonder is it going to be like this for ever. [Lynne, 1992]

The lack of interest shown by an intimate male partner was confirmation that one had become undesirable. Lynne has the public approval of marriage but experiences it intimately as a lack of validation. The cultural approval that she settled for is now not enough. She also feels powerless to do anything about it. Bartky (1990) argues that women may know that in the abstract they have little power to change politics and economics but what they feel is a power to change relationships and make an impact upon people, especially upon their intimate partners. It is what Bartky defines as a phenomenological presence, which, she argues, is how we inscribe and re-inscribe our subjection in the fabric of the ordinary. It was this that motivated many women into marriage and relationships. They believed they could exercise some control and power over their lives. They did femininity to generate security but for some the deal did not pay back. However, alternatives were considered to be worse.

Being single was experienced as feeling continually monitored by the local cultures of which they are a part, in which to be without a man is seen to be inadequate and undesirable. The feeling of inadequacy testifies to the power and pervasiveness of heterosexuality. Not all women felt culturally annihilated without a man and positions between desperation and indifference were occupied at different times. If they did not have any other external forms of validation (such as work, children) the need for confirmation grew greater. This was because the cultural stigma of being single in working-class cultures increased as they grew older. Women also found that at work they would be passed over for promotion and responsible jobs if they were not married. Fears of being 'left on the shelf' continued throughout the research. Age also meant they had fewer culturally validated ways of meeting potential partners and the numbers of friends to go out with decreased (as the friends were married). Hatred of 'playing the field' or 'being part of the meat market' (their terms) was a strong incentive to settle for inadequate partners.

For most of the women the white wedding was so central because it is the ultimate spectacle of heterosexual femininity which combined legal and cultural legitimacy with the promise of a potentially better economic life, potential emotional security, a respectable base for having children and confirmation of desirability. For some it offered the finale of the feminine masquerade, for others a respite from having to make feminine performances and for others it made their performances more regular, in which the public moves into the private. Marriage was a means of stating independence and signalling maturity. It was a day in which the woman was the centre of attention. This I realized, is why their weddings were such important memories and why each had a video, usually a very large photo album and remnants of the wedding, such as the dried bouquet in a frame on the wall. It was the day of validation, of legitimation, of being that which they have always felt distant from. This argument is visually illustrated in the film *Muriel's Wedding* (dir.: P.J. Hogan). To not be married is still a sign of cultural failure. In their local culture it signifies lack of desirability and it generates real problems about socializing. Lynn found that most people in their late twenties are in couples. It may be the combined effects of heterosexuality and couple culture which puts the pressure on women to find partners:

> I think the most difficult thing about being single, and don't get me wrong, I like my house and having my own way and doing what I want but the real problem is finding people to go out with. I'm sick of tagging along and they make you feel like a real fool and they talk to you as if they're doing you a favour and they all have their private little jokes and you're made to feel excluded. It's bloody couples. There's two women at the hospital and they're like, you know, you know together, and they're the same. I went out with them one night and I might well have not existed. Me, I'd rather stay in than go out with couples. It also sometimes makes you feel really lonely when you go out, when I go out with like the girls at work and they all, you know that they're all going back to someone at the end of the night and you're just going home to a cold house. I don't know it just makes you feel as if there's something wrong with you. I've even thought of going back with Sam just so I could go out and not feel like that. [Lynn, 1992]

Men are a waste of time. I haven't been out with anyone for four years. It's a waste of time. I'm too set in my ways. I want nice things and I'm not prepared to give them up. You wonder is it worth it with so many people splitting up. Now I would-n't go out with the type of guys who'd bad mouth you. I don't want to go out with a macho dickhead. I still want children . . . what I really hate though, like at work last week, I had to separate them, it's the couples who do their private life in front of you. It's like they're flaunting it. [Jane, 1992]

Sue and Anne were my best friends but then now because they've got Phil and Rod they all go out together in a foursome. They go off by themselves. They're not doing it on purpose, I know, but it hurts. [Sharon, 1992]

Not to be in a relationship with somebody is experienced as cultural exclusion. These women were aged 27 when these comments were made. They feel they have been left out of a cultural activity in which everyone else is involved and which is given greater social value than their own lives. Couple culture (especially heterosexual) makes it difficult for single women to occupy public space and for them to feel as valid as married women. Desirability is not their only concern, it is being given the same social value as those who are in relationships. This is why many women invest in men, not just for economic reasons but for cultural validation. Some of these men provide sustenance and safety. Some, of course, do not. Male partners can enable the construction of confidence generated from cultural validation, otherwise unavailable.

Conclusion

The concept of femininity is only partially adequate to encapsulate the experiences by which the women of the study occupied the category 'woman'. It is always over-layered with other categorizations such as class and race. Historically this is because working-class women (Black and White) have been positioned against femininity with the sexual. They were precisely what femininity was not. However, to claim respectability, disavowal of the sexual is necessary and constructions, displays and performances of feminine appearance and conduct are seen as necessary. The women are positioned at a distance from femininity but claim proximity to it. This ambivalent positioning informed their responses. The women made feminine performances appropriate to the situations they were in. These could be made across a range of sites, with differing value and potential (often produced through institutionalization (in the sexual division of labour; the legal system; the education system). These were not masquerades employed to generate distance (that was already guaranteed) but tactical deployments of forms of femininity which protected their investments and gained cultural approval and validations. Their attempts to 'pass' as feminine were always in jeopardy of being read by others as representative of authentic femininity. To not make these performances would have seriously endangered their bids for respectability. Their awareness of their positioning by default as sexual, vulgar, tarty, pathological and without value meant that they felt they had to continually prove that they were different.

Previously appearance was equated with conduct: to look was to be. This was resisted by the women for whom 'divine composure' was disregarded in favour of 'having a laugh'. They had knowledge and competencies to construct feminine performances but this was far removed from *being* feminine. They usually 'did' femininity when they thought it was necessary. They did not feel others had the power to judge their appearance, other than through respectability – so style and fashion (although ultimately coded by respectability) were also spaces where fun could be had, pleasure taken, validation given but also distinctions drawn. They did, however, feel economically compelled to appear feminine. They made investments in femininity because they had few other alternatives available to accrue cultural and economic resources. The consequences of not investing in femininity produced a range of responses from desperation to loneliness, few of which were experienced as positive. Femininity provided a cultural resource through which they could try to put a floor on their circumstances. To avoid jeopardizing their investments they sometimes colluded in its production. The investments that could be made were age and place specific, informed by textual mediations. They saw femininity as a structural inconvenience which was difficult to avoid. Femininity is not something that can be seen simply as physical appearance. It is an institutionalized sign that also operates as a form of cultural capital. McCall (1992) asks if gendered forms of cultural capital can ever function as profitable capital. Rarely, I would argue; they are more likely to operate as halts on losses. It is these processes of investment and experience that operated as a disincentive to the take up of feminism (see Chapter 8).

Their forays into femininity were immensely contradictory. Femininity offered a space for hedonism, autonomy, camaraderie, pleasure and fun whilst simultaneously regulating and generating insecurities. The women simulated and dissimulated but did not recognize themselves as feminine. They felt most comfortable with glamour because it enabled them to hold femininity and sexuality together in respectable performances and generate value in local circuits of exchange. It also provided a space for them to operate with attitude. This meant glamour could work at the level of subjectivity, whilst other forms of femininity were recognized to be the property of others. However, glamorous performances could be compromised by the desire to be seen and legitimated as desirable.

This suggests that femininity may indeed be an uninhabitable category, reproduced by White working-class women through necessity rather than volition, through their deployment of different forms of femininity. The women's performances did not engender identification because they did not recognize themselves addressed by the classed category of femininity. They do not know themselves as feminine. Aspects of femininity are, however, something which they have learnt to perform and from which they can sometimes take pleasure. The central problem with the reproduction of femininity was that there were few culturally valid and economically possible or potential alternatives available for enacting at a local level. The next chapter will explore how similar ambivalent recognitions occur in the way that the women experience categorizations of heterosexuality and occupy the category 'woman'.

Notes

1 Texts do not necessarily pre-date interpretation; they may be the encoding of forms of behaviour not previously produced as texts. Texts, however, are always produced with interests in mind (Venn, 1992) and, as Said (1984) argues, the relations of power and authority are what makes the production of texts possible.

2 This is made most obvious when larger or older women try and do femininity. Roseanne and Dawn French expose the ridiculousness of femininity in their magazine spreads in. *Vanity Fair.* Thanks Celia for this example.

3 Earlier in the seventeenth century dressing outside of one's class was legislated against (Creed, 1995).

4 See the 1975 radical feminist film *Take it Like a Man Ma'am* (dirs. Melle Knudsen, Elizabeth Rygard and Li Vilstrup) which brilliantly visualizes these points.

5 By producing a table Bourdieu (1986: Table 20, pp. 203–5) argues that working-class women are less likely to enter one of the occupations which most strictly demand conformity to the dominant notions of beauty and are less aware of the 'market' value of beauty. My research does not confirm his findings. The women of the study were acutely aware of the value of physical appearance. It was a site of significant investment.

6 This should not be surprising when we think of the pressures on the mothers themselves to display their respectability through appearance.

7 Jackie Stacey, in personal correspondence, notes how middle-class girls are discouraged by their mothers to display too much femininity. They have to display femininity with 'taste' and without sexuality.

8 It is likely that the labour can decrease when others can be paid to do it for you. Beauticians, who are most likely to be drawn from the working or lower middle-classes, have converted their feminine cultural capital to gain employment. They then service, mainly, middle-class women. This investment in feminine labour is not highly socially or economically valued.

9 They had few other pursuits in which to invest, having not been educated in the cultural capitals of middle-class leisure pursuits (see Savage et al., 1992)

10 Nor should dressing up as a means of generating collective identity and camaraderie be seen to be restricted to heterosexual women. See Blackman and Perry (1990) and Creed (1995).

11 O'Neill (1993) notes how these 'nights out with the girls' are a site for the pleasure of many women. The form differs depending on class, age, region, etc.

12 See also Thomson and Henderson (1994) on fag hags.

13 Middle-class women learn to mimic also, but it is unlikely that working-class women will be used as a legitimate source of their mimicry unless they want to mimic femininity with sexuality, thus reproducing working-class women as the site of the sexual.

14 This suggests a historical change in forms of class address through consumption. Partington (1990) notes how in 1950s Britain professional discourses attempted to confine working-class women's consumption practices to the realm of economic necessity, separate from the decoration, display and excess that defined middle-class femininity.

15 She notes how Princess Diana is never referred to as 'tarty' although she carries all the signs (from personal communication).

16 Desirability is an issue within both the institution of heterosexuality and in lesbian cultures.

7

Becoming Respectably Heterosexual

This chapter explores how the women become heterosexual. It examines how processes of recognition (non and mis-recognition), identification, disidentification and dissimulation produce subjectivity. Its central focus is how the category of respectability mediates positionings and responses to sexuality. It argues that the material and institutional are central components in the construction of a sexual subjectivity. Whereas the women were marginalized by class they should be normalized by heterosexuality (as none constructed an oppositional political identity from it during the research) yet they are not. This is because of the historical association of heterosexuality with respectability and dangerous perverse sexuality with Black and White working-class women *and* the lesbian. The chapter explores how the association of lesbianism with sex would make it difficult for the women to maintain distance from the sexed and simultaneously become associated with it. Heterosexuality produces simultaneously normalization and marginalization for working-class women.[1] It is another category they feel does not speak to them because they do not want to be classified as sexual. Respectability, as a discourse of normativity, is one way in which sexual practice is evaluated, distinctions drawn, legitimated and maintained between groups. This means that heterosexuality is not occupied equally precisely because it is mediated by respectability and some women are already, by class and race location, already categorized as non-respectable; it is another mechanism for the reproduction of difference and inequalities.

The chapter starts with a journey through the many definitions of sexuality. It does this to show that sexuality is not just discursive or a representation, but also a materiality which is institutionalized. It then explores how the historical production of sexual classifications were mapped onto distinctions of respectability by class and race associations: the category lesbian was produced through association with Black and White working-class women. The shame induced by recognizing oneself as sexed is explored. The third part of the chapter analyses how heterosexuality operates within the caring courses to show how institutionalization of heterosexuality is produced, especially through responses to it. The final section explores how a small group of (heterosexual) women masquerade as lesbians and analyses the implications of this for sexual identification. The chapter begins with comments produced by the women at the start of the research and ends with those made later. This is to show how they move through the processes of heterosexualizations.

Heterosexualities, sexualities and sexual practice are central sites for contestations about respectability. It is where the codes which have lain dormant in debates over the family and caring are made explicit. Kaplan (1992) shows how profoundly women's subjectivity is constructed through sexual categorization (although not necessarily sexual practice). She also shows how the discourses of maternal care and sexuality are often in contradiction with each other enabling motherhood and sexuality to be represented in opposition. Lesbian and gay sexuality is frequently set up in opposition, as threatening, to the family (as evidenced in Section 28 of the Local Government Act which became law in 1988 and laid down that a local authority should not promote homosexuality in any way and must not make homosexuality legitimate as a pretend family relationship). There is a great deal of slippage over definitions. Sexuality is at least: a form of institutional organization (as in heterosexuality); a regulative (public/internal) discourse; a linguistic unity; a representation; a practice/behaviour; an identity; a desire; a form of citizenship. The category can never capture all the desires, physicality and bodily sensations that lurk under academic representations.

The Contortions of Sexuality: What is it?

It is impossible to understand sexual organization, discourse, representation, practice and the values accorded to it without an understanding of historical contingency and location. Sedgwick (1991) notes the problems in trying to define what sex and sexuality actually are and how they relate to gender. Sexuality is also equally difficult to define ranging through the array of acts, expectations, narratives, pleasures, desires, knowledges and identity-formations also often classed 'sex':

> To note that, *something* legitimately called sex or sexuality is all over the experiential and conceptual map is to record a problem less resolvable than a necessary choice of analytic paradigms or a determinate slippage of semantic meaning; it is rather, I would say, true to quite a range of contemporary world views and intuitions to find that sex/sexuality *does* tend to represent the full spectrum of positions between the most intimate and the most social, the most predetermined and the most aleatory, the most physically rooted and the most symbolically infused, the most innate and the most learned, the most autonomous and the most relational traits of being. (1991: 29)

Sexuality is thus a categorization of many different things. It is, as Hussein (1981) notes, merely a name given to an historical artefact. Sexuality, Evans (1993) argues, has, most frequently, been theorized within two discourses – that of individual expression and that of regulation. What we experience as sexuality, Foucault (1979) argues, is both the product and process of its representation, if experience is understood as the correlation between fields of knowledge, types of normativity, and forms of subjectivity. We are born into heterosexuality as institution and dominant norm, just as we are into systems of gender, class and race. Structural positioning and access to discourses and meanings is already circumscribed by social location. Heterosexuality is where subject positions such as mother, wife, girlfriend, are defined and institutionalized through a process of iterability, a regularized and constrained repetition of norms, a ritualized production, into which we are implicated on a daily basis (Butler, 1993). Heterosexuality is continually given legitimacy through its repetition and through the silencing and delegitimation of any alternatives. We are always implicated in the organizing system of heterosexuality, even if we define ourselves against it. Heterosexuality is the acceptable, dominant and for some often the only known way of speaking sexuality.

Foucault defines sexuality as a form of verbalization, based on definitions of discursive appropriateness

> I try to make an archaeology of discourse about sexuality which is really the relationship between what we do, what we are obliged to do, what we are allowed to do, what we are forbidden to do in the field of sexuality and what we are allowed, forbidden, or obliged to say about our sexual behaviour. That's the point. It's not the problem of fantasy; it's a problem of verbalization. (Foucault in Kritzman, 1988: 8)

Hence sexuality becomes a matter of what can and cannot be said. Heterosexuality is an authorizing discourse, it gives validity to 'correct' forms of sexuality. The silencing of women on matters of sexuality has a long history: Jones (1987) notes how in 1559 Court Ladies in England were required to use euphemisms, constructed from male fantasies, to speak about sex.

Hetero/sexuality is also a matter of economic and institutional organization:

> Sexuality is inextricably tied to capitalism's requirements for reproduced labour of different values, the buoyant consumerism of the metropolitan economies and, as with all capitalist social relations, sexuality's material construction is effected not only directly through the market, but also mediated through the state's formal machineries and practices of citizenship, and in all these arenas sexuality is, albeit attenuated, a channel of class relations. (Evans, 1993: 36)

Hart (1994) argues that heterosexuality, as an institution, is also an economy that maintains White supremacy. She argues that this is evidenced in the history of reproductive legislation, and especially the more recent 'right-to-life' movement, which incites White middle-class women to reproduce and, paradoxically, restricts access to abortions for women of colour and working-class women.[2]

Heterosexuality can also be seen as a form of capital interlinked with other capitals through social networks and cultural knowledge. It is often necessary for entry into sexual divisions of labour (Adkins, 1995). Heterosexuality can confer privilege but only alongside other relations of inequality such as class, race and gender. The total volume of capital will depend on the amalgam of these different positions. The women of this study, like those of Batsleer's (1994) and Fine and Macpherson's (1994) did not have problems conceptualizing sexuality as economic, as that which is commodified, traded, imposed and resisted. For them sexuality is not an expression of their inner selves, but an expression of the unequal power relations in which they are located and struggle.

So, sexuality and gender are the product of representation and reiteration produced through various technologies, institutional organization and discourse, epistemologies and practices. They are material practices. The sexed and gendered subject is constructed across a multiplicity of discourses, positions and meanings, which are often in conflict with one another and are inherently contradictory but which are circumscribed through access. We do not all have equal access to positions in discourse.

Sexual Classifications: Race, Class and the Lesbian

Foucault (1979) notes how the process of constructing woman as first and foremost a sexual subject was itself a class-bound project. As Chapter 3 noted, respectability was a key signifier in the class struggles between the aristocracy and the bourgeoisie in which women's bodies, speech and responsibilities were mapped out and circumscribed. The political struggle to consign values of decadence and respectability has always been a strategy of producing, distancing, making dangerous and regulating. The dominant representations of the Victorian urban poor as sexually decadent, diseased and dangerous enabled the construction of political regulations to distance, control and contain (Stedman Jones, 1971).

The struggles in which the representational evaluation of displays of female sexuality became coded through respectability began as class and gender struggles but were later extended to race. Ware (1992) describes how modes of colonial White femininity were defined in relation to particular constructions of Black femininity and White masculinity. As the power of the English aristocracy declined and the decadent aristocratic woman was rendered inadequate as a signifier of threat to colonial power, new forms of knowledge from science, medicine and anthropology, were produced in an attempt to legitimate colonialism (see Fryer, 1984). These enabled the construction of a sexualized other which respectability could be measured against and distanced from. Both Black women and men were designated as the dangerous, atavistic sexual other. Definitions of sexuality became deeply linked to class and race because:

> Sex is regarded as that thing which *par excellence* is a threat to the moral order of Western civilization. Hence one is civilized at the expense of sexuality, and sexual at the expense of civilization. (Mercer and Julien, 1988: 107–8)

Display of sexuality came to be designated as a practice of the 'other', a practice of the uncivilized, the one without respectability. The moral discourses of the nineteenth century, which were initially organized around a strategy of class disciplining and regulation, became combined with race. The structuring of official discourses through a series of oppositions – vice/virtue, filth/cleanliness, animality/civilization – around whose polarities the labouring classes and women were once differentially constructed were now stretched to also designate Black peoples. In so doing the links and differences between Black and White working-class women, according to Gilman (1992), became more blurred in respect to sexuality: Black female sexuality became equated, in the nineteenth century, with White working-class prostitution. White middle-class women (as Chapter 6 showed) were able to locate themselves within a pure and proper femininity, precisely because Black and White working-class women were defined and designated as unpure, dangerous and sexual (Ware, 1992). The embodiment of purity in the middle-class White woman continues to be reproduced (Dyer, 1993).

Moreover, the category of the lesbian was mapped onto these classifications. Hart (1994) explores the discursive dilemma that was produced in the historical recognition of the lesbian. Naming the activity threatened to produce the category, and thereby to mark a site that could actively be assumed. She notes how the entry of the lesbian into discourse was a historical construct that not only pathologized and criminalized her but also displaced the threat of women's sexual 'deviance' onto women of colour and working-class women. One reason for the discursive act, she argues, was to maintain a category of 'woman' that was purified and unmixed with racial and class differences.[3]

Historically, Hart (1994) shows how the lesbian was sexed through association with the already sexed Black and White working-class woman, groups who through their distance from the feminine were classed as 'non-women' and as dangerous:[4]

> Lesbianism was recognized as prevalent among women of color and working-class women: foreclosure would 'properly' pathologize it in order to obviate the 'contagion' of the White, middle-class European female. (Hart, 1994: 14)

Through these discursive manoeuvres heterosexuality was associated with respectability and middle-class women predominantly positioned as heterosexual. The heterosexual was a category, alongside femininity, designed to 'other' working-class women.

Thus, the heterosexual subject is a particular sort of woman, not working class or Black, but respectable. This is very different from the homosexual subject which, White (1980) argues, has become *the* sign of sex. The lesbian subject has been defined as perverse, deviant, dangerous and contaminating (Merck, 1993; de Lauretis, 1994) and most definitely not respectable.[5] The normalizing function of heterosexuality works precisely by defining what it is not. For the women to take up a lesbian identity (rather than play with it) would mean to disinvest their gains in respectability. They would become everything they have been trying to escape from. Also, until the 1990s, representations of lesbianism were not associated with glamour; rather, as Chapter 8 shows, they were associated with drab, worthy, serious, mad, bad and dangerous feminists. These representations offered little appeal to women who had learnt to negotiate their sexuality through glamour, had fantasies of a better (more glamorous) world and who already felt that feminism was not speaking to them.

Paradoxically, however, whilst the lesbian is sexed through class and race associations, she has a (modern) parallel categorization as part of the bourgeoisie. This was produced from 1960s and 1970s counter culture where sexuality signified self-expression, a site of rebellion, and a form of individualistic choice (Marshall, 1981). Weeks (1981) notes, by the 1960s 'permissiveness' had become a political metaphor, marking a social and political divide. So, lesbianism is represented by both association with pathological class and race contagion and/or as bourgeois individualistic self-expression. Neither of which are designed to include or endear themselves to working-class women whose desire is for respectability. A double distancing is made possible, consolidated even further by the women's prior investments in caring, family and motherhood.

Shameful Recognitions

Regulation and containment of sexual practice, speech and display becomes another surveillance responsibility for those who are positioned through sexual distinction (Lees, 1986, 1993; Walkerdine, 1989). The intensive self-regulation of sexual relations and sexual conduct, which Elias (1982) identifies as psycho-social surveillance, a key characteristic of civilization, engenders shame. He demonstrates how shame produces the ultimate coercion because it produces defencelessness against the external construction of superiority. Recognition of othering produces shame; a legacy which remains. Shame, Bartky argues, is the distressed apprehension of the self as inadequate or diminished:

> It requires if not an actual audience before whom my deficiencies are paraded, then an internalized audience with the capacity to judge me, hence internalized standards of judgement. Further, shame requires the recognition that I *am*, in some important sense, as I am seen to be. (1990: 86)

Shame involves a recognition of the judgements of others and awareness of social norms: one measures oneself against the standards established by others. The discourse of shame is one of the most insidious means by which women come to recognize, regulate and control themselves through their bodies, what Bartky (1990) defines as perpetual attunement. Kathy, for instance, will not let anyone see her body:

> I still make sure the lights are turned off and that I can't be seen. It would just be awful. I think I wear more clothes in bed than out. I'd be useless at one night stands, they'd have to wait while I got dressed for it. [Kathy, 1986]

The heterosexual encounter forces Kathy to evaluate her own body, of which she is ashamed, so she hides it. This was not uncommon. A respectable and modest feminine reputation, for instance, requires women to construct a disembodied sexuality which, as Martin (1989) notes, results in women seeing their bodies as separated from themselves, in need of control (or cover). Measurements of respectability are the means by which evaluations and judgements are made about the appropriateness of speaking and displaying sexuality and bodies.

The activity of sex is also experienced with shame by some of the women. They feel that it is something they should not be associated with:

I've always felt that sex is dirty, like it's something that animals do. I mean it's really undignified and it makes you look at yourself and it's dead embarrassing. I remember thinking how could I let me do that to myself. I just felt really ashamed about the depths to which I'd sunk. [Ann, 1992]

I don't know how women can be interested in sex, you know you see all these women on the TV and in the cinema all passionate and that and I have to look away. It's like how can they do that in front of millions of people. I'd be really ashamed if it was me. It's bad enough in front of one person, I think that's bad enough, but not in public. [Julia, 1986]

Sexual practice and respectability seem to be at odds with each other, evoking shame in the women's responses. Shame, argues Sedgwick is 'a bad feeling attaching to what one is: one therefore is something, in experiencing shame':

Shame . . . generates and legitimates the place of identity – the question of identity – at the origin of the impulse to the performative, but does so without giving that identity-space the standing of an essence. It constitutes it as to-be-constituted, which is also to say, as already there for the (necessary, productive) misconstrual and misrecognition. (1993: 12)

Sex is shameful for Julia and Ann because for them it forces a recognition of what they are meant to be: sexualized working-class women. They make this recognition when they see other women speaking about sex. For Ann, investments in dignity have led her to disassociate from sex completely. To be ashamed here invokes the policing of themselves.[6] Suzanne occupies a contradictory position on her sexual practice, which is closely linked into how she feels about her body:

You know there's moments when I can suddenly see myself, it's as if there's another person there doing it, as if it's not me, because I look awful [laughs]. There I am all contorted with rolls of fat showing in a completely undignified position and I think 'is this me?' Sometimes it's so alarming that I have to stop. Like it shocks me to think it's me and how awful I look. Other times, maybe depending on how much I've had to drink, I just laugh at myself and get on with it. It does disturb me though. [Suzanne, 1992]

The momentary recognition of herself as a sexual subject and body is brought into view alongside frameworks of respectability and these generate momentary flashes of dissonance. Suzanne does not want to recognize herself as a sexual subject. Nor does she have a belief that she is entitled to be sexual. Like many other forms of entitlement she cannot see any access. This does not stop her completely, as it does with Ann and Julia, rather through feelings of shame she is able to hold herself together as respectable. This is one of the ways in which the practice of heterosexuality is lived as classed and gendered. The actual practice of sex occurs within a framework of recognitions of how women have already been socially positioned.

Griffin (1994) argues that the process of distancing from sexuality is consolidated further by what she calls the 'norm of niceness' which locates working-class (Black and White) women outside of it. Through this the signifiers of sexuality are dispersed into other signs such as loudness, vulgarity, bluntness and openness (see Fine and Macpherson, 1994), or as Ortner (1991) notes, through hairstyles and clothing. Being continually marked as sexual through a multitude of signifiers generates resistance to and difficult negotiations of sexuality. It also means that shame is not infrequent. Fixing through signification generates recognition and disidentification. This frequently occurred on the caring courses.

Educated to be Heterosexual

The framing of sexuality within education can be characterized by many different regulative methods. The first, Foucault (1979) identifies as the internal discourse of the institution. Historically, he argues, the organization of education was predicated upon the assumption that sexuality existed, that it was precocious, active and ever present. The second method of regulation involves the maintenance of heterosexuality through the process of exclusion and delegitimation of certain forms of sexuality alongside inclusion and control of others, as in the attempts by the state to legislate against homosexuality (Section 28) whilst also legislating for familial heterosexuality (Education (no. 2) Act, 1986).[7] These domains of constraint set limits not only on what is difficult to imagine but also what remains radically unthinkable, providing a temporal condition for the ritualized production of gender and sexuality (Butler, 1993).[8] This heterosexualizing process also occurs across other sites of social policy such as tax and social security. The third mechanism of regulation involves the prioritizing of heterosexual masculinity as the norm through the organizational structure and pedagogy of education. The provision of caring subject positions (as shown in Chapter 4), also regulates the expression of sexuality.

On the caring courses the women were directly educated to be heterosexual.[9] Heterosexuality was not only institutionalized through assumptions about 'proper and correct caring' but was also actively encouraged through discussion and inclusion of marriage as a topic across the curriculum. One student even designed and made her own wedding dress in the needlework class. Marriage was a designated topic in Health Care for the first year PCSC and Community Care students. An exam question asks them to discuss the relevant criteria when choosing a marriage partner. The teacher justifies the inclusion of such a topic, and the teaching which led to the information used in the answer, which involves both racist and class based assumptions, in the following way:

> Well I think it is important for them to think about it, some of them, you know the type, just go rushing into it, having babies before what's what and not going to be able to cope and it's the children that normally suffer, so I think it's important that you point out the difficulties in certain types of marriage, you know forces marriages or mixed marriages say, the insurmountable problems need to be explored to assess if they are able to handle such things. [Mrs S, Health Care Tutor, 1983]

The inclusion of marriage, coupled with the many comments about the organization of family life which takes marriage for granted, not only implies that marriage and heterosexuality are inevitable, but also emphasizes that marriage is the only acceptable future positioning, and the assumption is made that students are in need of basic advice to 'get it right'. Inherent within such comments is the implication that students are inadequate, immature, incompetent and incapable, in need of training in respectable heterosexuality and that working-class marriages are likely to be ill conceived and representative of future 'social problems'. Just as the history and organization of heterosexuality is class dependent so is the take-up. It is assumed that because they are White and working-class that they will be married. If they were Black and working-class the assumptions would be different (see Mac an Ghaill, 1988; Mirza, 1992). Marriage is, however, seen as a gendered substitute for the problem of unemployment and the inclusion of it in an educational organization is seen to compensate for the lack of educational value provided by the courses:

> Yes, I do sometimes worry about what I'm here for with unemployment facing the majority of students . . . I often wonder what will happen to them, but even now most of them are involved with boyfriends, they'll settle down quickly and have kids, it's not as if they're the career sort. [Graham, PCSC tutor, 1983]

The women clearly recognize the underlying messages about class, but not about heterosexuality, which is normalized rather than pathologized.

> Like Richard he's saying when we ask him to explain things, 'Oh it's not important you don't need to know, you'll be married and settled down and that' . . . and he thinks he's joking but you know that's what he means deep down, we know he thinks we're thick. [Lisa, PCSC O, 1983]

However, whilst the women are able to challenge class-based assumptions they are unlikely to challenge the inevitability of heterosexuality and marriage which represent potential economic security and provide cultural success and status. Heterosexuality is thus also produced through economic and cultural incentive. (At this stage they believed that men could offer economic security; later, as Chapter 5 shows, they became more cynical.)[10] Being engaged provided status just as being married was a signifier of respectability, responsibility, desirability and material security. The institution of marriage is also supported by ideologies of caring and romance which maintain that the 'deep and meaningful' relationships involved in marriage and family life are so special that they cannot be experienced elsewhere (McRobbie, 1978). Marriage is presented in the same way as family life was: as a matter of 'standards' and appropriate practice. To be 'left on the shelf' was considered shameful; it meant being recognized as a failure.

Heterosexuality is not only reproduced on a daily basis through inclusion in the curricula and assumptions about future marital status but also through the continual sexualizing of situations. A central feature of the women's educational experience involved developing tactics to deal with being positioned as sexual (see also Stanworth, 1981; Jones, 1985; Halson, 1989; Kelly, 1989; Mahony, 1989; Mac an Ghaill, 1994). In actually dealing with what is seen by the perpetrators of sexual harassment to be 'natural' and 'normal' behaviour the women become implicated in the normalization of heterosexuality, masculinity and the policing of their own behaviour. Although they are continually positioned by sexuality they refuse to be rendered powerless in this process, as the following comments suggest:

> I've just had it up to here with him, he gets on my nerves, always asking me about my boyfriend and trying to put his arms around me. He's a real dirty old bastard and when I came in and he said somat about whose bed had I got out of the wrong side of, well that was it, I just thought fuck it. I was so bloody angry . . . If I'd have opened me mouth to him though I don't know what'd've come out. [Karen, PCSC, 1983]

> He calls it counselling. I call it plain fucking nosy. I'd like to tell him where to get off but you can't, can you really? [Michelle, CC, 1983]

Such comments, indicative of many, suggest that during their time at college most of the women had to deal with intrusions and innuendoes about their supposed class-based (hetero)sexuality. They were forced to make these recognitions which are not uncommon in education: Halson (1989) notes how linguistic double meanings are a frequent and significant part of classroom interaction; contributing, by embarrassment and/or humour. Situations are heterosexualized at women's expense: women are not allowed to forget their heterosexual functions and the embodiment of positions of power/powerlessness that these contain (Holly, 1989; Mac an Ghaill, 1994). The regulation of themselves through displays of respectable caring is contradicted through being positioned as sexual. All the work they put into trying to construct a coherent caring identity is constantly undermined by assumptions about their sexual practice. So they are caught in an institutional situation ubiquitous with sexuality in which they must constantly demonstrate their distance and respectability.

Paradoxically, responses involve using their own (hetero)sexuality as a tactical resource.[11] Female sexuality as fun, empowering and pleasurable, aspects which momentarily escape regulation, are brought to use in the classroom. Flirting is a tactic the women use to avoid being positioned by others as sexual; it is seen as playful and non-direct. Flirting is always ambiguous, so can be denied if necessary. Yet flirting is also one of the ways that male teachers can establish familiarity with students whilst also controlling them. The women use flirtatious behaviour to turn situations to their own advantage, for example:

> It's odd how on the one hand they're our teachers and they're meant to be clever and that, but then you can wrap them round your little finger. You just do the seduction bit, you know all soft and helpless like, make them feel they're big and clever and everything. If you behave pathetic like, but look good too, you can get away with anything. I don't think I've handed in anything on time yet. [Alison, PHS, 1983]

> Yea like Tina, she just pretends to be all dizzy and confused with her little girl lost look, and they all fall for it. We all have a laugh about it, but it's not fair really, like only a few can get away with it, you know with Tina's looks. [Susan, PHS, 1983]

> Also if you pretend to fancy them and chat them up they'll treat you better, like better placements and that, it's stupid though. They're stupid to believe that girls

like us would ever fancy the likes of them . . . Like they've got nothing going for them . . . but it's survival isn't it? [Judy, PCSC, 1983]

Flirtation, however, is only an option for those who conform to stereotypical attractiveness. The implicit sexual market where exchanges are governed by estimations of relative value reappears. The teachers can provide educational capital, the women have corporeal capital; they are traded in relations of unequal exchange and power. Whilst control and humiliation of teachers is celebrated, it can also create resentments and divisions, as those who can trade are seen to benefit to the detriment of others. Flirtation entails the reproduction of traditional femininity (e.g. passivity, helplessness, dependency), the stretching of traditional femininity (e.g. directly chatting-up) and the reproduction of heterosexuality. When their sexualized tactics of flirting and fantasy fail them, the frequent daily humiliations of sexism that generate latent resentment lead to periodic explosions. These occur only when the women believe that the situation has become unbearable and that confrontation is worthwhile either to relieve the monotony of classroom life or to 'get their own back'.

Five women from the Community Care group and four from the Pre-Social Care group felt able to make regular confrontational stands, which sexualize classroom interaction, to embarrass and humiliate male teachers. Whilst they represent only a small proportion of those involved, once they had begun the challenge, many others joined in what can be seen as collective constructions in which others are relied upon to fill in the gaps. Indeed, it would be difficult for women to make such challenges on an individual basis which would locate them within the 'slag' category of feminine policing (Cowie and Lees, 1981; Lees, 1993). The following example from 1983 illustrates the form of the incident in the Community Care group:

God have you seen that [spoken really loudly for everyone to hear staring at a particular part of a male teacher's anatomy]. [Therese]

Bloody hell, what the heck could you do with that, not much. [Mandy]

Can't believe he's got kids with one that size you'd think he'd never be able to get it up. [Therese]

[to Graham, the teacher]: You've got kids haven't you how did you get them? Get someone else to do it for you? [Karen]

Bet he plays with it in his pocket. [Michelle]

I expect that's all it's good for. [Therese]

Whilst these incidents can be seen to be part of a general social activity, the comedy of the classroom situation, in which lessons are brought to a laughing and embarrassing standstill, they are also significant in terms of what they tell us about the use and construction of sexuality in the classroom as a means for control. Cunnison (1989) and Ramazanoglu (1987) demonstrate how male teachers use jokes about femininity to assert their authority over female teachers in schools and universities. Likewise, Mealyea (1989),

Westwood (1984) and Hearn (1985) demonstrate that humour is used as both a mechanism of status maintenance and a means for the dissipation of alienation. 'Having-a-laugh' which can be of central interest for both female and male students (Willis, 1977; Wolpe, 1988) can also be seen to be about questioning assumptions about gender and sexuality. Pessimistically, Dyer (1985) notes how comedy, as a technique to ridicule male sexualities by bringing insecurities onto the surface, always ends up by asserting as natural the prevalent social definition of that sexuality.

These outbursts also voice a vulgarity from which most of the women, in trying to generate their distance from sexuality, are at pains to disassociate themselves. Yet, very occasionally they feel safe enough to display sexual vulgarity when it is packaged as fun and justifiable. Paradoxically, they use vulgarity to retain dignity. However, not all of the women approve of this sort of challenge:

> I know why they do it and it's really funny sometimes – it's hard not to laugh, but I just wish they didn't have to be so crude. I just wish they could do it in a nicer way. [Anna, CC, 1983]

> I know, sometimes it's just dead embarrassing, like you can see Richard getting all flustered and that, and it's not fair really, he's not the worst. I think it goes a bit too far. [Manda, CC, 1983]

> There's just no need for it, they don't have to do it. I think it shows them up for what they are, crude. I didn't expect to see that sort of thing here. [Janet, CC, 1983]

Yet both Anna and Manda understand the reasons why such a response occurs, although they would prefer the use of different methods to achieve the expression of revenge and resentment. However, they want to establish a clear distinction between themselves and the other women. Janet does not feel it is justifiable and condemns such display locating herself firmly with respectability and away from expressions of direct sexuality. The direct articulation of aspects of sexuality is in contradiction to the discourse of femininity found in some women's magazines which show the reader how to care for, care about, and protect masculinity.[12] Yet they obviously only do this when they feel they have to or should.

Cohen (1982) would argue that the challenging responses of the women represent the survival tactics of every subordinate group, which neutralize the consequences of powerlessness without challenging the prerogatives of power. Yet these comments do make explicit the challenges to the repetitive sexualizing of education and the positioning of themselves as sexual, even if only momentarily; they are more than just reproductive contestations (Aggleton, 1987). These incidents attempt to both redesignate the object of the sexual discourse and the place of that object, hence the reference to 'putting them back in their place'. In the temporal conditions of education the process of iterability, the regularized and constrained repetition of norms, is destabilized (Butler, 1993). Foucault (1977a) argues that the power of institutional apparatuses can be sapped through the surreptitious reorganizing and undermining of power through a multitude of tactics that redistribute discursive space. The women felt no need to respond to the women teachers in the same way. Targets are only those who make visible displays of power and sexualize them. Distinctions of respectability are thus reproduced not only through the regulative structures but also through the responses that these generate.

However, the constraints, iterations and productions take on a different shape outside of the relatively safe space of the almost single-sex educational environment. Different subject positions are available for occupation which are far more closely self and other monitored and constrained. The explicit regulation, through internal organization and discourse, and the institution-alized relationships of authority and power in education are very different from the ubiquitous, diffuse, disorganized power that exists in the women's cultural environments. Sexuality is still organized through gender, race and class but is far less obviously externally regulated. Self-monitoring and regu-lation occur through reputation. Proving and maintaining respectability involves taking responsibility for the control of overt sexual display. Producing oneself as respectable becomes the means by which internal regu-lation and the specific policing of bodies occurs. The construction of heterosexual subjectivity is framed by, not only external constraints which can be put into effect through institutionalization, the policing of space and/or violence, but also through the positioning and negotiation of one's em-bodied 'self' *vis-à-vis* sexual classifications constructed through respectability. The following section concentrates on how women perform, produce and use het-erosexuality in the construction of themselves as non-sexual and sexual subjects: how they monitor themselves and engage in power relations.

Producing their own Sexuality

In the social spaces outside of college, discussions about sexuality take on a highly precarious manner. Their ability to directly speak sexuality to confront masculinity is compromised in exchanges with those they consider to be eco-nomically and culturally significant, such as prospective boyfriends, or by the cultural fear of reputational labels. The following conversation (from 1985) illustrates the extent to which the women who were involved in challenging male sexuality in the classroom are implicated in the surveillance of their own:

> *Mandy*: Like on the telly on Wednesday, these women were playing out problems and the like and one says to the man, she says . . . 'you've come too soon' . . . I couldn't believe my ears, I was dead embarrassed, how could she, how dare she, I could never do that to anyone.

> *Ruth*: A girl couldn't you know, say things like that, prostitutes could, but girls like us they couldn't.

> *Janet*: I hate it when people talk about things like this, it makes me really ashamed to think about what's expected of us women, I'd just rather not discuss it.

This distinction that is made between themselves, and others who enjoy and are in control of sex, suggests that they consider themselves to be relatively powerless in sexual encounters, resigned to manipulation. In contradiction to the previous provocative encounters, these statements suggest that women have more knowledge about masculinity than about their own sexuality. Although they can make challenges and directly confront masculinity within the safe space of the classroom, they are unable to challenge their own sexuality to the same extent due to the investments that they make in prospective heterosexual relationships to try to guarantee future security and to the lack of knowledge about their own bodies. For instance:

> No, don't be daft women don't have urges like men do, theirs are uncontrollable once they get going. [Ruth, PCSC, 1983]

> It's always the males, they're real randy sods. [Mandy, CC, 1983]

> Women only have them when they're turned on, you know if he's doing something to her. [Cindy, PCSC, 1983]

> Well I expect I've got feelings but I wouldn't go round hunting for someone, it wouldn't bother me much if I never had sex again, truthfully. [Ruth, PCSC, 1983]

> You must have had the whip it in, whip it out and wipe it type, it can be really good, I expect it's 'cos Mark were married once, he's divorced now, you know, he's older, he's got more idea, I think they only have an effect on you if you fancy them. [Lindy, PCSC, 1983]

This lack of belief in their own sexual feelings and lack of control over their own bodies is illustrative of how their positioning in heterosexuality ultimately informs and constrains their responses, suggesting that they do not feel as confident about their own sexuality as their previous resistance would lead us to believe. They distinguish between those 'types' who enjoy and are in control of sex, and themselves. These distinctions map onto the respectable and unrespectable women (Nead, 1988). Yet they also display a coded way of displaying sexual knowledge alongside condemnation of the sexual (even Ruth has had sex). Because experience of sex signifies maturity they want to show that they are mature and experienced, hence Lindy's comment. This implicates them in many contradictory moves which also involve the continual monitoring and self-surveillance of their own sexuality:

> *Bev*: Well what if you were in bed with someone and you didn't like what they were doing, would you say anything?

> *Therese*: God, no, never, no, I could never do that, you just couldn't it'd ruin everything it's like when they put their fingers inside you and you're meant to like it, you know they're looking at you and it hurts, you move away gradually like, you know squirm a bit to get them out, but God no I'd never be able to say anything, they'd think you were a real tart.

> *Ruth*: I wouldn't dare.

These responses, first made in 1983, did change over time and seemed to be influenced by experience and the conferral of respectability through marital status. In the follow-up interviews similar distinctions were drawn and surveillance and evaluation of themselves was still in place, particularly by single women. Unlike the women who had and remained married and who felt that their sexual respectability was established, the single women, feeling that it needed to be explained, constantly referenced their relationships. Emphasis was placed by most on the commitment and seriousness of these, although reference was sometimes made to what they perceived to be aberrations: 'flings' and one-night stands. Sarah, in particular, was most reflexive about her manoeuvrings through sexual conduct, power and identity:

> *Sarah*: I don't wait for men to pick me up, I'd wait for ever and still be a virgin. One guy came up to me in here [pub] last week and said 'do you want a fuck tonight'. I said that's no way to ask a lady [laughs]. Me and Cath we write lists and we grade them, we went into Queensgate with all the Rugby players and I'd slept with six of them. One actually asked me if I was embarrassed about my past. I used to have the biggest name in this town when I was 18.

> *Bev*: Did that get to you?

> *Sarah*: I ran away from it and went to Spain and then I made an effort. The problem is that everyone knows you round here, but I tell you if I ever got married my husband would have his wedding ring super glued on [laughs].

> *Bev*: Are you confident about your own sexuality?

> *Sarah*: I fake it.

> *Bev*: So it's not about you getting pleasure?

> *Sarah*: No, it's about making sure they enjoy it and come back for more. I can be a real evil bitch.

> *Bev*: So your own pleasure isn't important?

> *Sarah*: It's like a game. I don't like the thought of them thinking I'm bad at it and telling their friends . . . I just can't trust any of them. They tell you all this crap, I don't know why they do it, is it for their own egos? I just don't know. Sometimes I go home crying and can't take anymore, there is a hard front but underneath I'm really soft. I just want someone to put his arms around me and tell me it's all right. Believe me I'm really good until I've had a few wines and it all goes to pot. After I was badly hurt by John and Alan I went through a stage that when I drank I slept with somebody. It's bodily contact. I stopped a couple of months back. Stopped. Can't do this anymore. I slept with five guys in a week [laughs] I just stopped, couldn't do it and everybody gets to know about it, like in the pub they always talk about you to their mates. I'm not a nymphomaniac I must just be highly sexed. I didn't shag anybody when I went to Crete, mind you, I was just off it at the time. [1992]

Sarah's comments illuminate some of the self-constraints and constitutive elements to heterosexuality. Her sexual experience is framed through wider social categories such as reputation and respectability; sexuality is translated into heterosexual performance and Sarah is implicated in the evaluation of it through the standards established for her. She partially recognizes herself through the recognitions of others which she knows are not positive (hence her rebuttal 'I'm not a nymphomaniac') but she has sex because she wants to be seen as desirable. Her distance from and awareness of her performance enables temporary resistance to be made from the imposition of power. But the performance is unsustainable, as demonstrated in her despair 'can't take anymore'. It is not a parodic subversion; it is a defensive strategy.[13] Sarah has the knowledge that she is playing, that it is a game, an act, a performance, yet she also knows that she enters the heterosexual encounter already categorized as of lesser value as a woman with a sexual reputation and she continues to categorize herself. She is aware that she will be assessed on her heterosexual performance, also believing that the judgements she can make of the hetero-sexual encounter (such as the graded lists she makes with Cath) carry far less cultural value.[14] Sarah's heterosexual performance is, paradoxically, a tem-porary defence within heterosexuality against the ability of men to judge, classify and position her. Her knowledge that she is performing enables her to *feel* in control and retain some dignity. Her identity is not produced from this performance, rather, it is the recognitions that enable her to see herself not as heterosexual but as contradictorily un-respectable, powerless, desirable and in control. It is only the man that signifies heterosexuality; the processes of recognition potentially occur through all categorizations.

Sarah's representation of her sexual performance is mediated through the discourse of respectability, through the signifier of reputation. It is both biol-ogized through reference to a high sex drive and culturalized through reputation. Sarah is able to abdicate responsibility by blaming factors (wine) that take her out of her control. She desires to be desirable and wants bodily contact to confirm desirability but constantly eludes it through her own knowledge that she is performing and he is probably lying. The ability to authenticate desire is lost in the defensive power plays. She remains unsatis-fied and is constantly evaluating her own performance. By making the distinction between sexual pleasure and desire for desirability, sexual satis-faction is lost. Sexual pleasure is not the issue as power cannot be achieved in this context if it is. But the pleasure gained from having knowledge that enables distance from, and feeling in control of, heterosexual power relations is greater than the pleasure she may derive from sex itself.

This suggests that heterosexuality is not a homogeneous category and not occupied in the same way by all heterosexual women. Whilst heterosexuality is an organizing principle of sexual difference which is institutionalized, it can also be taken up in many diverse, contradictory and resistant ways, hence het-erosexualit*ies* (Hollway, 1984). The difference between Sarah and Sonya is enormous:

> For me I think of how much I know now to what I used to be like. If someone had said it was normal to have sex standing on your head I'd have probably believed them. I didn't know anything and my first boyfriend was just a fumbler. He was clueless. He was only 16 poor lad. But since leaving college and having two long serious relationships and I think 'cos they've both been older that I've learnt things. Like they were both married before me and I think they knew a lot. I think Mike's first wife must have been a real go-er. He used to say 'oh Sally used to like it like this' and at first this used to really piss me off. I was also a bit embarrassed, to tell the truth, well in fact shocked. Sometimes I used to think he was making things up just to tease me. He bought me loads of sexy knickers and things once because that was what she liked but I told him I wasn't wearing those they'd make me look like a right tart. But I think they both taught me lots. It's daft isn't it? men having to teach you . . . well not anymore. With Peter we now talk about things and I know what I like. It's just so much easier, I wish I'd known then what I know now. Then

I had the body for it. It's odd when you think like then I had the body and didn't know what to do with it, now the body's going and it works so much better but it looks far worse. I have to be careful now of the positions I get into [laughs] in case I drown him in fat and lose him. [Sonya, 1992]

Confidence gained through relationships and knowledge about body and sexual practice here make a difference to the use of performance (although the body is still seen to be problematic). Women who were able to negotiate and claim power in heterosexual relationships made less investment in male power and were less likely to generate defensive distancing strategies. This suggests that not all heterosexual femininity is by definition a performance, although it may be performed (as it was in Chapter 6). A performance requires conscious action, it is knowledgeably and consciously enacted.

Responses to Lesbianism

Some performances are obvious masquerades. One group of women when they were 19 years old masqueraded as lesbians. They were particularly confident in their bodies and appearance and spent a lot of social time together going clubbing. They all had cultural approval and respectability through 'steady' boyfriends.[15] They had moved into radical thinkability by using knowledge of lesbian appearances and non-sexual behaviour to play at being lesbian in heterosexual clubs:

Jenni: It's just for a laugh, it stops us getting hassled, it's a good laugh.

Sam: I don't know how we started it, it was just for a laugh, it keeps the creeps away, I've been called a 'fucking queer bitch' but you just laugh, most of the time you have a really good time, you're left alone. In fact the funniest time is when you go to the loo and all the women move away, that's a laugh in itself.

Mo: Yea, some guys they say 'you're a load of lezzies', but we just laugh, they're only jealous, like all men want to think they can have you. They don't like to think that you might not be there for them. It's good, we're there for ourselves.

Anita: We went up to Club K [Manchester gay club], it was brilliant, really wild and loads of gorgeous men, I love it, but it is funny we didn't do it up there, I don't know why, it just didn't seem right and if a woman got the wrong idea and came to chat me up I'd be scared shitless.

This ability to masquerade as lesbian, however, does not mean that they radically challenge the reproduction of heterosexuality. It is a temporally linked contestation in which nothing is jeopardized or lost in its performativity. It is used in a similar way to femininity – as a useful contextualized cultural resource: lesbianism used in the service of heterosexuality. These women want a safe, hassle-free space for women and have found a way of achieving it without great loss to themselves but by using space that others had created for themselves as 'safe'. The lesbian masquerade enables the elements of female friendship such as 'having a laugh' and talking and physical closeness to occur.[16] To achieve this they use gay and lesbian space without having to suffer any of the consequences of labelling, which they can easily laugh off, or structural inequalities. Mo is aware that women are expected to be there for men and uses lesbianism to construct a challenge to it – what other cultural resources could she use to make such an obvious social gesture? But equally they may know that they make themselves more heterosexually desirable by displaying overt lesbian sexuality.[17] Also, displaying overt sexuality with men would not only lead to a loss of respectability but in a dance club (at that time) be seen as inappropriate. A glamorous form of lesbianism (labelled 'Lipstick Lesbians', see Blackman and Perry, 1990), which has now become chic in some heterosexual clubs, enables straight women who are invested in glamour to 'pass' as lesbian. By using the gay club to look at men and classify them as gorgeous Anika safely practises her sexuality in a way that does not jeopardize her respectability (which would happen if she did it in straight clubs).

Their trying-on and wearing of lesbianism is not so different to the wearing of special club clothes, which they save for nights out and which have little bearing on their everyday. To date it has had little impact on the potential transformation of their heterosexuality. In fact it may even reinforce the boundaries between heterosexuality and lesbianism. Their performance is ambiguous but not necessarily as transformative as theories of the postmodern or queer may suggest, their playfulness enables their heterosexuality to remain intact whilst constructing a safe space for them as working-class women to be together and to touch each other without fear of redress. It enables an eroticizing of their friendship, a means to play at being sexual without incurring any loss, an ability to disclaim responsibility without the take up of a political identity.

Conclusion

Heterosexuality is institutionalized, reproduced in material practices, regulated and normalized through signification, consolidated through links with other forms of capital and enacted in performance. The struggles around sexuality were not fought through claims to identity but by negotiating power in everyday settings. Heterosexuality consolidates respectability. The women do not become heterosexual, rather, they are positioned by heterosexuality. In their identifications with respectability and caring they assume heterosexuality by default. Yet they refuse to be fixed. It is in their recognitions of this positioning that resistances are produced. Their recognitions of themselves as heterosexual are only made when they disassociate themselves from other sexed identities such as signifiers of working-classness and lesbianism. To be lesbian would only add to their being positioned as sexual which is what they were trying to distance themselves from. They do not take up the signifier, which, as Butler (1993) argues, is always a matter of taking-up that by which one is oneself already taken up, constituted, initiated. For working-class women invested in respectability it is very hard for them to take on a sexed identity (either lesbian or hetero) because it is precisely being sexed which they have been trying to avoid in their claims for respectability. The production of themselves as sexual subjects occurred in response to being sexualized and through the use of lesbian masquerade which enabled the construction of a safe-space, intimacy with other women and sexual display without condemnation or loss of their prior investments in respectability. Enactments of different performances which drew on sexuality were produced as defensive strategies *against* their being sexualized.

This chapter shows how the organization and practice of heterosexuality is put into effect in an institutional context. Specific forms of heterosexuality are produced in education by external legislative regulation, in which alternatives are delegitimated in an attempt to make them radically unthinkable. The education for heterosexuality is mediated by race, class, gender and place: it is assumed that the women will be poor, married, remain in Railtown and be a problem. The women were, however, able to challenge the internal discourse of the institution and the positioning of themselves as sexual by others by making gender power plays, which were put into effect through their sexualizing of situations through the occupation of masculine subject positions. This was only momentary because the discourses of morality, articulated through respectability, and achieved through the caring subjectivity, in which they had made investments, overdetermined the challenge. This was further consolidated by the investments the women made outside of the institutional setting and where the assessment of them as sexual subjects was more acute and potentially damaging.

It is the refusals to be rendered powerless in sexualized encounters (be they educational, social or intimate), when historically positioned as sexualized beings, circumscribed by limited position in discourse and being aware of the continual evaluations and distinctions produced through speaking or displaying sexuality, which were continually present over time and contexts.

Heterosexuality has been variously represented by forms of feminism as offering the possibilities of utopia (Soper, 1995), as a route to sexual freedom and as repressive and destructive, a form of eroticized degradation (Jeffreys, 1990). It has been seen as compulsive, an imperative, normalized and fixed. It has also been represented as a 'choice', yet choice is always limited to individualistic discourse which ignores all the material, institutional and discursive factors involved. How then can it change? One suggestion has been to denormalize the category of heterosexuality. However, this ignores the class and race connotations in-built into the concept. If certain groups are positioned as sexual (historically and through signifiers dispersed throughout culture) then attempts to name and fix them as heterosexual to generate awareness is doomed to failure. The working-class women of this chapter do not want to be categorized as sexed, and certainly do not want to be classified by others who have the potential to make distinctions and judgements. It may be far more effective to challenge homophobia than heterosexuality. When heterosexuality is such a strong marker of respectability it will always induce investments from those positioned at a distance from it and pathologized as a result.

Notes

1 Speaking of sexuality directly in a research context is often difficult: the research setting is mediated just as much through respectability as is the everyday experience of sexuality. Discussion of sexuality became more open as close friendships developed over the duration of the research with a small number of the women. I have chosen not to use some very emotional and intimate disclosures which when located in the context of cold analytical discussion appear as exploitative and voyeuristic.

2 This, Hart (1994) argues, becomes increasingly more apparent when analysing the campaigns of Operation Rescue, the US anti-abortion protesters who, often violently, campaign outside abortion centres. Phelan (1993) notes how members of this organization see themselves as performing missionary work, not dissimilar to that of the earlier colonialist project. This became apparent in the recent 'conversion' of Norma McCorvey (the woman named Jane Roe in the historic Roe v Wade judgment in 1973) who was 'baptized' by the leader of Operation Rescue, Rev. Philip Benham.

3 'The entrance of the lesbian into representation as a *negation* is coupled with her carrying the mark of aggression' (Hart, 1994: 11). She demonstrates how the shadow of the lesbian animates representations of violent women from Victorian times to present day.

4 Foucault (1977b) argues that women have always been defined through sex: some in opposition, some as sex.

5 Although Evans (1993) notes how the categories 'rough' and 'respectable' are transposed onto social classes and reproduced in *The Spartacus Guide* (1988), a guide to gay male tourism.

6 This is reversed in camp discourse, which by the comment 'shame on you' evokes that which should be seen as shameful but which is celebrated as challenge.

7 Evans (1993) maps out the enormous amount of legal enactments in the UK which have tried to define morality and allocate responsibility for it onto different social groups and bodies.

8 Butler notes the problems with social constructivist theories which suggest that sexual orientation is a matter of choice over sexual desires. She argues that sexual constructivism needs to take account of the domain of constraints without which a certain living and desiring being cannot make its way (1993: 94).

9 As Louise Allen (1993) points out, so are most women, but it does not always work (from personal communication).

10 The economic difference a man can make depends on where the women are situated in the first place. If they are unemployed a man is a financial disincentive and can lead to them losing their benefit. If they are employed a man can help them with mortgages; although an unemployed married man can severely reduce their income by becoming a 'dependant'. While they carefully avoided unemployed men, this did not guarantee that their partners, who initially offered economic incentives, did not become unemployed, as many did throughout the course of this study.

11 De Certeau (1988) draws a distinction between strategies and tactics. Strategies, he argues, have institutional positioning and are able to conceal the connections with power: hence, the strategic use of masculinity. Tactics have no institutional location and cannot capitalize on the advantages of such positioning. Rather, tactics constantly manipulate events to turn them into opportunities. Tactical options have more to do with constraints than possibilities. They are determined by the absence of power just as strategy is organized by the postulation of power.

12 Since the time of the research women's magazines have undergone a transformation in which autonomy and sexuality have become more explicit. The introduction of magazines like *More*, *Bite* and *For Women* suggest that women have a right to the expression of sexual desire and sexual needs. The downside of this is that women are expected to spend even more time on their bodies and to evaluate themselves through performance. Even *Just Seventeen* (aimed at a younger 12 to 16-year-old audience) has shown explicit diagrams of the clitoris and commentary on what to do with it.

13 Parody has been suggested as a strategy to disrupt the stable signifiers of heterosexuality. But these signifiers are always raced and classed and are often reproduced as such through parody. As Chapter 6 shows parody often reproduces the working class as the object of ridicule (Tyler, 1991).

14 This is completely opposite to a group of Black female rappers (BWP) and a group of young African-American women interviewed by Sharon Thompson (1990) who are aware of their power to expose as fraudulent displays of male power by making judgements about male sexual (and/or economic) performance; see Skeggs (1994b).

15 They went to different clubs with their boyfriends from when they were together. They were more adventurous without boyfriends.

16 See Chris Griffin (1994) for an account of the absences on work on friendship and sexuality.

17 Lesbianism is frequently marketed as a commodity for men's pleasure in traditional pornography and in tabloids such as the *Sport* and the *Sunday Sport*.

8

Refusing Recognition: Feminisms

Why should I be a feminist? [Sarah, 1992]

When Gramsci (1971) speaks about the consent that is given to power he analyses how it is predicated upon an assessment. This is based upon understandings and interpretations of experiences which have already occurred and an estimation of what is to be the likely outcome of the giving of consent. Feminism is assessed by the women of the study in a similar way. They related their knowledge of feminism (produced through representations and through everyday interactions) to their own investments and experience. This meant that recognizability and/or relevance were crucial factors in the assessment of feminism. The process by which they made assessments was dependent upon the contact they made with feminism and hence upon what sort of feminism was on offer and what access they had to it. Their positioning by and investments in class, femininity and heterosexuality (as shown in the previous chapters) informed their responses: experiences of inequality, harassment, abuse and feelings of injustice engendered an entry into feminist understandings, but experiences of being classed, having security and emotional affirmation, provided obstructions to entry into interpretative feminist frameworks. If their investments in being a multitude of caring, familial, respectable, glamorous, feminine, heterosexual selves are simultaneously held together they present a veritable resistance to acceptance of most discourses of feminism. If a feminist interpretation was made of a particular experience then other prior experiences were often reassessed. As this chapter will show the women did not recognize themselves as the subject 'woman' of most feminist discourse.

This chapter investigates the cultural representations of feminism which were available throughout the research and maps out how discursive positions were occupied, negotiated and resisted. The first part explores the major influences on the form feminism took in the 1980s and was produced after writing the second section. This is because it provides a framework for understanding the women's responses and the confusion they experienced about what feminism actually is. It was their fragmented and contradictory comments that led me to investigate what discursive frameworks were available for them. The first section maps out why feminism may produce such confusion, the second shows how it is known by the women and the third section explores how feminism speaks to and positions the women, providing them with interpretative frameworks by which they can understand their experiences. It asks who feminism is speaking to and discusses how feminism has come to be defined.

The women's responses are always historically located, the product of positioning and partiality. They are interpretations made at a local level of global issues and representations. For instance, at the start of the research the representations of anti-nuclear campaigns at Greenham Common influenced the women's perceptions of feminism. By the end of the research it was Madonna and the semi-clad women of Page Three.[1] Wicke argues that in the US the celebrity zone is the public sphere where feminism is now in most active play:

> This zone lies on the border of academic feminism, adjacent to it, sometimes invading it, at other times invaded by it . . . The celebrity zone is fed by streams flowing from civil society. (1994: 757)

Whilst this is less so the case in the UK, a great deal of feminism is mediated though celebrities such as Madonna, the comediennes French and Saunders, and celebrity feminists such as Germaine Greer and Camille Paglia.[2] These are the forms of representation to which the women had access.

Just as we have textually mediated femininities we also have textually mediated feminism. Their knowledge is produced from the unequal material relations in which they are inscribed. It is produced from the interpretations they make of their experiences in relation to the frameworks which are available to them. Their positionings inform their responses to feminism. The feminisms that I live with on a daily basis are practically unrecognizable to the women of the research, for I have different social and discursive positions to occupy, different knowledges and investments. Time is a central constraint on the women's involvement in different forms of feminism and access to knowledge about feminism is another. There were also limitations on the space to practise feminism. The last section of Chapter 6 showed how space *not* to be feminine was severely restricted and stigmatized. Here I discuss how the space to *be* feminist is similarly constrained.

So What is Feminism?

It is almost impossible to hold on to one watertight definition of feminism. When feminists speak of women, Alcoff (1988) argues, they often seem to presuppose that they know what women are. This is one of the central definitional problems. Feminism and feminist theory often assumes women, without a specificity and often with little knowledge and understanding of the differences between women (Riley, 1987). This has led, as noted in Chapter 2, to only some women's experiences becoming the basis for feminist theorizing. Feminism has never been universal, even though it has been soundly criticized for the pretence to be so (see, for example, Black feminist critiques in *Feminist Review*, no. 22, 1986). It has always been partial, being spoken by specific interest groups, and usually by those with class and race privilege (see Fuss, 1989; Ware, 1992).

In the 1970s in the UK attempts were made to develop feminism as a representative movement with a clear agenda which included: equal pay for equal jobs; equal educational provision; free 24 hour nurseries; abortion on demand; free contraception; a woman's right to control her own fertility.[3] Since this time hard battles have been fought and different fragments have developed (Segal, 1987; Ramazanoglu, 1989). The diversification of feminism is a product of its influence and success. It now exists across a range of sites and forms such as the popular, in local community activism and within academia and in different guises.

Ramazanoglu (1989) argues that there is a gap between the theory which explains women's lives and the experience of living women's lives. The debates within academic feminism are themselves fragmented, straddling a range of disciplines and ranging from research on policy initiatives, which have a direct link to women's everyday lives, to the more abstract debates over, say, epistemology. Often, the more theoretically sophisticated feminist analysis becomes in the academy, the less likely it is able to speak to women outside of it.[4] The debates that rage between postmodern and materialist feminism occupy a completely different space to that occupied by the women of this research. Feminist knowledge has been produced but it has only been distributed selectively. The women of the research do not have access to academic feminism and if they did it would not be easily accessible because of differences in educational capital. Access to knowledge about feminism is central to understanding how the women respond to, resist and take up feminism.

Part of the problem in Britain, as noted by Coward, is that there is not a clearly articulated discourse which can be identified as feminist:

> There is too much awareness amongst British women of differences between economic groups, too much reluctance to promote already over-privileged women at the expense of others, and too much concern with the complex social and economic realities amongst which most women move to allow a simple set of women's demands. (1994: 13)

There is not a 'woman's position' on the leading issues of the day. We are not even certain what the term 'woman' means anymore (Riley, 1987). Fragmentation, dispersal and the marketability and notoriety of certain aspects of feminism means that the women only have limited and partial knowledge about feminism.[5] Griffin (1989) argues that because feminism is not a unitary category with readily identifiable boundaries and consistent sets of ideas, this creates problems for identification. It is, she argues, a contested space, a category under continual dispute and negotiation.

Douglas (1994) argues that this may be not only a result of the many different types of feminism available but also a product of schizophrenic media coverage. By tracing the US media campaigns from the 1950s (and there are strong UK parallels) she presents a picture of media disarray in which feminism is simultaneously legitimated and trivialized and many contradictory positions offered. Television attempts to understand feminism through tentatively trying to find an angle and simultaneously trying to contain any threat. It is underpinned by a fear of dismissing feminism completely and thereby being out of touch. This, Douglas argues, produces a form of feminism that is, effectively, a pastiche. She demonstrates how the media utilize binary divisions to set up women against feminism. One mechanism was the establishment of feminism with grotesque women against the non-feminists who were defined as refined and respectable women. The use of terms such as 'feminazi' indicates the vitriol that is poured onto feminists.[6]

The statement 'I'm not a feminist but', Griffin (1989) argues, is a way of speaking feminism without making an identification with it. It may display a refusal to be fixed as feminist, but may also be a sign of the inability to position oneself as feminist because of confusing and contradictory messages about what feminism actually is. As Douglas (1994) argues, there are as many ways of becoming a feminist as there are of becoming a woman. Fragmentation has provided many different ways for women to be feminist, although the positivity of diversity is rarely represented. So in order to know how women can make identifications with feminism we need to know what is on offer and what subject positions are available for occupation. The next section documents the representations and feminist discourses in circulation at the time of the research

Available Feminist Discourse

During the period of the research different events influenced the representations of feminism: the first was Greenham Common; the second was the continual electoral success of Margaret Thatcher; the third was the proliferation of popular feminism and the fourth was the Miners' Strike. These marked out contradictory bases for feminism. Thatcherism, for example, provided the conditions for the development of 'corporate feminism' but the same period also generated working-class women's resistance through the Miners' Strike.

Greenham Common was the site for the location of an American Cruise Missile base in the South of England. A group of women organized a peace camp outside of the gates in 1981, which became women only in 1982 and which today still exists. The media coverage of Greenham, as A. Young (1990) notes, was based on a mythology which centred on the fact that the protesters were *women* and that aspects of their womanhood were *deviant*. Young (1990) recounts how the women's peace protest was represented as a criminal activity. It was the women-only aspect that came in for greatest coverage (in the tabloids) and greatest attack: the women, they claimed, were 'man-haters'. This, they argued, was signified through the women's clothing which – rather than being seen as functional clothing for those living in tents and cold conditions – was noted for its anti-femininity and lesbianism. A. Young (1990) recounts the story of the *Express*'s 'undercover girl' whose reportage warned men not to let women near the camp for fear that they might 'go gay'. A veritable moral panic around women's sexuality was generated and this appears in confused form in the comments of the women. Feminism, in this case, entered into and fed upon prior discourses about womanhood and deviance.

Out of this came the popular association of feminisms with the image, identified by Kelly and Breinlinger (ud.) in their research on women's perceptions of feminism, of the 'loony, lefty, lesbian madwoman'.

Also of significance during the course of the research was the presence of Margaret Thatcher who was marketed to women in the 1979 and 1984 election campaigns as 'a housewife'. She specifically addressed women through rhetoric on the family (Thatcher, 1982). During the long period of Conservative rule the values of individualism, meritocracy and self-help came to permeate the discourse of the popular (Hall, 1983).[7] Margaret Thatcher embodied what Loach (1987) identifies as 'female triumphalism', an ability to triumph over others whilst still retaining qualities of femininity. This ability was, however, individualist rather than collective (McNeil, 1991). The rhetoric of motherhood was promoted simultaneously as the economic conditions were made worse for working-class mothers (Wilson, 1987; Franklin et al., 1991).

The Thatcher emphasis on the 'special' nurturing and mothering values, Segal (1987) argues, fed into a 'new feminism'. She sees this 'new feminism' to be a particular manifestation of radical feminism which defined women as virtuous and men as vicious, engendering a clear discourse of difference. This puritanical feminism, she argues, provided a series of prescriptive behavioural (and clothing) codes (see Wilson, 1986) in which women's conduct and appearance was monitored. Although Thatcherism did not pick up on the vicious men angle which defined men as a completely different species and heterosexual women as colluding with the enemy, it was able to market sameness without difference (Segal, 1987).[8] The depiction of feminists as men-haters impacted upon the women's understandings of feminism as did fragments of individualistic discourse.

The 1980s witnessed a consistent media discrediting of left-wing initiatives, as part of Thatcher's policy to eradicate socialism from Britain. Discrediting occurred, first, under the guise of attacks on the 'loony left' for policies of anti-racism and anti-sexism, then later, under 'critiques' of political correctness. Feminism was trivialized and was associated with petty behaviour such as slamming doors in men's faces and language campaigns to eradicate 'man' in language use.

Pathological representations of feminism ran simultaneously alongside the rhetoric of individualism promoted by the Thatcher government. Discourses of entitlement also entered the equation. Once the prerogative of a feminist agenda, which claimed entitlement to equal pay and so on, entitlement became part of an ideological package associated with the rights of the consumer (Skeggs, 1995c). Judith Stacey (1988) uses the term 'post-feminism' to describe the movement from social entitlement to an individualistic discourse of entitlement.[9] She argues that the depoliticization of many of the central goals of second wave feminism are influenced by the Protestant notion of free individual will. Post-feminism, according to Stacey, describes the assumptions of entitlement to decent work and decent home and applies to the lives of millions of American women who would be quick to distance themselves from the label of 'feminist' but believe in equality at work. Entitlement beliefs predicated on individualistic lifestyle are consolidated by the contradictory nature of popular feminism which feeds easily into the rhetoric of individualism in which women are presented as having choice and as not being judged by others:

> In the early 1980s Feminism fell victim to its proscriptive legacy which dictated certain codes around dress, fashion and sexuality. Being a feminist had come to say more about what you didn't do – eat meat, fuck men, wear make up – than what you did do. It is no surprise that 'eighties girl' is more attracted by the rhetoric of *laissez-faire* freedom that is so seductively presented by the Right. (Stuart, 1990: 32)

A sense of entitlement, however, was not an element in the cultural capital of the women. Their conceivability structures did not enable them to think that they were entitled to many things. They rarely saw themselves as individuals with rights and had not been positioned historically to do so. This is not dissimilar to Oakley's (1974) research on housework which documented how middle-class women tended to base their self-concept on individualism whereas working-class women defined themselves through their domestic roles.

Stuart (1990) suggests that the 1980s represent a time period when popular feminism became separated from professional and academic feminism. Popular feminism, she argues, is the feminism which can be marketed. It is the sort that pervades our common sense, but also the sort which is ironic, playful and glamorous. I watched *Desperately Seeking Susan* (dir. Susan Seidleman) with a group of the women who took enormous, noisy delight in the control displayed by the Madonna character. The research was also marked by proto-feminist pop such as Cyndi Lauper's 'Girls Just Wanna Have Fun' and 'Sisters are Doing it For Themselves' by Annie Lennox and Aretha Franklin. These popular moments marked sites of pleasure where the women felt vindicated for collectively being positioned as women. Yet, Benn (1994) argues that in Britain we have witnessed a change of emphasis from feminism as a politics of collective struggle to feminism as a form of image dominated success.

McRobbie (1991) shows how a wider range of feminist ideas entered the realms of common sense in the 1980s. These ideas do not just exist at the site of the popular, she argues, but have become embedded in our taken for grantedness. Rapp (1988) suggests, paradoxically, that it is the taken for grantedness of some of feminism's aims that is the greatest victory and simultaneously the greatest problem. The taken for granted, she argues, does not happen all at once, nor is it all of one piece or even inevitable; rather, it occurs in non-synchronous fragments.

However, it is the ability to pull out the individualist aspects – such as sexual power, autonomy, respect, self-esteem, entitlement – of feminism and make them marketable which has helped to generate these contradictory effects. These aspects give feminism a popular front which provides selective appeal and reaches across class and race divides by speaking to the desire to be autonomous, powerful, confident, glamorous, and so on. But while it does this it detaches feminism from the social and the systemic. It reduces feminism to the solitary individual and linkages across difference and distinction and any sense of collective responsibility are made invisible.[10] Restricted representations come to represent the whole. Feminism becomes only that which offers personal power, autonomy and independence.[11] Or, obversely, as that which is mad, bad or dangerous. Popular feminism has been hailed as the site of change, but it may also have the opposite effect; it may be the site of obfuscation where links between individual and collective are blocked, in which individualism is seen as the only form of address, which is not recognized by many women as speaking to them.

Yet whilst the individualistic marketing of feminism was being established (and in the 1990s is consolidated through the feminisms of Camille Paglia and Kate Rophie who set up earlier feminism as whinging and victim producing)[12] the 1984 Miners' Strike was also taking place. The Miners' Strike began in Britain in 1984 following an orchestrated attempt by the Thatcher government to destroy the Miners' Union, which was the strongest trade union in Britain and which had been (partially) responsible for bringing down the prior Conservative government. The Thatcher government attempted to close down coal mines and make thousands of miners redundant. The NUM (National Union of Mineworkers) responded with a strike. After a year with no respite and with a dirty tricks campaign which included government funding for the establishment of an alternative miners' union – the UDM (the Union of Democratic Mineworkers) – the miners were being criminalized and starved. In an effort to provide support their wives became involved and organized food provisions and campaigns to keep the strike going. Admiration for these women did not diminish throughout the course of the research. There was not a single woman in the whole study who did not support the Miners' strike. It is from these contradictory sources of feminism, from these cultural, historical, economic and social conditions that the knowledge and available discursive frameworks were formed.

Therefore at the time of the research the women were offered a mixture of mad, bad, loony women alongside powerful successful (community and corporate) women and female triumphalism, denigration and individualism. These contradictions and multiple-feminist representations are picked up by the women when they try and position themselves in relation to feminism and to understand what feminism means, as the next section will demonstrate.

The following responses need to be read as productions in which I am the dialogic other, the designated feminist. The women knew of my feminism (and for some I became the representative of feminism) but unlike their responses to class, they did not see feminism as something which had the power to position them as completely inadequate or lacking in value.

Confusing Feminisms

Fragments of feminist discourse appear in their responses as they position themselves in relation to the questions and the discourses offered in the first section.[13] The question was 'What does feminism mean to you?'

I've never been one. I just do what I want. I don't preach about it. I'm into Amnesty and the ANC but I wouldn't go to those rallies. I wouldn't even go on a miner's march although I did queue for ages to sign the petition. This government is totally knackered but I think the media is pushing this Royal thing too far, they've got no chance now [reference to Prince Charles and Princess Diana divorce]. I like Princess Di . . . I'm strong mind you. I say don't patronize me when people try to talk down to me and lie to me. I won't take no shit. It's like when guys they say Sarah you're gorgeous, you've got a good personality, well then why won't they go out with me? You just can't afford to leave what you've got now, nothing's safe. If I leave there now what have I got? Nothing, back on the dole and I don't want to be back on the dole at 30. [Sarah, 1992]

Sarah's answer continually moves around: feminism is thought of initially as political involvement, as something which has to be displayed, as something which you join and in which you participate; then it shifts back into the personal in which the contradictions of feeling strong but not desirable are explored. Feminism here becomes a matter of control over one's life. It then moves back to the public sphere and feelings of economic security. It is as if feminism implies change so that Sarah feels she needs to change jobs to designate herself a feminist. The fear of change and scepticism about the possibility of change also featured in the research by Kelly and Breinlinger (ud.). They suggest that feminism is equated with making changes which in the political climate of the 1980s was impossible to perceive by many women.

The same question was asked of Linda who immediately equated feminism with anti-pornography:

I'm really not into pornography. I can be very straight sometimes. I think Page Three degrades women, why are women expected to do that? What is the difference between a women and a man? But I think it's degrading. Now Mary Whitehouse she's a pain in the arse. If people don't like things they don't need to watch. I don't mind porn existing I just couldn't watch it in front of a man – I'd just laugh. My friend at work had video parties, all porn with animals and that. She's been told off for laughing. She laughs all the way through. The people who use it have to be weird in themselves. [Linda, 1992]

Linda displays a clear distaste for pornography and the inequalities it visualizes but she is concerned to disassociate herself from the censoring, puritanical position which is signified here by Mary Whitehouse (president of The Listeners and Viewers Association which monitors media output for sex and violence and continually calls for censorship). Linda wants to show that she is anti-censorship. Her ambivalence may have been generated through the tabloid newspaper the *Sun* which she reads on an occasional basis and which ran a long campaign in the mid-1980s against feminist 'spoilsports'. Holland (1987) demonstrates how, through narrative devices, the *Sun* makes a particular class address to women, and in so doing defines feminists as moralists, patronizers and condescending middle-class educators who are determined to spoil the fun, miss the joke and see sex as degrading for women. It is this designation of feminism as moralist and anti-humorous which Holland thinks is particularly difficult to challenge. To take up an anti-Page Three position would mean being positioned with the serious, the boring, the educated and the pretentious who spoil the enjoyment of others. The women had learnt ways of dismissing any feminist debate of a serious nature:

> Are you ranting again? [humorously said by Jane C in response to a comment I made about inequality] [1983]

and:

> Why don't you just accept you're never going to be equal and get on with your life and enjoy it. It's no use moaning all the time. [Sharon, 1985]

Feminism is here positioned as anti-pleasurable, boring and serious. It is associated with whinging and passivity.[14] In this context it is not surprising that Linda makes it clear that she does not want to occupy this position by maintaining that she does not mind porn existing and that it can be seen to be a laugh. However, she simultaneously feels degraded by it. This emerges even more clearly from the second part of her answer:

> I think it's nice for women to get equal parts to a certain extent but I also think it's nice for a man to open doors for you so they don't, instead of letting go and your nose is knocked off. I think feminine does have a lot of parts in your life I just go along with the way things are . . . The only thing as regards feminism that annoys me so much, I mean not that I read a lot of papers and look at the pictures, I don't really, particularly, but what annoys me is you get a Page Three girl but where do you get the man? I mean I'm not particularly bothered to look at it but it does annoy me, where's the man? Where is he? [Linda, 1992]

Here a slippage is made between the feminine and feminism. Feminism implies difference whereas the feminine is part of the way things are. In the first part of Linda's commentary, she rejects the feminist discourse of difference, yet it is her belief in the lack of difference that generates her outrage at Page Three. She sees no reason why women should be made to do things that men are not. This suggests that Linda is clearly angered by inequalities but she also wants men to behave in particular ways, and as occurs later in other comments the opening of doors is seen to be a significant sign of respect. Men confirm respectability by showing respect.

Angela's response is significantly different. She sees feminism to be about strong women:

> *Angela*: Er . . . in a way I suppose it makes you . . . you want to look like a woman . . . I don't think it's awful. It's strong. I'm a strong woman I've always had the leadership in me. I'm determined if I want something I'll go at it, even if I can't. A lot of it is to do with children . . . I think of somebody strong, looking like a woman, acting like a woman . . . er . . . I think of somebody headstrong. On the surface they are but you don't know about underneath. People who can achieve like people who say I can get that job, they go and get it. I wouldn't classify myself as a feminist.

> *Bev*: Why not?

> *Angela*: Don't know I've never thought about it before. I don't know what else to say. That's my answer. [1992]

Angela sees feminism to be associated with differences between men and women and thinks that only strong women are feminists. The confused start as she works out her position on the issue suggests that she is working with a visual image which displays strength, but which may not be about looking like a woman. So the emphasis is then placed on appearance. A feminist is someone who looks like a woman, a strong woman, therefore not feminine. But then she doubts the façade of appearances; people may be vulnerable underneath. Feminism then becomes associated with women from another social group: those who achieve. From the beginnings of an association with feminism – 'It's strong', 'I'm strong' – Angela moves into a position of disidentification. Feminism is for those who achieve. It is this realization, I suggest, which makes her refuse to discuss the issue any further with such vehemence. By asking the question I forced an act of recognition. Angela, who is very comfortable seeing herself as a strong woman, does not recognize herself as a strong woman who also achieves things. (If you refer back to Chapter 5, it is Angela who is having to deal with bailiffs.) Her knowledge of her own positioning influences her understanding. Angela measures herself against her perceptions concluding that feminists don't look, or do things, like herself. She sees herself as different, not just from men, but from feminists too. Compare this with a comment she made earlier in the research which was part of a conversation totally unconnected to feminism:

> People think I'm dead strong and capable because I'm determined and if I think something is right I'll say so. I'll speak my mind. Never mind all this 'stand by your man' bollocks, if he's crap I'll tell him. I'm not one of those women who'll let people walk all over them. I've got a good job, good money, good parents. I'm independent now and it's the best way to be. I'm not prepared to be treated like a pile of shite anymore . . . People have to respect me. I'll treat them with respect if they do the same to me.[15] [Angela, 1986]

Here Angela articulates a feminist sensibility: resistance to abuse, being independent, strong and prepared to stick up for herself. She has a strong sense of self-worth. Yet none of this is framed by feminism (nor, obviously, femininity). She behaves in a way which is recognizably feminist but does not recognize herself as such. She is a strong woman, made, by my questioning, to recognize herself as less strong when she realized that she did not fit into a framework of feminism informed by middle-class values of achievement. Feminism is a recognition of difference, a difference from other women with different forms of capitals.

Mary also associates feminism with strength:

> *Mary*: At first it means billboards and shouting and all that militant stuff and then when I think about it, it means women being more in control, women being more in control of their lives.

> *Bev*: Are you a feminist?

> *Mary*: I'm not a feminist at the moment. I'm desperate for control and feel that I've lost all my control. I thought you stupid cow what have you done.

> *Bev*: If you were in control would you see yourself as a feminist?

> *Mary*: Yes, probably, but I can't see it happening for a while. [1992]

For Mary the image of a feminist is someone who is always in control of her life. Mary has no ideological resistances to feminism, and would wear the label if she felt in control, but she does not. The individualistic discourse of autonomy, independence and control, so effectively marketed through women's magazines such as *Cosmopolitan* and heralded as popular feminism, has led Mary to measure herself against it and find herself wanting. The fantasies of independence, autonomy and self-esteem are not associated with the reality of Mary's life which she feels is out of control. Feminism is seen to require control and the achievement of power which is very hard to live up to; vulnerability, lack of autonomy, dependence and lack of control are embedded in the daily lives of most of us. To measure oneself in terms of control is surely a hard punishment, but also a very effective way of generating distance from identifications with feminism. Popular feminism has generated disidentifications. It is through interpretations of their situation and their experiences that recognitions and disidentifications are enabled from feminism: they cannot see themselves as feminists. Feminism does not fit into their conceivability structures; it cannot be envisaged. It is not part of their imaginary.

Jane C has interpreted feminism in a less personal way, which enables her to articulate what Stacey (1988) identifies as post-feminism:

Bev: When I say the word feminism what does it mean to you?

Jane C: Rights, equal opps, things like that.

Bev: Do you see yourself as a feminist?

Jane C: I like to see equal rights and equal pay and things like that, I suppose so. If two of you are working why can't the husband share the ironing, cleaning and cooking? I don't see why I should obey as they say, he'd have to go and obey somebody else [laughter]. I suppose I am in a way but I won't say . . . I'm not really heavy on the subject but I'll turn around and say you male chauvinist pig, you know, bits. But there again I was working with all women. [1992]

Like Linda, Jane C implies that there is a seriousness associated with feminism: 'I'm not really heavy'. She sees feminism to be about equality at a public and private level. She feels she has been protected from sexism at work by working with women and is prepared to speak out and challenge sexist behaviour. The refusal to obey occurred in many of the women's comments and was most likely provoked by the Royal Wedding of Prince Charles and Lady Diana Spencer and the publicity surrounding the deletion of obey from their wedding vows. Although Jane C is prepared to see herself as a feminist she cannot bring herself to complete the labelling. She counteracts her reluctance to identify as feminist with an example of her feminist behaviour.

For Jane McD feminism is seen to be outside of her social space. It is something associated with those who use a different language:

Bev: What does feminism mean to you?

Jane McD: I'm not very good on big words. I suppose I would think that feminism is . . . er . . . people who want to have women's rights and all that and that sort of thing. People who don't do what I do, stay at home with the kids. I suppose it's opposite to that but I may have them mixed up. I believe in women's rights in some ways but they go too far, it's like anything, like people complaining about coloureds, yes they should have rights but it goes over the top. Like a situation where you can advertise a job for a Black person but not for a white person. I think it's the same in the sense that they go over the top don't they? Yes I think you should have your rights, should be able to vote and do jobs men do if that suits you, if you're capable of doing it, but I don't think there should be favouritism. In the Police Force there's favouritism for women, women get maternity leave but men don't get paternity leave. [1992]

Unlike Angela, Jane McD does not see feminism necessarily associated with women like her who are full-time mothers. For her feminism is not an identity based on attitude and affiliation but on social role. Like Linda she finds the term confusing. But she knows that feminism has a connection to extremism, hence the comments about going too far. The trivializing of feminism appears to have been effective; it makes dismissal possible for those with only limited knowledge about feminism. Jane McD reiterates the rhetoric of the popular press because this is all she knows about feminism. Even women's rights are translated into those for men. She performs a textual mediation by interpreting this discourse through her experience of being married to a policeman who, when she had her children, was not entitled to take time off work. As a result rights become acts of favouritism.[16] They are not something which she sees herself possessing. It is this reductionism which is produced when women have limited access to feminism. Jane McD is not totally resistant; rather, she does not see it applying or having any benefits to herself, only disadvantages.

Direct Resistances to Feminism

Janice, however, is outraged:

> *Janice*: I'm not one of these for burning their bra or anything. Like I'm quite disgusted that they've let women into the church now. I think it's nice for a man to be a vicar. I wouldn't like a woman to marry me. I'd be put off by that.
>
> *Bev*: Why?
>
> *Janice*: Because it's nice. Like when we got married. I'm just a bit old fashioned. I wanted obey not that I do obey but I said it.
>
> *Bev*: Let's get this right, you want the traditions but you're not going to obey?
>
> *Janice*: Yes we joke about and he says you have to obey. I see myself as a strong woman and I think I deserve equal pay. It's just I don't like the idea of women marrying. I think I'm just old fashioned and traditional. Maybe it's because my sisters are a lot older. [1992]

Janice believes in equal pay and sees herself as a strong woman but she also wants to keep to traditions and be told to obey (whether she will or not is a different matter and knowing Janice this is unlikely). Here, religious beliefs and traditions interfere strongly with Janice's perceptions of herself. Her comment also suggests, a point applicable to all the women above, that feminism is not practised as a coherent continuous framework for understanding. It operates in fragments, appropriate for some places and not for others. It is not central to their recognition and production of themselves. It just does not figure as a form of identification. Nor does it figure as a necessary disidentification, something to be resisted (like class). It is not seen to be something they feel positioned by or appropriate to their lives, unlike femininity which could be used by the women to feel good about themselves, or at least to enable them to avoid un-pleasure.[17] Even the feminism with the 'feel good' factor has generated insecurities, operating as yet another standard that cannot be achieved.

The resistances of Lucy and Cindy are of a completely different order:

> *Lucy*: I'm not the sort of person feminists would want me to be part of. For a start I'm happily married, then I have two children and one's a boy and I love them all. I'm not going to get rid of my husband or little boy just because they're men. It's just rot. In fact our Julie is far more trouble. I think it's girls, we were talking about this this morning, it's the girls these days that are all the trouble. You should see her knock him about if she gets the chance.

> *Bev*: Why do you think you'd have to get rid of your son and husband?

> *Lucy*: It was our Samantha she was telling me about this nursery in London where they've banned boys from, she said that even at the baths you couldn't take your sons into the women's with you. I said well that's stupid, but she said it's true, she'd read about it in the paper and, you know, feminists have always hated men. I just think what are the boys, more like, what are the mothers meant to do when they go swimming? A 2-year-old couldn't get changed in the men's by himself, it's ridiculous. [1992]

> I'm just not that sort of person. I'm not a lesbian for a start and I really like men. I mean really like them, you know everything about them [laughs]. I like the door being opened for me, basically I like to be treated like a lady. I want all the nice things. I want to be able to tell all my mates about the nice things and compare notes and that. Yea we diss men, all the time, I said sometimes that's all we talk about, but it's a laugh. They're harmless. [Cindy, 1992]

Lucy and Cindy have clear images of what they think a feminist should be and they know they are not this sort of person. They associate feminism with lesbianism and make disidentifications by affirming their relationships to men. Lucy's comment draws from the trivialization of feminism in the tabloids (it must be true I read it in a paper). Whilst we know about the millions of critical and resistant media readers (see, for instance: Seiter et al. (1989) and Barker and Beezer (1992)) there are also those whose prior experiences and knowledge do not enable them to counteract the information about feminism which is offered. (This, Hartmann and Husband (1974) argue, is precisely how the media reproduces racism.) Lucy's sister, Samantha, spoke with authority and from the bits of knowledge Lucy already has about feminism it seemed entirely plausible.

Cindy believes that feminism would deprive her from talking about men and having a laugh with her friends. It is seen to be morally censorious. Which, as Constance Penley (1993) would argue, is not surprising. Her research suggests that it is the puritanical, anti-sexual, anti-glamour stance attributed to feminism through the publicity successes of anti-pornographers, such as Catherine MacKinnon and Andrea Dworkin, and their links (through the Meese Commission)[18] with the fundamentalist Christian Right in the US, which has alienated many young women. A similar resistance is documented in Britain by Hunt (1990). It needs to be remembered (from all the previous chapters) that these women feel the constant pressure of judgements of others. The last thing they want to do is embrace another position of moral authoritarianism. They do not want to be judged by other women. The difference between the ease of embrace of feminism by two middle-class white women (documented by Hobsbawm and Macpherson, 1989), and the women of this study are phenomenal. The cultural capital of the middle-class women predisposed them towards feminism, whereas the opposite is the case for the working-class women of this study. Resisting being an object of surveillance and judgement is one of their major daily struggles.

It is on the issue of affiliations with men and refusal to be morally judged by others that these White working-class women share their resistance to feminism with their Black counterparts. The women invested in positive relationships with men do not recognize or identify with the unequal, oppressive and abusive relationships identified by feminism. Cathy and Jane take a different position on men to Cindy. Rather than seeing men for fun and pleasure, they see them as suffering from inequality:

> You know what really disturbs me about feminism and I guess the real reason why I wouldn't want to be a feminist is the way it's so anti-men. It just doesn't make sense all this stuff about men as evil oppressors and that. I look at Kevin, and I think, well, my dad too and his brother, it's like what have they got going for them. They've no future. They've no job, they're miserable, they don't know what to do with themselves. I worry if Kevin can keep going you know he keeps saying he's got nothing to live for and no hope. And he's meant to be strong and in control and all that. All I see is a desperately unhappy, sad, pathetic boy. It's rubbish they just don't know what they're talking about. They live on another planet. [Cathy, 1986] [Kevin was Cathy's ex-boyfriend with whom she remained in contact. He committed suicide in 1988. He had been unemployed for five years.]

> I'm not down with all that man hating nonsense. Most of the men I know are the same as us. In fact, now in this area, we were saying before, there's more women getting jobs now than men. It's the women who are in control. They can't do much without any money. [Jane, 1988]

Their allegiances with men of their social class means that they see feminism as resolutely middle class. The representations of patriarchy as all oppressive and men as always powerful does not resonate with their experiences, although allegiances may be produced as much through dependency and inequality as through empathy and pity. The representations do not offer a dialogic bridge that can be crossed (cf. Pearce, 1994). Like Angela, Jane McD and Mary, feminism is for another sort of woman: a 'woman' with whom they do not identify. As Fuss (1989) argues, one of the problems with the term woman is that as theorists we always have to specify which sort of woman we mean; it seems these women do it automatically. As Jean so clearly articulates:

> *Jean*: Feminism is for women like you, you know the sort who read things, like that paper there [reference to the *Guardian*]. It's for those who only have themselves to worry about.

Bev: What do you mean?

Jean: Well if you had a family and that you'd not have time to worry about yourself and your job and getting better rights for yourself and that because you'd be worrying about normal things like the shopping and cooking and getting all that done.

Bev: But if you had better pay and things wouldn't you have less worries?

Jean: Yes, but that's for the sort of jobs you do. Like most part-time jobs they pay shit wages whatever and if you ask for more money they sack you. You can only ask for better things when you're able to. It's like if I said to my boss you're sexually harassing me, he'd tell me to fuck off . . . I'd be out like a shot. Yea, I do think it's right that we have these issues to think about, but as per usual it's always the best off that benefit and then they come and say hey we need you to support us. They can fuck off. [1986]

Here we have the logical conclusion to the marketing of popular individualistic feminism: feminism is seen to be selfish, a prerogative of the privileged, something that benefits those in different economic, social and cultural circumstances. There is a fatalism in Jean's acceptance that before any change will occur you have to be in the right place to instigate it. But there is also anger. Jean is aware that feminism can offer benefits from which she is still excluded. By asking the question I become representative of the patronizing, privileged, policing authority of feminism. Her comments are not dissimilar to the resistance articulated to white feminism by Black women which have been well documented (Joseph and Lewis, 1981; Amos and Parmar, 1984; Bryan et al., 1985; Spillers, 1984; Bhavnani, 1989; hooks, 1989).

For Feminism

Feminism, however, can speak to working-class women when it provides an interpretative framework for the experiences they are having. It is then often articulated through a heroic or conversion narrative. Feminism becomes the explanatory factor which can extend across the totality of their experiences. It is through events such as domestic violence and rape that feminism speaks across difference and connections are made. For instance:

Yea, I'm definitely down with feminism. You must think that's really funny now. I remember having that big argument with you at college. Do you remember I turned up with a black eye and I remember saying, it's dead embarrassing now, but I'm sure you'll remember . . . I said to you, well, I told you it was Dave and I said it's 'cos he's jealous and really he must have loved me loads to get that jealous and you said it wasn't about love and I was livid. I thought of course it was and you just couldn't see it and you didn't know him. Well, as you know I married him. It was disastrous. Don't you dare say 'I told you so' [laughs]. When he was fine it was OK. He was lovely, paid me loads of attention, he was really affectionate, bought me little cuddly toys and that. But then he could just turn. You never knew when it was coming. Well, it was always after a drink, but sometimes he'd be really sexy after a drink so you never knew which way he was going to turn. I was a wreck by the end, we just had to get out. You just never knew when you were going to get it and I didn't really care about me, but I didn't think it was good for our James. We left and went to the battered women's place at X. They helped get us sorted out and got us this place. It's not brilliant, I know, but anyway what I'm trying to say is that it was just talking to women in the refuge and you start to think and realize you're not the only one and it's not you and, you were right, its not about love but it's about power. I came to feel he always had power over me and I used to just respond to him and stopped being me. It was all for him. There was a woman down at the Centre and she talked to me about all these things, about all the power men have over you and you don't even know about it at the time. Loads of women are blind to it. They say stupid things like 'he loves me really' but he doesn't [laughs]. He just wants to control you. [Felice, 1992]

For Felice the coming together of feminist explanatory frameworks with her experience enables her to re-evaluate her relationship. As these insights are used to explain events her previous understandings come under scrutiny and are no longer considered to be plausible. It is also about timing. When I provided a challenge to Felice's investments in Dave when she was at college she resisted. At that time she had a greater investment in being loved and culturally validated. As the amount of abuse increased over time her investments no longer were enough. She began to disinvest. Her concern for her son along with her own fear enabled her to leave and it was the contact with women at the refuge that enabled her to see things differently. Her narrative of overcoming adversity is told as a power struggle in which she comes out as a woman with some control. The feminist explanation enables her to rescue a sense of dignity and self-worth.

Many of the women's experiences and responses could be classified as feminist, if they are not forced to fit a coherent and consistent framework. They are often momentary responses to local conditions rather than the wearing of an identity (which does not in itself produce feminist responses). In many ways their public, collectivist behaviour could be seen to be more feminist than the individualism of some academic feminists who do make the identification. Many of the women are involved in struggles over their working practices, struggles which produce a feminist analysis:

I'd never go back into caring. It was the worst mistake of my life. I'm taking them through a court case. I've got the support of the union. I'm expecting about £35,000 from the industrial tribunal if it ever gets finished. They just feel they can treat women like shit and nobody will do owt about it because they need the work. Since leaving I've found out that it's nearly always the women at the bottom and the men at the top and they just expect you to do anything because they have the power. [Michelle, 1992]

Michelle's account is less of a heroic narrative than one of revenge. Her work experience was so intolerable that she had to leave. It was only through union involvement that she came to realize that the exploitative practices in institutional caring could be generalized to other women. This involvement makes possible the connection into feminist understandings. However, whereas Felice re-evaluated the whole of her life on the basis of feminist explanations, Michelle just uses it to understand her work experiences. As Chapter 6 showed, her investments in femininity are still high; the ability to make links into all of her experiences has not occurred because of this. The level of discontents and types of experience effects the connections that are made. Both

Felice's and Michelle's openness towards feminism is made when they recognize themselves as survivors of abusive relations.

For those who support and identify with the Miners' Strike different feminist recognitions are made:

> I think they're brilliant. It's like all these women who've been stuck at home for ages have suddenly decided to fight for their rights. It's just brilliant. I'd do the same. We went down to the club when they had him out of *Coronation Street* on, you know, Vera's husband, Jack Duckworth, it was a benefit for the miners and we gave them money. Mind you he wasn't exactly supportive to women with his jokes and that. But I think what they're doing is right. [Paula, 1985]

> It's the women who've kept it all going. If it had have been down to the men they'd have gone back ages ago. It's the women who are organized and holding it all together. I don't know all the ins and outs of it all but I think that they're protecting their communities. There's so much unemployment, they're fighting for the last chance. It's the only chance they have left to protect their families, like all their futures. [Sue, 1984]

> I'd do what they did if I'd have been a miner's wife. It's only right, the government were trying to starve them back to work. It's not right. They were only protecting their families. [June, 1985]

Here identification is not made on the basis of being a woman, or of a survivor of abuse, but by being a member of a family and a community with a livelihood to fight for. It is a more general connection which does not rely on discourses of difference, on being judged by others, on disinvestments in men and families *and* which does not involve enormous amounts of change when they are trying continually to generate security. Rather, it is to fight from where one is positioned with cultural approval, which suggests how central class is. Feminism needs to find an address for class solidarity even if it is not expressed as such by the women. Perceived injustice, as Breinlinger and Kelly (1994) argue, is an important trigger for activating feminist change, and as all the above comments testify, it is injustice that has enabled their discursive shifts, their movements into other interpretative frameworks. But some movements demand more of women than others. A movement into middle-class White feminism may involve the complete loss of all that has been invested in, a loss of the only cultural capital they have and know, a movement into a place where they are unlikely to have respect. Doane (1989) argues that it may ultimately be the case that all feminist positions are in some sense uninhabitable or only uncomfortably inhabited. For these women it certainly feels that way.

Although clearly not identifying or recognizing themselves as feminist, the women are involved in many struggles which could be seen to be feminist: over the use of space, constructing safe areas for their children to play, organizing campaigns to save a local nursery and challenging sexist behaviour. Most are outraged at the negative representations of women in the media. They display a lot of anger at the expectations which are made on the basis of gender. This anger remained even as the issues changed: when they were younger it was about domestic responsibility, education and appearance; it later became about childcare, mothering and the labour market. They also knew that they experienced inequality. As Fine and Macpherson (1994) note, feminist scholars often forget the amount of daily struggle and resistance in which women are engaged.

Feminism may, however, offer a fantasy of a better life. The popularizing of fragments may enable feminism to present the plausibility of different ways of being:

> I used to think that being a feminist meant that you had to be ugly and shouting and all that. But now I think that's daft. Now it means to me not being a doormat, standing up for yourself – you have to, nobody else will. I love the woman on that car ad. Like she comes home and he ignores her so she just gets, she just thinks, stuff that I'm off, and she gets in her car and drives off. That's how I feel. I wish I could just drive off . . . What sort of car have you got? [Sarah, 1992]

If feminism could offer the promise of a better life and/or escape it could counteract the harsh realities which have to be lived.

Conclusion

Chapter 6 analysed the investments that the women felt they had to make in femininity. As working-class women femininity was a means of gaining cultural approval, of being seen to be respectable and as a way of putting a floor on their economic circumstances. Femininity provided rewards against degradation and had the potential for gaining economic and emotional security. The cultural (and often economic) consequences of not investing in femininity produced a range of responses from desperation to loneliness, few of which were experienced as positive. Not to look or be feminine carried enormous cultural costs. The subject positions of femininity worked to contradict those of feminism. It is the processes of investment and the textual mediations of femininity that operate alongside other resistances as disincentives to the take-up of feminism.

Another disincentive to identifying as feminist was that they firstly had to identify as 'woman' and because woman was inseparable from working-class-woman they spent most of their time trying to disidentify (see Chapter 5).[19] They did not recognize themselves as the 'woman' of much feminist address and they did not want, yet again, to be positioned as other to it and judged as lacking. Nor did they position themselves in an individualistic discourse, a discourse into which a great deal of feminism has been located, which ignores the power relations that the women struggle against daily (Fox-Genovese, 1991). They did not recognize feminism as an identification they could make. They rarely gave their consent to feminism because they were rarely addressed, recruited or asked.

Their take-up of feminism was also disturbed through the contradictory and confusing representations available to which the women had access. These were historically dependent and fed into their prior experiences and understandings. Overall, the women had little knowledge about feminisms. What they did know was a product of the contradictory and confusing discourses

transmitted through popular culture, which had simultaneously provided discursive strategies for dismissal. These fragmentary understandings rarely
offered any positive representations to which they could aspire. Even the
marketable, positive elements of feminism, such as autonomy and independence, were experienced as standards which they were unlikely to achieve,
established for women who were different from them.

Most forms of feminism were seen to offer few incentives, especially in
comparison to the use that could be made of femininity; feminism could not
offer similar economic security, cultural approval or (even, for most) emotional support. As Sarah asked at the beginning: feminism, what's in it for
her? And what does she stand to lose? Feminism was seen to come at a far
higher cost than femininity. Feminism would incur disinvestments and potential losses. Representational associations meant that feminism was seen to be
a signifier of undesirability, pretension, seriousness and being boring, that is,
what they perceived to be middle class and what they did not want to be. It
was seen as a moralizing, judgemental discourse which spoke to other sorts of
women. Feminism could not endear them to anyone within their cultural
groupings and worked as a strong disincentive to camaraderie. It was also
seen to represent change that could not be guaranteed as desirable. Most
had neither the time nor the space to engage with what they saw to be feminism. Feminism, unlike femininity, did not offer access or movement into
respectability.

Knowledge of feminism, however, was useful for interpreting bad experiences. This is where feminism has a particularly useful function to name
problems, experiences, oppressions and imagine changes. The conclusion
from this seems to be that women have to have bad experiences before feminism is seen as a useful interpretative device for understanding their positions.
The up-side of this could be that most women have bad experiences for which
feminism can provide a collectivized explanation. But the problem is how
many women see or hear these explanatory frameworks or come into contact
with feminist agencies. Also, this contact has to occur at the right time otherwise it will not be acknowledged. If feminism is only associated with bad
experiences how can it be seen as something positive that is worth knowing
about? Feminism is here divided between an explanatory discourse and an
identity. The women did not make identifications but found some feminist
explanations useful.

The solutions I propose are not novel and have been tried but perhaps
they need reiterating. They are addressed primarily to academic feminists
who need to take seriously their own dictum that all knowledge is situated. Is
it possible or even reasonable for middle-class women to ask working-class
women to make disinvestments which could exacerbate their disadvantages?
Why should women incur losses on their cultural capital to inhabit a position
that they recognize as belonging to others, the dialogic other who have the
power to make negative evaluations of them?

Studies which make up feminist theory need to address just who is the
subject 'woman' of their knowledge. The concept woman as Butler (1992)

argues needs to be re-signified. Recognition is crucial if action is to be taken. Feminism has to take into account history, economic realities, social positions, cultural representations, popular discourse and cultural investments. Specificity about context and an understanding of the differential access women have to forms of capital and knowledge will be helpful.

Second, we need to think how connections can be made to many different groups of women: do interpretative frameworks provide access to enable crossing the dialogic bridge? We may need to embrace other struggles which do not signify women, but which make connections to women (as did the Miners' Strike). Access to feminism is a critical issue; we may need to ask 'where is feminism' rather than assuming that it exists.

Third, we may need to be more circumspect about popular feminism: how do we replace individualistic understandings with those that take account of the social (and economic) and how do we give these a public voice? (This argument applies also to a great deal of feminist theorizing which appears unlocated.) But also how do we work with the inroads that popular feminism has made? Feminism has to continue naming and providing frameworks of interpretation for everyday experiences of injustice in a way which is interesting and appealing and can embrace fragmentary forms of feminist activity rather than searching for a feminist purity, avoiding what Haraway (1990) notes as the totalizing and imperialist forms of naming. The last thing working-class women need are further negative classifications of othering.

Sensitivity to these issues may enable less purity and more politics, more constructive campaigns that take seriously the differences *and* inequalities that exist between women, which need addressing rather than assuming. Butler (1992) asks what are the possibilities of politicizing disidentification and experiences of misrecognition and how are we to interpret the disidentifications produced by and through the very signifier that holds out the promise of solidarity? She argues that the failure of identification may itself be the point of departure for a more democratizing affirmation of internal difference. The subject of feminism should not be normalized, 'othered', made invisible or made to feel inadequate. She is classed just as she is raced and sexed. This is recognized by the women of the research so why not by many feminist scholars?

Notes

1 In Britain the *Sun* newspaper has photographs of topless women on its page three. A campaign was established by Clare Short, Labour Member of Parliament, to ban Page Three. She received hundreds of letters from women in support (see Short, 1991).

2 See O'Sullivan (1995) for an excellent analysis of the promotion of Camille Paglia. Also, Skeggs (1993) and Lloyd (1993) for analysis of Madonna and popular feminism.

3 A similar history is documented in the USA; see Fox-Genovese (1991) and Douglas (1994).

4 This is often a product of the technical specificity of the language used.

5 Knowledge is always partial, as Haraway (1990) notes, but some knowledge is more partial than others. Access to and availability of feminism acted on the partiality of their knowledge productions.

6 Thanks to Jackie Cook for bringing this term to my attention. It has wider circulation in Australia and the US but still exists in the UK.

7 Thatcherism offered an individualized address to the working class through consumption and paradoxically citizenship.

8 I share the same reservations as McNeil (1991) for seeing Thatcherism as a coherent ideological project: it was not as Callinicos (1989) notes.

9 This definition of post feminism is very different from that used in the media to signify that feminism is over. See Modleski (1991) for critique.

10 This lack of collective struggle and focus on individualism was reproduced within feminism in the movement towards identity politics; see Adams (1989) and Parmar (1989).

11 Sunder Rajan (1993) notes a similar trend with the representation of Indian women: individualism is framed as feminist self assertion.

12 The *Guardian*, usually a liberal newspaper, celebrated 1994 International Women's Day with a vitriolic article by Catherine Bennett on feminism which lamented the underdevelopment of British feminism and the advancement of individualistic US feminism represented by Paglia et al.

13 The comments were produced from women who I taught at the beginning of the research and followed through until 1992. The majority of sessions had an explicitly feminist angle (I taught Sociology) and they knew I was a feminist. Their comments suggest, first, that the power of the researcher has been overestimated and, second, that when they were younger feminism meant even less to them than it does now.

14 It was these already established reactionary positions in to which Camille Paglia and Kate Rophie could fit.

15 Respect is a regular demand from groups who rarely get it (see McCall, 1994), highly visible in Black music, especially by Black women such as Adeva and Aretha Franklin.

16 This comment was made two years after the case of Alison Halford, a Police Inspector, who brought a charge of sex discrimination against Merseyside Police Authority claiming they had continually blocked her promotion. Their response was to open proceedings against her alleging misconduct. It was settled out of court after the High Court ruled that the Authority had acted unfairly. This suggests Jane McD's response is very much a product of her experience not of her knowledge of the Police Force.

17 Robins (1994) argues, from Freud, that avoiding un-pleasure is probably a greater motivation than finding pleasure.

18 The Meese commission was a federal investigatory commission appointed in May 1985 to investigate the effects of pornography in the US; see Segal and McIntosh (1992) for review.

19 This could be particularly problematic, for as Rich (1979) claims, part of becoming a feminist is the hermeneutic enterprise of discovering identity as a woman.

9

Conclusions

In this book it has been impossible to convey the warmth, humour and sharpness of the women involved, to represent accurately the intensity of the research experience, to show the brilliant conversations, the shared confidences, the difficult dilemmas, the camaraderie and the great and painful times that were all part of its production. There are also limits on the representation of the women's heterogeneity. This is a book about issues in feminist and cultural theory rather than a description of the lives of the women. It was motivated by my suspicion of the impossibility of femininity and ubiquity of class. It developed through a general scepticism about the categories we deploy on a daily basis in academia. Inadequate understandings are unlikely to motivate political change. The women fuelled my scepticism and it was their insights, energy and refusals that enabled me to produce this critique. It was their unswerving commitment to respectability which compelled me to investigate why it was such an issue. I hope this book has shown why.

The historical generation of the representations of the working class to signify all that is mad, bad and dangerous, reproduced through academic analysis and popular culture, produces legacies and signs through which those who inhabit the category can be recognized. It was this recognition the women wished to deflect by cloaking themselves in respectability. Sunder Rajan notes:

> The concept of representation is useful precisely because and to the extent that it can serve a mediating function between the two positions, neither foundationalist (privileging 'reality') nor superstructural (privileging 'culture'), not denying the category of the real, or essentialising it as some pregiven metaphysical ground for representation . . . Our understanding of the problems of 'real' women cannot lie outside the 'imagined' constructs in and through which women emerge as subjects. (1993: 9–10)

The women of this study emerge as subjects through the nexus of structures, power relations and capital transfers which produce frameworks of representations and values which establish what it is to be a White working-class woman. This is why it is illuminating to engage with representation as a domain with its own substantial political reality and effects (Rose, 1987). The representations the women were positioned by were not those of reality but autonomous and paradigmatic conceptual structures produced by others whose social and representational position was very different. The representations of working-class women (historically and contemporary) are more likely to be products of fear, desire and projection than of knowledge and understanding.

Being and Becoming Classed

Class was completely central to the lives of the women. It was not only structural, in the sense that the division of labour organized what economic opportunities were available for them, or institutional, in that the education system was designed on this basis and operated to allocate them into this unequal division of labour, but also operated through a multitude of operations of capital transformations and trading. By using Bourdieu's (1979, 1986, 1987, 1989) metaphors of capital and space the study mapped how a group of White working-class women were born into structures of inequality which provided differential amounts of capital which circumscribed their movements through social space. These movements were not imposed but put into effect by the women who utilized the forms of capital to which they had access in an attempt to put a floor on their circumstances. They did not have access to the sort of capital that could be capitalized upon, that is, those forms of capital which are convertible in an institutional system, such as the cultural capital of the middle classes, which can be converted and traded-up through education and employment into symbolic capital and economic reward. They made the most of what they had but it rarely offered good trading potential. They were in the process of continually halting losses rather than trading-up and accruing extra value. The investments they made often closed down other ways of being; so when they made investments in caring this closed off their possibilities for focusing on themselves rather than others. To discontinue their caring investments would have engendered potentially great losses with few alternative venues for further investment. For many it was all they had as an alternative to unemployment. Lack of alternatives was one of the central features of being working class; they rarely had the potential to re-valorize their classed subjectivities.

Investments, however, always incurred personal costs; some investments in femininity ensured that their bodies were the object of exchange. Their claims for respectability were movements in systems of value which they entered at a disadvantage in which access to positive valuations were limited or closed, but in which they were forever trying to make the best out of limited resources. The women entered trading arenas which were established in the interests of and benefit for others. They were able to generate their own local trading arenas with their own distinctions, but these barely influenced the supra-local arenas for capital exchange and conferral of legitimacy. Sometimes desire for value reproduced the very distinctions they were trying to avoid. Respectability was used to make the movement in and out of the local, to increase their tradable assets, to generate distance from the representation of them as pathological and to claim legitimacy outside and inside the local. It was used to show that they were worthy, that they have value and that they should not be written off. Respectability was also invoked *against* the numerous implicit sexual trading arenas which they entered. The education system and the labour market provide the most obvious examples, but they were always conscious of their marking by (hetero)sexuality in most situations.

It was argued that the most fundamental marker of class was that of exclusion. The women were excluded from positions in the labour market, the education system, from forms of cultural capital and from trading arenas. They were delegitimated through associations of non-respectability. The way class was experienced was through affectivity, as a 'structure of feeling' (cf. Williams, 1961, 1977). This is the emotional politics of class fuelled by insecurity, doubt, indignation and resentment (but also lived with pleasure and irreverence). These affective responses presuppose an imagined (and sometimes real) superior other that enabled them to police themselves and open out every aspect of their lives, their bodies, their appearance, their homes, their caring practices and their emotional attachments to others, to judgement and scrutiny. They were never able to feel comfortable with themselves, always convinced that others will find something about them wanting and undesirable. Their pathologization through contemporary representations serves to continually confirm this discomfort. This was especially acute when they recognized themselves and felt themselves recognizable as that which they were hoping to avoid: the shameful recognitions of themselves as sexual generated disturbances for the production of themselves as respectable. Shame was produced as a result of their consciousness of their 'place' – through the mismatch of their dispositions and positions. But there were also times when they were able to resist the negative valuing by others. Their attempts to claim respectability locked them into systems of self-regulation and monitoring, producing themselves as governable subjects.

Public and 'Individual' Subjective Productions

The women produce themselves as particular sorts of 'women' in relation to public narratives of what it means to be a working-class woman. Their subjectivity is dialogic. It requires a knowledge of where they think they should be, where they think they can be, of that which they can conceive and see as plausible and how they are positioned. They do not produce themselves in relation to individualistic narratives. They feel their lives are very public, very social and hence open to scrutiny. They can only authorize their place in public narratives at the local level. This book is not an account of how individuals make themselves but how they cannot fail to make themselves in particular ways. In this research the women are not the originators of their identities but are located in temporal processes of subjective construction (Bhabha, 1994). There are limitations on how they can be. Within these constraints they deploy many constructive and creative strategies to generate a sense of themselves with value.

A great deal of the women's time is taken up with surviving or openly enjoying life rather than with introspection. This is how the metaphors of depth, and hence shallowness are invoked: the women live at the surface, in public, because their subjectivity is produced from and for public knowledge. They do not feel a possessive relationship to their subjectivity although they do often feel compelled to prove they are not what they may be assumed to be by others. To live visibly is to construct oneself publicly through relations with others rather than to spend time on oneself. Claiming respectability is a public characterization. Theirs is a different ethical motivation. Their self exist for and in close relation to others. Their reflexivity occurs through others. Their care of the self and the technologies they work on the self are not for self-mastery, as Foucault (1988) would suggest, but to generate dignity, deflect degradation *and* help others. They make a gift of caring for others; a gift, Diprose (1994) argues, is about the dispersal of their identity to others. They do not do the work on themselves and others just for themselves: they are neither selfish nor altruistic. They have a different take on subjectivity.

The individualism which is assumed in a great deal of theorizing on subjectivity is the product of, and in the interests of, privileged groups in very specific historical and national circumstances. The project of the self is a Western bourgeois project:[1]

> Most Indians do not reveal themselves because it does not occur to them that they have unique selves to reveal. (Gearing, 1970: 146)

Concepts of individualism legitimate powerful groups and render other groups unworthy of the designation 'individual'. Discourses of individualism have long been deployed in the service of political rhetoric to differentiate groups on the basis of inequality (Abercrombie et al., 1986). 'Individuals' are the product of privilege, who can occupy the economic and cultural conditions which enable them to do the work on the self. The 'individual' is part of a very different class project to the one these women are involved in. The project of the individual developed from and in relation to the category of the person and the category of the self; all of which Mauss (1985) notes, implied self-knowledge. This is why many theories of subjectivity did not apply throughout the study; they were produced from within the discourse of individualism, a discourse to which the women have only had limited access (through the material 'incentives' of Thatcherism). Many theories of subjectivity were designed for a different body in different circumstances, a body which occupies social space and is able to move through it in very different ways. The women did not assume that their bodies were valuable, that they had entitlements or that they were even interesting. The women's ontological security was found precisely not in being an 'individual' but in 'fitting-in'. The discourse of individualism was not taken up because it was not recognized as available or addressed to them. The way they lived sexuality is a case in point. It was more about tradings in power and accruing local exchange value than about an expression of their inner selves. They do not have access to the egocentric preoccupations which are the prerogative of a different class. What they did know of them they identified as pretentious.

Another challenge to traditional theories of the subject is made through the women's exercise of responsibility which was opposite to the traditional form of individual responsibility outlined by Mauss (1985) in his discussion of the development of the concept of the self. Rather than being the free, autonomous, independent selves which he suggests accompany the modern self (and on which modernist theories of justice and morality are built), their selves were full of duty and obligation generated through their relationships to others rather than legally enforced (although recent legislation such as the Children's Act and Community Care Acts legalizes some of their previous social obligations).[2] Here I am not romanticizing the kinship networks of the working class but rather suggesting that historically they have been so excluded from full citizenship which promoted discourses of individualism that they have never been positioned by it in the same way as the middle classes (Lister, 1990; Pateman, 1988; Walby, 1994). Working-class women have always been seen *not* to embody the individualism which was crucial to the construction of concepts of personhood and self (see Taylor, 1989) but to be the mass against which individualism is constructed. These highlight the problematic issues of a study such as this whose focus is subjectivity. The women do subjectivity differently: incorporating the self-regulative elements outlined by Foucault (1988) and Rose (1989) but few of the self-mastery and self-care elements previously assumed. Their subjectivity is not part of a discourse of individualism; rather, it is part of a discourse of dialogism and connection.

It is often assumed that the link between the individual and the social is through identification. This link, the study suggests, is precarious and lived in many different ways. The women spend more time either not recognizing the identifications which it is assumed that they make (e.g. class, femininity or heterosexuality) or disidentifying. Recognition had to occur for identifications to be made and the women either did not recognize themselves or did not want to recognize themselves as the categories of identification that were available to them. Recognition, refusal to recognize, partial recognitions, disidentification, dissimulation and identification are part of the same process and may occur simultaneously or not at all. The women worked to be recognized as caring and respectable which has repercussions for how they refuse and mis/recognize and dis/identify as sexed (hetero) and gendered (femininity and feminism). Their different types of recognition were context specific and sometimes temporal, changing over time, space and place. The production of themselves for recognition was deployed strategically. In working dialogically to produce themselves for others they came to recognize themselves as certain sorts of 'subjects'.

Refusal to be recognized meant a great deal of energy was spent displaying that they *are not* that which is expected. This operates simultaneously with *being* and *becoming*. They act and posture *as if they were* even when they know they are not (especially in the case of femininity). Performativity was only one of many techniques deployed in the processes of identification and was not always done to make or ensure identification. Some caring and feminine performances were made out of necessity: femininity, for example, was seen by some of the women as a structural inconvenience, something which they could not avoid; they had to 'do' femininity to avoid the consequences of not being feminine. Performances do not automatically lead to the comfortable take-up of that position; rather, it may be a straightforward acting out of a necessary performance. Just because the women *appeared* to be feminine does not mean that they *are*: they were very good at constructing appearances and they had many other dispositions which were less apparent and counteracted their appearance.

The performances they made to display their respectability were, however, consolidated across a range of sites: their feminine appearance was complemented and reinforced by their caring behaviour. Their caring performances were translated into forms of subjectivity through the discursive conflation of caring *for* with caring *about*. Whilst sometimes distance could be made between the two behaviours, when their performances were institutionally legitimated (as was the case with caring) the distance became lessened. Institutional legitimation was a powerful incentive for the take up of performed subjectivity. Performances of subjectivity always occurred against a backdrop of power relations, in specific arenas, in which values could be consolidated, investments made and capitals lost and/or enhanced. These conditions impacted upon the status, value and significance of the performances. Their attempts to 'pass' were not made from a position of ironic reverence; rather, they wanted to appear as something different. They did not want to *be* middle class even though some of these performative passings come to take on a quality of being. The processes of being and becoming are held together with processes of not being and refusal. Their passing attempts suggest that they are not becoming less working class, but because they remain as attempts, they remain working-class.

Their refusal to be fixed by historically generated representational and social positionings was a major feature of the study, suggesting the temporality and instability not only of identification but also of the concepts and signs that define what identification actually means.[3]

The women do not have coherent identities. When I identify them as White working-class women I impose categories onto them which they use very differently to produce their own subjectivity. I identify their positioning in economic, social and discursive relations *not* their subjectivity. This is why identity politics only works as a politics and not a form of subjectivity. Subjectivities are not produced as coherent categories. The women's refusal of fixity is an admission of its impossibility. To fix the women is to project my desire for fixity onto them: they always refuse it.

Useful Categorization, Useful Knowledge

This suggests that we need to be more circumspect about how we approach universalizing theories of subjectivity and identity. In fact this book calls for a greater critical reflexivity of many of the central concepts of feminist and cultural theory. Many of these are barely adequate to conceptualize the lives of working-class (Black and White) women: they were not designed with them in mind.

This book has shown how the category 'woman' is lived and intimately experienced as a form of subjectivity inhabited through other categories. Through the overlaying of categories the term 'woman' always comes with a specific form of class address: for the women of the study the address of the feminine is not heard, the address to the sexual woman is not acknowledged and the address of the feminist woman is not recognized. Overlaying always occurs in a nexus of power relations in which valuations of different types of women are made. Categories of singular identity are always uninhabitable because they assume a coherence, a homogeneity and fixity over time and space. They were, however, useful in this book as provisional abstractions in moving towards the concrete level, for interrogating the assumptions that underpin the different categorizations of 'woman' and for exploring why the lack of fit occurs.

Unpacking the category femininity was useful as an exercise in seeing how the women were constrained in the interpretations, appearances, performances and movements that they could make. This suggests that the concepts are not necessarily redundant but rather that they may need continual modification and grounding to understand the specificities of lived experience. Refusal by the women to inhabit the category of class did not mean that it was abandoned. Rather, it was investigated to see why disidentifications were made and the political consequences of this. Different forms of address are needed if working-class women are to hear the politics of feminism, lesbian and gay issues and socialism. As Butler argues:

> If 'women' within political discourse can never fully describe that which it names, that is neither because the category simply refers without describing nor because 'women' are the lost referent, that which 'does not exist', but because the term marks a dense intersection of social relations that cannot be summarized through the terms of identity. (1993: 218)

We also need concepts that do have explanatory value for those to whom they are meant to apply, concepts that can encapsulate experiences otherwise unnamed. This is because in so doing they can create what Code (1995) identifies as rhetorical space, so that experiences cannot be dismissed as illegitimate just because they are not known by those who have the power to effect judgements on others. This leads to more responsible knowledge and representations. Certain theories tilt the explanatory balance of power in favour of those they are being used for. The concept of cultural capital, for instance, shifts power and agency back into the hands of those who have restricted access to it. It helps explain why some groups are not in the position to formulate academic concepts. Some concepts do not impose their frameworks onto lived experience but are generated from it: respectability was a case in point.

In the 1980s with the demise of class analysis and lack of attention given to the material-structural features of people's lives and the concomitant rise of the 'psy' professions, we find the emergence of an authorizing narrative of emotional trauma in which singular difficult experiences come to account for the whole personality. What this study shows is that it is not the singular but the unremitting emotional distress generated by the doubts and insecurities of living class that working-class women endure on a daily basis. The only authorizing narrative they have to explain their identities is pathology. This lack of a symbolically legitimate authorizing narrative means it is difficult to understand which experiences count towards subjective construction (and which are considered worthy of having). Whereas an event can produce explanations of identity, the mundane reiterative everyday experiences of living degradation and negative value positioning often cannot. Those experiences are rarely considered worthy of study and knowing. However, this study has shown that it is precisely the everyday negotiations of the mundane that do matter, that are formative, that do count and that these mundane experiences are a product of systematic inequality. They are not free-floating emotional experiences. They are profoundly located in structural organization. They may not be authorized, often un-eventful (and rarely spectacular) but as this study shows they do matter and they are constitutive.

This means that we should not abandon the study of experience. Rather, we need to rework it to explore how subjects are produced and produce themselves through their different experiences, exploring how different processes produce experience, which ones matter, which are authorized and how interpretation is central to productions. Experience relates to theory, not only in terms of how it can be encapsulated, but by showing how the subjectivity and the experiences of the knowledge producers inform the knowledge productions. Many of the concepts we have to work with are produced from those who just do not know about the experiences and interpretations of others and can only speak to those who occupy similar positions to themselves. Just as subjects are produced through experience so are theorists. The experiences of the theorist are the means by which the theorist becomes a knowing subject and these are significant to understanding the theoretical debates in which we engage, as are the experiences of those we study.

Listening and hearing others is important for the production of accountable and responsible knowledge. This suggests that questions of methodology underpin all theoretical productions: questions of who we hear, how we listen, who we are accountable to, who we address and how we address them are central methodological and political issues. Theories of working-class women are just as likely to represent them as pathological as are popular representations if questions of methodology are not addressed. The working class are constantly aware of the dialogic other who have the power to make judgements about them. Privileged academics might produce more rigorous theory if they imagined a dialogic working-class other, one that does and will make judgements about the adequacy and applicability of their arguments.

Similarly working-class women need to put into effect the(ir) realization that the dialogic and real other who makes judgements is not justified in doing so. The energies invested in deflecting perceived difference could be put to more effective use. To do so, however, would mean to see class as a basis for challenge, not shame, and sexuality as something in which to take pleasure and control rather than to feel judged by or compelled to act out. Different political articulations need to take the specificities of 'real' lives into account in order to work out which forms of analysis and address can and cannot cross the dialogic bridge.

To study class should create a displacement of the categories of knowledge themselves. It should mark the production of different rhetorical spaces, generating a space where women like those of the study can be heard *and* listened to, at least where they can no longer be ignored. These are not just a group of women studied in isolation; their experiences and interpretations challenge many assumptions reproduced through feminist theory. I hope they can no longer be ignored, made invisible, deconstructed to irrelevance, dismissed as part of a redundant concept, or pathologized as just another 'social problem'. To silence these women through theoretical debate, which can conveniently ignore their inability to fit either their social positions or the categorizations designed for others, is to commit yet another act of symbolic violence.

And Finally . . .

I will always be indebted to the women; they now operate as my dialogic other enabling me – I hope – to counteract pretentious theory and the judgements of others in the academy who rarely question their entitlements. The women enabled me to understand why a great deal of feminist and cultural theory did not feel right and that a great deal of feminist theorizing depends on recognition. They taught me that the most substantive understandings are situated productions.

> I also reminded myself that it would probably not be worth the trouble of making books if they failed to teach the author something he hadn't known before, if they didn't lead to unforeseen places and if they didn't disperse one toward a strange and new relation with himself. The pain and the pleasure of the book is to be an experience. (Foucault, 1986: Preface)

In his usual male egocentric, 'all knowledge is for self mastery' style, Foucault (1986) here addresses the basis for this book. It taught me things I did not know and made me rethink my politics, my forms of address, political strategies and my understanding that difference is more than a descriptor waiting to be filled: inequality proliferates on a daily basis.

But, even more importantly, I hope the women of the book realize that they have made a contribution to academic debate, that they are of great value, that they have been listened to and taken seriously. Without them these debates could not have taken place. Theirs, I think, is a substantial contribution and one which I hope has ramifications beyond the confines of this book. It is also to recognise that the power relations identified in this book and lived out through respectability occur in most daily interactions. As Willis (1977) notes, to contract out of the messy business of day-to-day problems is to deny the active, contested nature of social and cultural reproduction. To take, rather than abdicate, responsibility for the judgements that are made, the legitimations enacted and the power produced may ulti-mately make a difference at the cultural level where structural relations are figured and enacted. We can recognize our position in these relations of power and do something about it. For a start we can generate a politics which takes into account the experiences of the women we hope to address. To not do so is to produce irresponsible knowledge.

Notes

1 Donzelot (1979), Walkerdine and Lucey (1989) and Rose (1989) have noted how the project of the self came to dominate the modern episteme of the West and was institutionalized through the 'psy professions' which enabled the techniques of the self to be authorized and legitimated.
2 As Foucault (1979) argues, the law increasingly operates as a norm in a continuum of appa-ratuses.
3 See Barker (1989) for an excellent critique of the historical and contemporary problems with the concept of identification.

Bibliography

Abercrombie, N., Hill, S. and Turner, B. (1986) *Sovereign Individuals of Capitalism*. London: Allen and Unwin.

Abrams, M., Gerard, D. and Timms, N. (eds) (1985) *Values and Social Change in Britain*. London: Macmillan.

Adams, M.L. (1989) 'There's No Place Like Home: On the Place of Identity in Feminist Politics', *Feminist Review*. 31: 22–34.

Adkins, L. (1995) *Gendered Work: Sexuality, Family and the Labour Market*. Buckingham: Open University Press.

Aggleton, P. (1987) *Rebels Without a Cause: Middle-Class Youth and the Transition from School to Work*. Lewes: Falmer.

Alcoff, L. (1988) 'Cultural Feminism versus Post-Structuralism: The Identity Crisis in Feminist Theory', *Signs: Journal of Women in Culture and Society*, 13: 31: 405–36.

Althusser, L. (1971) *Lenin and Philosophy and Other Essays*. London: New Left Books.

Amos, V. and Parmar, P. (1984) 'Challenging Imperialist Feminism', *Feminist Review*, 17: 3–19.

Ang, I. (1994) 'On Not Speaking Chinese: Postmodern Ethnicity and the Politics of Diaspora', *New Formations*, 24: 1–19.

Appadurai, A. (1988) 'Putting Hierarchy in its Place', *Cultural Anthropology*, 3: 1: 36–49.

Arber, S. and Ginn, J. (1992) 'Research Note: Class and Caring – A Forgotten Dimension', *Sociology*, 26: 4: 619–35.

Archer, M. (1982) 'Morphogenesis versus Structuration: on Combining Structures and Action', *British Journal of Sociology*, 33: 4: 455–97.

Armstrong, N. and Tennenhouse, L. (1987) (eds) *The Ideology of Conduct: Essays in Literature and the History of Sexuality*. London: Methuen.

Bakhtin, M. (1984) *Rabelais and His World*, trans. H. Iswolsky. Bloomington: Indiana University Press.

Baldwin, S. (1993) *Myth of Community Care*. London: Chapman Hall.

Banks, M., Bates, I., Breakwell, G., Bynner, J., Emler, N., Jamieson, L. and Roberts, K. (1992) *Careers and Identities*. Buckingham: Open University Press.

Barker, M. (1989) *Comics: An Ideology of Power*. Manchester: Manchester University Press.

Barker, M. and Beezer, A. (1992) (eds) *Reading into Cultural Studies*. London: Routledge.

Bar On, B.-A. (1993) 'Marginality and Epistemic Privilege', in L. Alcoff and E. Potter (eds) *Feminist Epistemologies*. London: Routledge. pp. 83–101

Barrett, M. and McIntosh, M. (1982) *The Anti-Social Family*. London: Verso/NLB.

Bartky, S.L. (1990) *Femininity and Domination: Studies in the Phenomenology of Oppression*. London: Routledge.

Batsleer, J. (1994) 'It's All Right for You to Talk: Minding the Gap Between Feminist Theory and Youth Work Practice in Relation to Lesbian Identification'. Paper presented to BSA 'Sexualities in Social Context', April. Preston.

Bayley Report (1973) *Mental Handicap and Community Care*. London: Routledge Kegan and Paul.

Bayley Report (1978) *Community-Oriented Systems of Care*. Berkhamsted: The Volunteer Centre.

Bell, V.A. (1935) 'Junior Instruction Centres and their Future', from Horne, J. (1983) 'Youth Unemployment Programmes: A Historical Account of the Development of "Dole Colleges"', in D. Gleeson (ed.) *Youth Training and the Search for Work*. London: Routledge and Kegan Paul. pp. 309–31.

Benn, M. (1994) 'The Everywoman Interview', *Everywoman*, March, 101: 16–20.

Bennett, C. (1993) 'Sheep in Need of a Shepherdess', *Guardian*, 8 March. pp. 2–3.

Benzevale, M., Judge, K. and Whitehead, M. (1995) *Tackling Health Inequalities: An Agenda for Action*. Poole, Dorset: BEBC.

Berger, J. (1980) *About Looking*. London: Writers and Readers Publishing Cooperative.

Berger, J. and Luckmann, T. (1971) *The Social Construction of Reality*. Harmondsworth: Penguin.

Bhabha, H. (1994) *The Location of Culture*. London: Routledge.

Bhavnani, K.-K. (1989) 'Complexity, Activism, Optimism: Kum-Kum Bhavnani Interviews Angela Y Davis', *Feminist Review*, 31: 66–82.

Bhavnani, K.-K. (1994) 'Tracing the Contours: Feminist Research and Feminist Objectivity', in H. Afshar and M. Maynard (eds) *The Dynamics of 'Race' and Gender: Some Feminist Interventions*. London: Taylor and Francis. pp. 26–41.

Black Report (1982) *Inequalities in Health*, ed. P. Townsend and N. Davidson. Harmondsworth: Penguin.

Blackman, I. and Perry, K. (1990) 'Skirting the Issue: Lesbian Fashion for the 1990s', *Feminist Review*, 34: 67–79.

Bloustein, G. (1994) 'Strike a Pose: Teenage Girls, Performance and the Creation of Cultural Space'. Paper presented to 'Console-ing Passions', Tucson, Arizona. 21–4 April.

Blunden, G. (1983) 'Our Women are Expected to Become . . . Women and Girls in Further Education in England at the Turn of the Century', in London Feminist History Group (eds) *Sexual Dynamics of History*. London: The Women's Press. pp. 87–107.

Board of Education (1903) *School Training for the Deterioration of Women*. Special Report. London: HMSO.

Board of Education (1904) Report of the Inter-Departmental Committee on Physical Deterioration. Code 2175. London: HMSO.

Boudon, R. (1974) *Education, Opportunity and Social Inequality*. London: John Wiley.

Bourdieu, P. (1977) *Outline of a Theory of Practice*. Cambridge: Cambridge University Press.

Bourdieu, P. (1979) 'Symbolic Power', *Critique of Anthropology*, 4: 77–85.

Bourdieu, P. (1986) *Distinction: A Social Critique of the Judgement of Taste*. London: Routledge.

Bourdieu, P. (1987) 'What Makes a Social Class? On the Theoretical and Practical Existence of Groups', *Berkeley Journal of Sociology*, 1–17.

Bourdieu, P. (1989) 'Social Space and Symbolic Power', *Sociological Theory*, 7: 14–25.

Bourke, J. (1994) *Working Class Cultures in Britain: 1890–1960*. London: Routledge.

Brah, A. (1992) 'Difference, Diversity and Differentiation', in J. Donald and A. Rattansi (eds) *'Race', Culture and Difference*. Sage: London. pp. 126–49

Breinlinger, S. and Kelly, K. (1994) 'Women's Responses to Status Inequality: A Test of Social Identity Theory', *Psychology of Women Quarterly*, 18: 1–16.

Brenner, J. and Ramas, M. (1984) 'Rethinking Women's Oppression', *New Left Review*, 144: 33–72.

Breugel, I. (1979) 'Women as a Reserve Army of Labour', *Feminist Review*, 3: 12–23.

Brunsdon, C. (1991) 'Pedagogies of the Feminine: Feminist Teaching and Women's Genres', *Screen*, 32: 4: 364–82.

Bryan, B., Dadzie, S., and Scafe, S. (1985) *The Heart of the Race: Black Women's Lives in Britain*. London: Virago.

Burman, S. (1979) *Fit Work for Women*. London: Croom Helm.

Butler, J. (1990) *Gender Trouble: Feminism and the Subversion of Identity*. London: Routledge.

Butler, J. (1992) 'Contingent Foundations: Feminism and the Question of "Postmodernism"', in J. Butler and J. Scott (eds) *Feminists Theorise the Political*. London: Routledge. pp. 3–22.

Butler, J. (1993) *Bodies that Matter: On the Discursive Limits of 'Sex'*. London: Routledge.

Calhoun, C. (ed.) (1994) *Social Theory and the Politics of Identity*. Oxford: Blackwell.

Callinicos, A. (1989) *Against Postmodernism: A Marxist Critique*. Cambridge: Polity.

Callinicos, A. (1995) *Theories and Narratives: Reflections on the Philosophy of History*. Cambridge: Polity.

Carter, E. (1984) 'Alice in Consumer Wonderland', in A. McRobbie and M. Nava (eds) *Gender and Generation*. London: Macmillan. pp. 185–215.

Carter, E. (1990) 'Design, Class and Lifestyle: A West Berlin Perspective', *Magazine of Cultural Studies*, 2, 8–11 October.

(charles), h. (1992) 'Whiteness', in H. Hinds, A. Phoenix and J. Stacey (eds) *Working Out: New Directions in Women's Studies*. Lewes: Falmer. pp. 29–36.

Charles, N. (1990) 'Women and Class – a Problematic Relationship', *Sociological Review*, 38: 43–89.

Cixous, H. (1980) 'The Laugh of the Medusa', trans. K. Cohen and P. Cohen, in E. Marks and I. de Courtivron (eds) *New French Feminisms*. Brighton: Harvester. pp. 90–9.

Clifford, J. (1992) 'Traveling Cultures', in L. Grossberg, C. Nelson and P. Treichler (eds) *Cultural Studies*. London: Routledge. pp. 96–117.

Code, L. (1987) *Epistemic Responsibility*. Hanover, New Hampshire: University Press of New England.

Code, L. (1988) 'Experience, Knowing, Responsibility', in M. Griffiths and M. Whitford (eds) *Feminist Perspectives in Philosophy*. London: Macmillan. pp. 187–205.

Code, L. (1995) *Rhetorical Spaces: Essays on Gendered Locations*. London: Routledge.

Cohen, A.P. (1994) *Self-Consciousness: An Alternative Anthropology of Identity*. London: Routledge.

Cohen, P. (1982) 'School for the Dole', *New Socialist*, Jan/Feb: 3–4.

Collins, H.M. (1983) 'The Meaning of Lies: Accounts of Action and Participatory Research', in G.N. Gilbert and P. Abell (eds) *Accounts and Action*. Aldershot: Gower. pp. 69–77.

Comte, A. (1853) *The Positive Philosophy of Auguste Comte*, trans. H. Martineau. London: Chapman.

Connell, R.W. (1989) 'Cool Guys, Swots and Wimps: The Interplay of Masculinity and Education', *Oxford Review of Education*, 15: 3: 291–303.

Connell, R.W., Ashenden, D.J., Kessler, S. and Dowsett, G.W. (1982) *Making the Difference*. Sydney: Allen and Unwin.

Coote, A. and Campbell, B. (1987) *Sweet Freedom*. Oxford: Blackwell.

Coward, R. (1994) 'Is It Time for a Reawakening?', *Everywoman*, March, 101: 12–14.

Cowie, C. and Lees, S. (1981) 'Slags or Drags', *Feminist Review*, 9: 17–33.

Creed, B. (1995) 'Lesbian Bodies: Tribades, Tomboys and Tarts', in E. Grosz and E. Probyn (eds) *Sexy Bodies: The Strange Carnalities of Feminism*. London: Routledge. pp. 86–104.

Crompton, R. (1993) *Class and Stratification: An Introduction to Current Debates*. Cambridge: Polity.

Crosby, C. (1992) 'Dealing with Difference', in J. Butler and J. Scott (eds) *Feminists Theorise the Political*. London: Routledge. pp. 130–44.

Crossman, R. (1975) *The Diaries of a Cabinet Minister: Vol. One: Minister of Housing*. London: Hamish Hamilton and Jonathan Cape.

Crowther Report (1959) *Fifteen to Eighteen: A Report of the Central Advisory Council*, Vols 1–3. London: HMSO.

Cunnison, S. (1989) 'Gender Joking in the Classroom', in S. Acker (ed.) *Teachers, Gender and Careers*. Lewes: Falmer. pp. 151–71.

David, M. (1980) *The State, the Family and Education*. London: Routledge and Kegan Paul.

Davis, A.Y. (1981) *Women, Race and Class*. London: The Women's Press.

Davis, A.Y. (1995) 'I Used to be Your Sweet Mama: Ideology, Sexuality and Domesticity in the Blues of Gertrude "Ma" Rainey and Bessie Smith', in E. Grosz and E. Probyn (eds) *Sexy Bodies: The Strange Carnalities of Feminism*. London: Routledge. pp. 231–66.

de Certeau, M. (1988) *The Practice of Everyday Life*. London: University of California Press.

Deem, R. (1981) 'State Policy and Ideology in the Education of Women 1944–1980', *British Journal of Sociology of Education*, 12: 2: 131–44.

de Groot, J. (1989) '"Sex" and "Race": the Construction of Language and Image in the Nineteenth Century', in S. Mendus and J. Rendall (eds) *Sexuality and Subordination*. London: Routledge. pp. 89–128.

de Lauretis, T. (1984) *Alice Doesn't: Feminism, Semiotics, Cinema*. London: Routledge.

de Lauretis, T. (1988) 'Are You Experienced – An Interview with Theresa de Lauretis by Anu Koivunen', *Lahikuva*, 4: 33–4.

de Lauretis, T. (1994) *The Practice of Love: Lesbian Sexuality and Perverse Desire*. Bloomington: Indiana University Press.

Deleuze, G. (1986) Nomadology: *The War Machine*. Chicago: Semiotext(e).

Department of Health (1990) *Community Care in the Next Decade*. London: HMSO.

Diprose, R. (1994) *The Bodies of Women: Ethics, Embodiment and Sexual Difference*. London: Routledge.

Doane, M.A. (1982) 'Film and Masquerade: Theorising the Female Spectator', *Screen*, 23: 3–4: 74–88.

Doane, M.A. (1989) *The Desire to Desire: The Women's Film of the 1940s*. London: Macmillan.

Dominguez, V.R. (1994) 'A Taste for the "Other": Intellectual Complicity in Racializing Practices', *Current Anthropology*, 35: 4: 333–8.

Donald, J. (1985) 'Beacons of the Future: Schooling, Subjection and Subjectification', in V. Beechey and J. Donald (eds) *Subjectivity and Social Relations*. Milton Keynes: Open University Press. pp. 214–50.

Donzelot, J. (1979) *The Policing of Families: Welfare versus the State*. London: Hutchinson.

Douglas, M. (1988) *Purity and Danger: An Analysis of the Concepts of Pollution and Taboo*. New York: Ark Paperbacks.

Douglas, S.J. (1994) *Where the Girls Are: Growing Up Female with the Mass Media*. London: Penguin.

Duneier, M. (1992) *Slim's Table: Race, Respectability and Masculinity*. Chicago: University of Chicago Press.

Durham, M. (1991) *Sex and Politics: The Family and Morality in the Thatcher Years*. Basingstoke: Macmillan.

Dyer, R. (1985) 'Male Sexuality in the Media', in A. Metcalf and M. Humphries (eds) *The Sexuality of Men*. London: Pluto. pp. 28–44.

Dyer, R. (1993) 'A White Star', *Sight & Sound*, 3: 8: 22–4.

Dyhouse, C. (1976) 'Social Darwinistic Ideas and the Development of Women's Education in England, 1880–1920', *History of Education*, 5: 2: 41–58.

Dyhouse, C. (1977) 'Good Wives and Little Mothers: Social Anxieties and the School-Girls' Curriculum 1890–1920', *Oxford Review of Education*, 3: 1: 21–35.

Eagleton, T. (1987) 'The Politics of Subjectivity', in L. Appignanesi (ed.) *Identity: The Real Me*. ICA Document 6. pp. 47–8.

Edsall, T. (1984) *The New Politics of Inequality*. New York: Norton.

Edwards, R. (1990) 'Connecting Method and Epistemology: A White Woman Interviewing Black Women', *Women's Studies International Forum*, 13: 477–90.

Elias, N. (1982) *Power and Civility: The Civilising Process*, Vol. 2. New York: Pantheon Books.

Ellsworth, E. (1989) 'Why Doesn't This Feel Empowering? Working Through the Repressive Myths of Critical Pedagogy', *Harvard Educational Review*, 59: 3: 297–324.

Engels, F. (1844/1958) *The Condition of the Working-Class in England*. St Albans, Herts: Panther.

Engels, F. (1953) *Marx–Engels on Britain*. Moscow: Progress Publishers.

Evans, D. (1993) *Sexual Citizenship: The Material Construction of Sexualities*. London: Routledge.

Fabian, J. (1990) *Power and Performance: Ethnographic Explorations through Proverbial Wisdom and Theater in Shaba, Zaire*. Madison: University of Wisconsin Press.

Fildes, S. (1983) 'The Inevitability of Theory', *Feminist Review*, 14 : 62–70.

Finch, L. (1993) *The Classing Gaze: Sexuality, Class and Surveillance*. St Leonards, NSW, Australia: Allen and Unwin.

Finch, J. and Groves, D. (1980) 'Community Care and the Family: A Case for Equal Opportunities', *International Social Policy*, Cambridge: Cambridge University Press. pp. 487–511.

Fine, M. and Macpherson, P. (1994) 'Over Dinner: Feminism and Adolescent Female Bodies', in H.L. Radtke and H.J. Stam (eds) *Power/Gender: Social Relations in Theory and Practice*. London: Sage. pp. 219–47.

Finkelstein, J. (1991) *The Fashioned Self*. Cambridge: Polity.

Finn, D., Grant, N. and Johnson, R. (1977) 'Social Democracy, Education and the Crisis', *Working Papers in Cultural Studies*, 10. Birmingham: CCCS.

Forrester, J. (1987) 'A Brief History of the Subject', in L. Appignanesi (ed.) *Identity: The Real Me*. ICA Documents, 6: 13–17.

Foucault, M. (1974) *The Archaeology of Knowledge*. London: Tavistock.

Foucault, M. (1977a) *Discipline and Punish: The Birth of the Prison*. London: Allen Lane/Penguin.

Foucault, M. (1977b) 'Power and Sex: Discussion between M. Foucault and B.H. Levy', *Telos*, 32: 152–61.

Foucault, M. (1979) *The History of Sexuality: Volume One, an Introduction*. London: Penguin.

Foucualt, M. (1986) *The Use of Pleasure*, trans. R. Hurley. Harmondsworth: Penguin.

Foucault, M. (1988) 'The Ethic of Care for the Self as a Practice of Freedom', in J. Bernauer and D. Ramussen (eds) *The Final Foucault*. Cambridge, MA: MIT Press.

Fox-Genovese, E. (1991) *Feminism Without Illusions: A Critique of Individualism*. Chapel Hill: University of North Carolina Press.

Franklin, S. (1991) 'Fetal Fascinations: New Dimensions to the Medical–Scientific Construction of Fetal Personhood', in S. Franklin, C. Lury and J. Stacey (1991) (eds) *Off Centre: Feminism and Cultural Studies*. London: HarperCollins. pp. 190–206.

Franklin, S., Lury, C. and Stacey, J. (1991) (eds) *Off Centre: Feminism and Cultural Studies*. London: HarperCollins.

Fraser, N. (1995) 'From Redistribution to Recognition? Dilemmas of Justice in a "Post-Socialist" Age', *New Left Review*, 212: 68–94.

Frazer, E. (1989) 'Feminist Talk and Talking about Feminism: Teenage Girls' Discourses of Gender', *Oxford Review of Education*, 15: 3: 281–90.

Frazer, E. (1992) 'Talking about Gender, Race and Class', in D. Cameron, E. Frazer, P. Harvey, M.B.H. Rampton and K. Richardson (eds) *Researching Language: Issues on Power and Method*. London: Routledge. pp. 90–112.

Fryer, P. (1984) *Staying Power: The History of Black People in Britain*. London: Pluto.

Fuss, D. (1989) *Essentially Speaking: Feminism, Nature and Difference*. London: Routledge.

Game, A. (1991) *Undoing the Social: Towards a Deconstructive Sociology*. Milton Keynes: Open University Press.

Garfinkel, H. (1967) *Studies in Ethnomethodology*. New York: Prentice Hall.

Gearing, F.O. (1970) *The Face of the Fox*. Chicago: Aldine.

Gilman, S.L. (1990) '"I'm Down on Whores": Race and Gender in Victorian London', in D.T. Goldberg (ed.) *Anatomy of Racism*. Minneapolis: University of Minnesota Press. pp. 146–70.

Gilman, S.L. (1992) 'Black Bodies, White Bodies: Towards an Iconography of Female Sexuality in Late Ninteenth Century Art, Medicine and Literature', in J. Donald and A. Rattansi (eds) *'Race', Culture and Difference*. London: Sage. pp. 171–98.

Gilroy, P. (1990) 'One Nation Under a Groove: The Cultural Politics of "Race" and Racism in Britain', in D.T. Goldberg (ed.) *Anatomy of Racism*. Minneapolis: University of Minnesota Press. pp. 263–83.

Gittings, D. (1985) 'Inside and Outside Marriage', *Feminist Review*, 14: 22–35.

Glendinning, C. (1992) *The Costs of Informal Care: Looking Inside the Household*. London: HMSO.

Goffman, E. (1959) *The Presentation of Self in Everyday Life*. Harmondsworth: Pelican.

Goldthorpe, J. (1983) 'Women and Class Analysis: in Defence of the Conventional View', *Sociology*, 11: 2: 465–88.

Goldthorpe, J. and Marshall, G. (1992) 'The Promising Future of Class Analysis: A Response to Recent Critiques', *Sociology*, 26: 3: 381–400.

Gouldner, A.W. (1964) 'Anti-Minotaur: The Myth of a Value Free Sociology', in I.L. Horowitz (ed.) *The New Sociology*. New York: Oxford University Press.

Graetz, B. (1991) 'The Class Location of Families: A Refined Classification and Analysis', *Sociology*, 25: 1: 101–19.

Gramsci, A. (1971) *Selections from the Prison Notebooks of Antonio Gramsci*, eds Q. Hoare and G. Nowell–Smith. London: Lawrence and Wishart.

Gray, A. (1992) *Video Playtime: The Gendering of a Leisure Technology*. London: Routledge.

Gray, R. (1976) *The Labour Aristocracy in Victorian Edinburgh*. Oxford: Oxford University Press.

Griffin, C. (1980) *Feminist Ethnography*. Birmingham. Stencilled paper, CCCS.

Griffin, C. (1985) *Typical Girls: Young Women from School to the Job Market*. London: Routledge.

Griffin, C. (1989) '"I'm not a Women's Libber, but . . .": Feminism, Consciousness and Identity', in S. Skevington and D. Baker (eds) *The Social Identity of Women*. London: Sage. pp. 173–93.

Griffin, C. (1994) 'Absences that Matter: Constructions of Sexuality in Studies of Young Women's Friendship Groups'. Paper presented to BSA 'Sexualities in Social Context'. Preston. March.

Griffiths, M. and Whitford, M. (1988) *Feminist Perspectives in Philosophy*. London: Macmillan.

Grossberg, L. (1988) *It's A Sin: Essays on Postmodernism, Politics, Culture*. New York: Power Publications.

Hall, C. (1979) 'The Early Formation of Victorian Domestic Ideology', in S. Burman (ed.) *Fit Work for Women*. London: Croom Helm. pp. 15–33.

Hall, S. (1983) 'The Great Moving Right Show', in S. Hall and M. Jacques (eds) *The Politics of Thatcherism*. London: Lawrence and Wishart. pp. 19–40.

Hall, S. (1987) 'Identity Documents', in L. Appignanesi (ed.) *Identity: The Real Me*. ICA Document 6. pp. 44–7.

Hall, S. and Jefferson, T. (eds) (1976) *Resistance Through Rituals: Youth Subcultures in Post-war Britain*. London: Hutchinson.

Halson, J. (1989) 'The Sexual Harassment of Young Women', in L. Holly (ed.) *Girls and Sexuality: Teaching and Learning*. Milton Keynes: Open University Press. pp. 130–43.

Haraway, D. (1990) 'A Manifesto for Cyborgs: Science, Technology and Socialist Feminism in the 1980s', in L. Nicholson (ed.) *Feminism/Postmodernism*. London: Routledge. pp. 190–233.

Haraway, D. (1991) *Simians, Cyborgs, and Women: The Reinvention of Nature*. London: Free Association Books.

Harding, S. (1983) 'Why Has the Sex/Gender System Become Visible Only Now', in S. Harding and M. Hintikka (eds) *Discovering Reality: Feminist Perspectives on Epistemology, Metaphysics, Methodology and Philosophy of Science*. Dordrecht: Reidel. pp. 311–24.

Harding, S. (1991) *Whose Science, Whose Knowledge? Thinking from Women's Lives*. Milton Keynes: Open University Press.

Hart, L. (1994) *Fatal Women: Lesbian Sexuality and the Mark of Aggression*. London: Routledge.

Hartmann, P. and Husband, C. (1974) *Racism and the Mass Media*. London: Davis Poynter.

Hartsock, N. (1987) 'The Feminist Standpoint: Developing the Ground for a Specifically Feminist Historical Materialism', in S. Harding (ed.) *Feminism and Methodology*. Milton Keynes: Open University Press. pp. 157–80.

Harvey, D. (1993) 'Class Relations, Social Justice and the Politics of Difference', in M. Keith and S. Pile (eds) *Place and the Politics of Identity*. London: Routledge. pp. 41–66.

Hastrup, K. (in press) 'Beyond Words: On the Limits of Writing in Anthropology', in E. Archetti (ed.) *The Multiplicity of Writing Social Anthropology*. Oslo: Oslo University Press.

Hearn, J. (1985) 'Patriarchy, Professionalisation and the Semi-Professions', in C. Ungerson (ed.) *Women and Social Policy*. London: Macmillan. pp. 190–209.

Heath, S. (1982) *The Sexual Fix*. London: Macmillan.

Hennessy, R. (1993) *Materialist Feminism and the Politics of Discourse*. London: Routledge.

Henriques, J., Hollway, E., Urwin, C., Venn, C. and Walkerdine, V. (1984) *Changing the Subject: Psychology, Social Regulation and Subjectivity*. London: Methuen.

Hill, J. (1986) *Sex, Class and Realism: British Cinema 1956–1963*. London: British Film Institute.

Hill, O. (1877) *Our Common Land*. London: Macmillan.

Hill-Collins, P. (1990) *Black Feminist Thought: Knowledge, Consciousness and the Politics of Empowerment*. London: Routledge.

Hobsbawm, J. and Macpherson, J. (1989) 'Younger Women and Feminism: A Kaleidoscope of Old and New', *Feminist Review*, 31: 135–40.

Hoch, P. (1979) *White Hero Black Beast: Racism, Sexism and the Mask of Masculinity*. London: Pluto.

Holland, J., Ramazanoglu, C., Sharpe, S., and Thomson, R. (1991) *Pressured Pleasure: Young Women and the Negotiation of Sexual Boundaries*. WRAP paper 7. London: The Tufnell Press.

Holland, P. (1987) 'The Page Three Girl Speaks to Women Too', in R. Betterton (ed.) *Looking On: Images of Femininity in the Visual Arts and the Media*. London: Pandora. pp. 105–20.

Hollander, A. (1988) *Seeing Through Clothes*. London: Penguin.

Hollway, W. (1984) 'Women's Power in Heterosexual Sex', *Women's Studies International Forum*, 7: 1: 63–8.

Holly, L. (ed.) (1989) *Girls and Sexuality: Teaching and Learning*. Milton Keynes: Open University Press.

Holton, R. and Turner, B. (1989) *Max Weber on Economy and Society*. London: Routledge.

Holton, R. and Turner, B. (1994) 'Debate and Pseudo-debate in Class Analysis: Some Unpromising Aspects of Goldthorpe and Marshall's Defence', *Sociology*, 28: 3: 799–804.

hooks, b. (1989) *Talking Back: Thinking Feminist, Thinking Black*. London: South End Press.

Horne, J. (1983) 'Youth Unemployment Programmes: A Historical Account of the Development of "Dole Colleges"', in D. Gleeson (ed.) *Youth Training and the Search for Work*. London: Routledge and Kegan Paul. pp. 309–31.

Humphries, J. (1977) 'Class Struggle and the Persistence of the Working-Class Family', *Cambridge Journal of Economics*, 1: 241–58.

Hunt, M. (1990) 'The De-eroticisation of Women's Liberation: Social Purity Movements and the Revolutionary Feminism of Sheila Jeffreys', *Feminist Review*, 34: 23–47.

Hussein, A. (1981) 'Foucault's History of Sexuality', *m/f*, 7: 169–91.

Irigaray, L. (1985) *This Sex Which Is Not One*, trans. C. Porter with C. Burke. Ithaca and New York: Cornell University Press.

Jackson, R. (1988) *Fantasy: The Literature of Subversion*. London: Methuen.

Jagger, A. (1983) *Feminist Politics and Human Nature*. Brighton: Harvester.

Jeffreys, S. (1990) *Anticlimax: A Feminist Perspective on the Sexual Revolution*. London: The Women's Press.

Johnson, R. (1979) 'Popular Politics, Education and the State', *Popular Culture 7–8* Open University Unit. Milton Keynes: Open University.

Johnson, R. (1982) 'Reading for the Best Marx: History-Writing and Historical Abstraction', in CCCS (eds) *Making Histories: Studies in History Writing and Politics*. London: Hutchinson. pp. 153–205.

Jones, A.R. (1987) 'Nets and Bridles: Early Modern Conduct Books and Sixteenth Century Women's Lyrics', in N. Armstrong and L. Tennenhouse (eds) *The Ideology of Conduct: Essays in Literature and the History of Sexuality*. London: Methuen. pp. 39–73.

Jones, C. (1985) 'Sexual Tyranny in Mixed Schools', in G. Weiner (ed.) *Just a Bunch of Girls*. Milton Keynes: Open University Press. pp. 26–40.

Jordan, G. and Weedon, C. (1995) *Cultural Politics: Class, Gender, Race and the Postmodern World*. Cambridge: Blackwell.

Joseph Rowntree Foundation (1995) *Inquiry into Income and Wealth*. York: Joseph Rowntree Foundation.

Joseph, G. and Lewis, J. (1981) *Common Differences: Conflicts in Black and White Feminist Perspectives*. New York: Anchor Press/Doubleday.

Kaplan, E.A. (1992) *Motherhood and Representation: The Mother in Popular Culture and Melodrama*. London: Routledge.

Keat, R. and Urry, J. (1975) *Social Theory as Science*. London: Routledge and Kegan Paul.

Kelly, C. and Breinlinger, S. (1995) 'Identity and Injustice: Exploring Women's Participation in Collective Action', *Journal of Community and Applied Social Psychology*, 5: 41–57.

Kelly, C. and Breinlinger, S. (n.d.) *Involvement in Women's Groups and Campaigns: Why Women Do or Don't Get Involved*. Report for Research Participants. Department of Psychology, Birkbeck College, London University.

Kelly, L. (1989) 'Our Issues, Our Analysis: Two Decades of Work on Sexual Violence', in C. Jones and P. Mahony (eds) *Learning our Lines: Sexuality and Social Control in Education*. London: The Women's Press. pp. 129–57.

Kitzinger, C. (1994) 'Validating Women's Experience', paper presented to 'Women's Studies Network Conference', Portsmouth. July.

Knapp, M. (1992) *Care in the Community*, Evaluation by Personal Social Services Research Unit, University of Kent: Canterbury.

Koedt, A. (1973) *The Myth of the Vaginal Orgasm*. New York: Quadrangle.

Kritzman, L.D. (1988) *Michel Foucault: Politics, Philosophy and Culture; Interviews and Other Writings 1977–1984*. New York: Routledge.

Kuhn, A. (1982) *Women's Pictures: Feminism and Cinema*. London: Routledge and Kegan Paul.

Kuhn, A. (1988) *Cinema, Censorship and Sexuality, 1909–1925*. London: Routledge and Kegan Paul.

Kuhn, A. (1995) *Family Secrets: Acts of Memory and Imagination*. London: Verso.

Lacan, J. (1977) *Ecrits: A Selection*. London: Tavistock.

Lamont, M. (1992) *Money, Morals and Manners: The Culture of the French and the American Upper Middle-Class*. Chicago: University of Chicago Press.

Lash, S. and Urry, J. (1987) *The End of Organised Capitalism*. Cambridge: Polity.

Lash, S. and Urry, J. (1994) *Economies of Signs and Space*. London: Sage.

Lazreg, M. (1994) 'Women's Experience and Feminist Epistemology: A Critical Neo-Rationalist Approach', in K. Lennon and M. Whitford (eds) *Knowing the Difference: Feminist Perspectives in Epistemology*. London: Routledge. pp. 45–63.

Lees, S. (1986) *Losing Out*. London: Hutchinson.

Lees, S. (1993) *Sugar and Spice: Sexuality and Adolescent Girls*. London: Penguin.

Lendhardt, G. (1975) 'On the Relationship Between the Education System and Capitalist Work Organisation', *Kapitalistate*, 3.

Lennon, K. and Whitford, M. (eds) (1994) *Knowing the Difference: Feminist Perspectives in Epistemology*. London: Routledge.

Lister, R (1990) 'Women, Economic Dependency and Citizenship', *Journal of Social Policy*, 19: 4: 445–66.

Lloyd, F. (ed.) (1993) *Madonna*. London: Batsford.

Lloyd, G. (1984) *The Man of Reason: 'Male' and 'Female' in Western Philosophy*. London: Methuen.

Loach, L. (1987) 'Can Feminism Survive a Third Term', *Feminist Review*, 27: 24–36.

Lorde, A. (1984) *Sister Outsider*. New York: Crossing Press.

Lury, C. (1993) *Cultural Rights: Technology, Legality and Personality*. London: Routledge.

Lury, C. (1997) *Possessive Individualism*. London: Routledge.

Lyotard, J. (1984) *The Postmodern Condition: A Report on Knowledge*, trans. G. Bennington and B. Massumi. Manchester: Manchester University Press.

Mac an Ghaill, M. (1988) *Young Gifted and Black: Student Teacher Relations in the Schooling of Black Youth*. Milton Keynes: Open University Press.

Mac an Ghaill, M. (1994) *The Making of Men: Masculinities, Sexualities and Schooling*. Buckingham: Open University Press.

McCall, L. (1992) 'Does Gender *Fit*? Bourdieu, Feminism and Conceptions of Social Order', *Theory and Society*, 21: 837–67.

McCall, N. (1994) *Makes Me Wanna Holler: A Young Black Man in America*. New York: Vintage.

McClintock, A. (1995) *Imperial Leather: Race, Gender and Sexuality in the Colonial Context*. London: Routledge.

McIntosh, M. (1984) 'The Family, Regulation and the Public Sphere', in G. McLennan, D. Held and S. Hall (eds) *State and Society in Contemporary Britain*. Cambridge: Polity. pp. 204–41.

MacKinnon, C. (1983) 'Feminism, Marxism, Method and the State: Towards a Feminist Jurisprudence', *Signs*, 8: 4: 6635–58.

McNay, L. (1992) *Foucault and Feminism*. Cambridge: Polity.

McNeil, M. (1991) 'Making and Not Making the Difference: The Gender Politics of

Thatcherism', in S. Franklin, C. Lury and J. Stacey, (eds) *Off-Centre: Feminism and Cultural Studies*. London: HarperCollins. pp. 221–41.

Macpherson, C.B. (1962) *The Political Theory of Possessive Individualism*. Oxford: Oxford University Press.

McRobbie, A. (1978) 'Working Class Girls and the Culture of Femininity', in Women's Studies Group (eds) *Women Take Issue: Aspects of Women's Subordination*. London: Hutchinson/ CCCS. pp. 96–109.

McRobbie, A. (1982) 'The Politics of Feminist Research: Between Talk, Text and Action', *Feminist Review*, 12: 46–59.

McRobbie, A. (1984) 'Dance and Social Fantasy', in A. McRobbie and M. Nava (eds) *Gender and Generation*. London: Macmillan. pp. 130–62.

McRobbie, A. (1989) 'Second-Hand Dresses and the Role of the Ragmarket', in A. McRobbie (ed.) *Zoot Suits and Second Hand Dresses: An Anthology of Fashion and Music*. London: Macmillan. pp. 23–50.

McRobbie, A. (1991) *Feminism and Youth Culture: From Jackie to Just Seventeen*. London: Macmillan.

McRobbie, A. and Garber, J. (1976) 'Girls and Subcultures', in S. Hall and T. Jefferson (eds) *Resistance Through Rituals*. London: Hutchinson. pp. 209–23.

Mahony, P. (1989) 'Sexual Violence in Mixed Schools', in C. Jones and P. Mahony (eds) *Learning our Lines: Sexuality and Social Control in Education*. London: The Women's Press. pp. 157–91.

Mannheim, K. (1936/1960) *Ideology and Utopia*. London: Routledge and Kegan Paul.

Marcus, G.E. (1986) 'Contemporary Problems of Ethnography in the Modern World System', in J. Clifford and G.E. Marcus (eds) *Writing Culture: The Poetics and Politics of Ethnography*. Berkeley: University of California Press. pp. 105–93.

Marcus, G.E. (1992) 'Past, Present and Emergent Identities: Requirements for Ethnographies of Late Twentieth-Century Modernity World-Wide', in S. Lash and J. Friedman (eds) *Modernity and Identity*. Oxford: Blackwell. pp. 309–31.

Marks, P. (1976) 'Femininity in the Classroom: An Account of Changing Attitudes', in J. Mitchell and A. Oakley (eds) *The Rights and Wrongs of Women*. Harmondsworth: Penguin. pp. 176–99.

Marshall, J. (1981) 'Pansies, Perverts and Macho Men', in K. Plummer (ed.) *The Making of the Modern Homosexual*. London: Hutchinson.

Martin, E. (1989) *The Woman in the Body*. London: Routledge.

Maurice, Rev. F.D. (ed.) (1855) *Lectures to Ladies on Practical Subjects*. Cambridge: Macmillan.

Mauss, M. (1985) in M. Carrithers, S. Collins and S. Lukes (eds) *The Category of the Person*. Cambridge: Cambridge University Press.

Maynard, M. (1994) '"Race", Gender and the Concept of "Difference" in Feminist Thought', in H. Afshar and M. Maynard (eds) *The Dynamics of 'Race' and Gender: Some Feminist Interventions*. London: Taylor and Francis. pp. 9–26.

Mealyea, R. (1989) 'Humour as a Coping Strategy in the Transition from Tradesperson to Teacher', *British Journal of Sociology of Education*, 19: 3: 311–33.

Mercer, K. and Julien, I. (1988) 'Race, Sexual Politics and Black Masculinity: A Dossier', in R. Chapman and J. Rutherford (eds) *Male Order: Unwrapping Masculinity*. London: Lawrence and Wishart. pp. 97–165.

Merck, M. (1993) *Perversions: Deviant Readings*. London: Virago.

Mirza, H. (1992) *Young, Female and Black*. London: Routledge.

Modleski, T. (1984) *Loving with a Vengeance: Mass Produced Fantasies for Women*. London: Methuen.

Modleski, T. (1991) *Feminism Without Women: Culture and Criticism in a 'Postfeminist' Age*. London: Routledge.

Mohanty, C.T. (1984) 'Under Western Eyes: Feminist Scholarship and Colonial Discourse', *Boundry*, 2: 3: 12/13: 333–58.

Moi, T. (1991) 'Appropriating Bourdieu: Feminist Theory and Pierre Bourdieu's Sociology of Culture', *New Literary History*, 22: 1017–49.

Morgan, H.L. (1877) *Ancient Society*. New York.

Moye, A. (1985) 'Pornography', in A. Metcalf and M. Humphries (eds) *The Sexuality of Men*. London. Pluto. pp. 44–70.

National Health Services Act (1946) London: HMSO.

Nead, L. (1988) *Myths of Sexuality: Representations of Women in Victorian Britain*. Oxford: Blackwell.

Newman, G. (1906) *Infant Mortality: A Social Problem*. London.

Oakley, A. (1974) *The Sociology of Housework*. Oxford: Martin Robertson.

O'Neill, G. (1993) *A Night Out With The Girls: Women Having A Good Time*. London: The Women's Press.

Ortner, S. (1991) 'Reading America: Preliminary Notes on Class and Culture', in G.R. Fox (ed.) *Recapturing Anthropology: Working in the Present*. Santa Fe, NM: School of American Research Press. pp. 163–91.

O'Sullivan, S. (1995) 'On *Sex, Art and American Culture* by Camille Paglia', *Feminist Review*, Spring, 49: 108–15.

Parker, R.A. (1980) 'The State of Care', *The Richard M. Titmuss Memorial Lecture 1979–1980*. Joint (J.D.C.) Israel Brookdale Institute of Gerontology and Adult Human Development in Israel.

Parmar, P. (1989) 'Other Kinds of Dreams', *Feminist Review*, 31: 55–66.

Partington, A. (1990) 'Consumption Practices as the Production and Articulation of Differences: Rethinking Working-Class Femininity in 1950s Britain', unpublished PhD dissertation. University of Birmingham.

Pateman, C. (1988) *The Sexual Contract*. Cambridge: Polity.

Pearce, L. (1994) *Reading Dialogics*. London: Edward Arnold.

Pearce, L. (1995) Personal communication with the author. 9 December.

Penley, C. (1993) 'Pornography, Pleasure and Pedagogy'. Plenary address to 'Console-ing Passions Conference', University of Southern California, Los Angeles, April.

Phelan, P. (1993) *Unmarked: The Politics of Performance*. London: Routledge.

Pollock, G. (1989) *Vision and Difference: Femininity, Feminism and the Histories of Art*. London: Routledge.

Popular Memory Group (1982) 'Popular Memory, Theory, Politics, Method', in R. Johnson, G. McLennan, B. Schwarz and D. Sutton (eds) *Making Histories: Studies in History, Writing and Politics*. London: Hutchinson.

Poovey, M. (1984) *The Proper Lady and the Woman Writer: Ideology as Style in the Works of Mary Wollstonecraft, Mary Shelley, and Jane Austen*. Chicago: University of Chicago Press.

Press, A. (1990) 'Class, Gender and the Female Viewer: Women's Responses to *Dynasty*', in M.E. Brown (ed.) *Television and Women's Culture: The Politics of the Popular*. London: Sage. pp. 158–83.

Press, A. (1991) *Women Watching Television: Gender, Class and Generation in the American Television Experience*. Philadelphia: University of Pennsylvania Press.

Probyn, E. (1990) 'Travels in the Postmodern: Making Sense of the Local', in L.J. Nicholson (ed.) *Feminism/Postmodernism*. London: Routledge. pp.176–90.

Probyn, E. (1993a) 'True Voices and Real People: The "Problem" of the Autobiographical in Cultural Studies', in V. Blundell, J. Shepherd and I. Taylor (eds) *Relocating Cultural Studies*. London: Routledge. pp. 105–22.

Probyn, E. (1993b) *Sexing the Self: Gendered Positions in Cultural Studies*. London: Routledge.

Prohashka, F.R. (1974) 'Women in English Philanthropy 1790–1830', *International Review of Social History*, XIX: 3: 434–9.

Radner, H. (1995) *Shopping Around: Feminine Culture and the Pursuit of Pleasure*. London: Routledge.

Radway, J. (1987) *Reading the Romance*. London: Verso.

Ramazanoglu, C. (1987) 'Sex and Violence in Academic Life or You Can't Keep a Good Woman Down', in J. Hanmer and M. Maynard (eds) *Women, Violence and Social Control*. London: Macmillan. pp. 61–75.

Ramazanoglu, C. (1989) *Feminism and the Contradictions of Oppression*. London: Routledge.

Rapp, R. (1988) 'Is the Legacy of Second Wave Feminism Post-Feminism?', *Socialist Review*, 97: 31–7.

Rapp, R., Ross, E. and R. Bridenthal (1979) 'Examining Family History', *Feminist Studies*, 5: 1: 174–200.

Rich, A. (1979) *On Lies, Secrets and Silences: Selected Prose 1966–1978*. New York: Horton.

Riley, D. (1987) 'Does a Sex have a History? "Women and Feminism"', *New Formations*, 1: 35–45.

Robins, K. (1994) 'Forces of Consumption: From the Symbolic to the Psychotic', *Media, Culture and Society*, 16: 449–68.

Root, A. (1984) 'Return of the Nanny', *New Socialist*, 22 December: 16–19.

Rose, J. (1987) 'The State of the Subject (II): The Institution of Feminism', *Critical Quarterly*, 29: 4. Winter: 9–15.

Rose, N. (1989) *Governing the Soul: The Shaping of the Private Self*. London: Routledge.

Rowe, K. (1995) *The Unruly Woman: Gender and the Genres of Laughter*. Austin: University of Texas Press.

Said, E. (1984) *The World, the Text and the Critic*. London: Faber and Faber.

Savage, M. (1992) 'Women's Expertise, Men's Authority: Gendered Organisations and the Contemporary Middle-Classes', in M. Savage and A. Witz (eds) *Gender and Bureaucracy*. Oxford. Blackwell. Reprinted in *Sociological Review*, pp. 124–51.

Savage, M., Barlow, J., Dickens, P. and Feilding, T. (1992) *Property, Bureaucracy and Culture: Middle-Class Formation in Contemporary Britain*. London: Routledge.

Sayer, A. (1995) 'Notes on Objectivity', *Social Sciences Training Programme Handbook: 1995*. Lancaster: Lancaster University Social Science Faculty publication.

Sayer, A. and Walker, R. (1992) *The New Social Economy: Reworking the Division of Labour*. Oxford: Blackwell.

Scheff, T. (1994) 'Emotions and Identity: A Theory of Ethnic Nationalism', in C. Calhoun (ed.) *Social Theory and the Politics of Identity*. Oxford: Blackwell. pp. 277–304.

Scheman, N. (1993) *Engenderings: Constructions of Knowledge, Authority and Privilege*. London: Routledge.

Scott, J. (1992) 'Experience', in J. Butler and J. Scott (eds) *Feminists Theorise the Political*. London: Routledge. pp. 22–41.

Sedgwick, E.K. (1991) *Epistemology of the Closet*. Hemel Hempstead, Herts: Harvester Wheatsheaf.

Sedgwick, E.K. (1993) 'Queer Performativity: Henry James's *The Art of the Novel*', *GLQ: A Journal of Lesbian and Gay Studies*, 1.1, Spring: pp. 1–16.

Seebohm Report (1968) *Report of the Committee on Local Authority and Allied Personal Services*, Cmnd 3703. London: HMSO.

Segal, L. (1983) 'The Heat in the Kitchen', in S. Hall and M. Jacques (eds) *The Politics of Thatcherism*. London: Lawrence Wishart. pp. 207–16.

Segal, L. (1987) *Is the Future Female: Troubled Thoughts on Contemporary Feminism*. London: Virago.

Segal, L. (1991) 'Whose Left: Socialism, Feminism and the Future', *New Left Review*, 185: 81–91.

Segal, L. and M. McIntosh (eds) (1992) *Sex Exposed: Sexuality and the Pornography Debate*. London: Virago.

Seiter, E., Borchers, H., Kreutzner, G. and Warth, E.-M. (eds) (1989) *Remote Control: Television Audiences and Cultural Power*. London: Routledge.

Sennett, R. and Cobb, J. (1977) *The Hidden Injuries of Class*. Cambridge: Cambridge University Press.

Sherratt, N. (1983) 'Girls, Jobs and Glamour', *Feminist Review*, 15: 47–62.

Short, C. (1991) *Dear Clare, This is What Women Feel about Page Three* (letters edited and selected by Kiri Tunks and Diane Hutchinson). London: Radius.

Skeggs, B. (1986) *Young Women and Further Education: A Case Study of Young Women's Experience of Caring Courses in a Local College*, unpublished PhD dissertation. University of Keele.

Skeggs, B. (1991a) 'A Spanking Good Time', *Magazine of Cultural Studies*, Spring, 3: 28–33.

Skeggs, B. (1991b) 'Challenging Masculinity and Using Sexuality', *British Journal of Sociology of Education*, 12: 2: 127–41.

Skeggs, B. (1991c) 'Postmodernism: What is all the Fuss About?', *British Journal of Sociology of Education*, 12: 2: 255–79.

Skeggs, B. (1992) 'The Cultural Production of "Learning to Labour"', in A. Beezer and M. Barker (eds) *Reading into Cultural Studies*. London: Routledge. pp. 181–96.

Skeggs, B. (1993) 'For Women Only', in F. Lloyd (ed.) *Madonna*. London: Batsford Press. pp. 271–81.

Skeggs, B. (1994a) 'Theories of Masculinities', in P. Ahokes, M. Lahti and J. Sihvonen (eds) *Discourse of Masculinity*. Jyuaskylan Nykykultluria: Tutkimusyksikio (Finnish/English publication). pp. 13–36.

Skeggs, B. (1994b) 'Situating the Production of Feminist Ethnography', in M. Maynard and J. Purvis (eds) *Researching Women's Lives from a Feminist Perspective*. London: Taylor and Francis. pp. 72–93.

Skeggs, B. (1994c) 'Refusing to be Civilised: "Race", Sexuality and Power', in H. Afshar and M. Maynard (eds) *The Dynamics of Race, and Gender*. London: Taylor and Francis. pp. 106–27.

Skeggs, B. (1994d) 'The Limits of Neutrality: Feminist Research and the ERA', in B. Troyna and D. Halpin (eds) *Researching Educational Policy: Ethical and Methodological Issues*. Lewes: Falmer. pp. 115–35.

Skeggs, B. (1995a) 'Introduction: Processes in Feminist Cultural Theory', in B. Skeggs (ed.) *Feminist Cultural Theory: Production and Process*. Manchester: Manchester University Press. pp. 1–33.

Skeggs, B. (1995b) 'Theorising, Ethics and Representation in Feminist Ethnography', in B. Skeggs (ed.) *Feminist Cultural Theory: Production and Process*. Manchester: Manchester University Press. pp. 190–207.

Skeggs, B (1995c) 'Entitlement Cultures and Institutional Constraints: Women's Studies in the UK in the 1990s', *Women's Studies International Forum*, 18: 4: 475–85.

Smith, D.E. (1988) 'Femininity as Discourse', in L.G. Roman, L.K. Christian-Smith and E. Ellsworth (eds) *Becoming Feminine: The Politics of Popular Culture*. Lewes: Falmer Press. pp. 37–60.

Smith, N. and Katz, C. (1993) 'Grounding Metaphor: Towards a Spacialised Politics', in M. Keith and S. Pile (eds) *Place and the Politics of Identity*. London: Routledge. pp. 67–83.

Song, M. and Parker, D. (1995) 'Cultural Identity: Disclosing Commonality and Difference in In-Depth Interviewing', *Sociology*, 29: 2: 241–57.

Soper, K. (1995) 'Heterosexual Utopianism', *Radical Philosophy*, 69: 5–15.

Spallone, P. (1989) *Beyond Conception: The New Politics of Reproduction*. London: Macmillan.

Spelman, E. (1988) *Inessential Woman: Problems of Exclusion in Feminist Thought*. London: The Women's Press.

Spillers, H.J. (1984) 'Interstices: A Small Drama of Words', in C. Vance (ed.) *Pleasure and Danger: Exploring Female Sexuality*. London: Pandora. pp. 73–101.

Spivak, G.C. (1990) *The Post-Colonial Critic: Interviews, Strategies, Dialogues*, ed. Sarah Harassym. London: Routledge.

Stacey, J. (1994) *Star Gazing: Hollywood Cinema and Female Spectatorship*. London: Routledge.

Stacey, Judith. (1987) 'Sexism by a Subtler Name: Postindustrial Conditions and Postfeminist Consciousness in the Silicon Valley', *Socialist Review*, 17: 6: 7–28.

Stacey, Judith. (1988) *Brave New Families*. New York: Basic Books.

Stacey, M. (1975) *Power, Resistance and Change*. London: Routledge and Kegan Paul.

Stanworth, M. (1981) *Gender and Schooling: A Study of Sexual Divisions in the Classroom*. London: WRRC.

Stanworth, M. (1984) 'Women and Class Analysis: A Reply to Goldthorpe', *Sociology*, 18: 2: 153–71.

Stanworth, M. (1987) *Reproductive Technologies: Gender, Motherhood and Medicine*. Cambridge: Polity.

Stedman Jones, G. (1971) *Outcast London: A Study in the Relationship Between Classes in Victorian Society*. Oxford: Clarendon.

Steedman, C. (1986) *Landscape for a Good Woman: A Story of Two Lives*. London: Virago.

Strathern, M. (1992) *After Nature: English Kinship in the Late Twentieth Century*. Cambridge: Cambridge University Press.

Stuart, A. (1990) 'Feminism: Dead or Alive', in J. Rutherford (ed.) *Identity: Community, Culture, Difference*. London: Lawrence and Wishart. pp. 28–43.

Summers, A. (1979) 'A Home from Home – Women's Philanthropic Work in the 19th Century', in S. Burman (ed.) *Fit Work For Women*. London: Croom Helm. pp. 33–64

Summers, A. (1981) *Working with People*. London: Cassell.

Sunder Rajan, R. (1993) *Real and Imagined Women: Gender, Culture and Postcolonialism*. London: Routledge.

Taylor, C. (1989) *Sources of the Self: The Making of the Modern Identity*. Cambridge: Cambridge University Press.

Taylor, C. (1994) 'The Politics of Recognition', in D.T. Goldberg (ed.) *Multiculturalism: A Critical Reader*. Oxford: Blackwell. pp. 75–106.

Thatcher, M. (1982) 'Women in a Changing World', Press Office, Downing Street, July 1982.

Thompson, S. (1990) '"Drastic Entertainments": Teenage Mothers' Signifying Narratives', in F. Ginsburg and A. Lowenhaupt-Tsing (eds) *Uncertain Terms: Negotiating Gender in American Culture*. Boston: Beacon Press. pp. 269–81.

Thomson, R. and Henderson, S. (1994) 'Faghag: Thinking Sexual Identity as Process'. Paper given to British Sociological Conference, 'Sexualities in Social Context'. Preston. March.

Tilt, E. (1852) *Elements of Health and Principles of Female Hygiene*. London.

Treichler, P. (1986) 'Teaching Feminist Theory', in C. Nelson (ed.) *Theory in the Classroom*. Chicago: University of Illinois Press. pp. 57–79.

Tolson, A. (1977) *The Limits of Masculinity*. London: Tavistock.

Tyler, C.-A. (1991) 'Boys Will be Girls: The Politics of Gay Drag', in D. Fuss (ed.) *Inside Out: Lesbian Theories, Gay Theories*. London: Routledge. pp. 32–71.

Ungerson, C. (1982) 'Women and Caring: Skills, Tasks and Taboos'. Paper presented to British Sociology Conference. Manchester. April.

Ungerson, C. (1987) *Policy is Personal: Sex, Gender and Informal Care*. London: Tavistock.

Venn, C. (1992) 'Subjectivity, Ideology and Difference: Recovering Otherness', *New Formations*, Spring: 16: 40–61.

Visweswaran, K. (1994) *Fictions of Feminist Ethnography*. Minneapolis: University of Minnesota Press.

Walby, S. (1994) 'Is Citizenship Gendered?', *Sociology*, 28: 2: 379–95.

Walker, A. (ed.) (1982) *Community Care: The Family, the State and Social Policy*. Oxford: Martin Robertson/Blackwell.

Walkerdine, V. (1984) 'Some Day My Prince Will Come', in A. McRobbie and M. Nava (eds) *Gender and Generation*. London: Macmillan. pp. 162–85.

Walkerdine, V. (1987) *Surveillance, Subjectivity and Struggle: Lessons from Pedagogic and Domestic Practices*. Centre for Humanistic Studies: University of Minnesota.

Walkerdine, V. (1988) *The Mastery of Reason: Cognitive Development and the Production of Rationality*. London: Routledge.

Walkerdine, V. (1989) 'Femininity as Performance', *Oxford Review of Education*, 15: 3: 267–79

Walkerdine, V. (1990) *Schoolgirl Fictions*. London: Verso.

Walkerdine, V. and Lucey, H. (1989) *Democracy in the Kitchen: Regulating Mothers and Socialising Daughters*. London: Virago.

Wallace, M. (1993) 'Negative Images: Towards a Black Feminist Cultural Criticism', in S. During (ed.) *The Cultural Studies Reader*. London: Routledge. pp. 118–35.

Waquant, L.J.D. (1993) 'From Ruling Class to Field of Power: An Interview with Pierre Bourdieu on La Noblesse d'état', *Theory, Culture and Society*, 10, 19–44.

Warde, A. (1994) 'Employment Relations or Assets: An Alternative Basis of Class Analysis', Paper presented to Lancaster Regionalism Group, 13.12.94. Lancaster University.

Ware, V. (1992) *Beyond The Pale: White Women, Racism and History*. London: Verso.

Watt, I. (1957) *The Rise of the Novel*. London: Chatto and Windus.

Wearing, B. (1984) *The Ideology of Motherhood*. Sydney: Allen and Unwin.

Weber, M. (1949) *The Methodology of the Social Sciences*, trans. E.A. Shils and H.A. Finch. New York: The Free Press.

Weed, E. (1989) *Coming to Terms: Feminism, Theory, Politics*. London: Routledge.

Weeks, J. (1981) *Sex, Politics and Society: The Regulation of Sexuality Since 1800*. London: Longman.

Westwood, S. (1984) *All Day and Everyday: Factory and Family in the Making of Women's Lives*. London: Pluto.

Whelehan, I. (1995) *Modern Feminist Thought: From Second Wave to 'Post-Feminism'*. Edinburgh: Edinburgh University Press.

White, E. (1980) *States of Desire*. London: Andre Deutsch.

Whitford, M. (1988) 'Luce Irigaray's Critique of Rationality', in M. Griffiths and M. Whitford (eds) *Feminist Perspectives in Philosophy*. London: Macmillan. pp. 109–31.

Wicke, J. (1994) 'Celebrity Material: Materialist Feminism and the Culture of Celebrity', in T. Moi and J. Radway (eds) 'Materialist Feminism'. *The South Atlantic Quarterly*, Fall, 93: 4: 751–79. (Special Edition)

Williams, P. (1991) *The Alchemy of Race and Rights: Diary of a Law Professor*. Cambridge, MA: Harvard University Press.

Williams, R. (1961) *Culture and Society 1780–1950*. Harmondsworth: Penguin.

Williams, R. (1973) 'Base and Superstructure in Marxist Cultural Theory', *New Left Review*, 82: 3–16.

Williams, R. (1977) *Marxism and Literature*. Oxford: Oxford University Press.

Willis, P. (1977) *Learning to Labour: How Working Class Kids get Working Class Jobs*. Farnbrough, Hants: Saxon House.

Willis, P. (1979) 'Shop Floor Culture, Masculinity and the Wage Form', in J. Clarke, C. Critcher and R. Johnson (eds) *Working Class Culture*. London: Hutchinson.

Wilson, E. (with A. Weir) (1986) *Hidden Agendas: Theory, Politics and Experience in the Women's Movement*. London: Tavistock.

Wilson, E. (1987) 'Thatcherism and Women: After Seven Years', in R. Miliband, L. Panitch and J. Saville (eds) *Socialist Register*. London: Merlin Press. pp. 199–235.

Wilson, E. (1991) 'Feminism Without Illusions', *New Left Review*, 190: 119–27.

Winch, P. (1958) *The Idea of Social Science, and its Relation to Philosophy*. London: Routledge and Kegan Paul.

Winship, J. (1983) '"Options – for the way you want to live now", or a Magazine for Superwoman', *Theory, Culture and Society*, 1: 3: 44–65.

Winship, J. (1985) '*A Girl Needs to Get Street-Wise*: Magazines for the 1980s', *Feminist Review*, 21: 25–47.

Wolfenden Committee (1978) *The Future of Voluntary Organisations*. London: Croom Helm.

Wolff, J. (1995) *Resident Alien: Feminist Cultural Criticism*. Cambridge: Polity.

Wolpe, A.-M. (1975) 'The Official Ideology of Girl's Education', in M. Flude and J. Ahier (eds) *Educability, Schools and Ideology*. London. Croom Helm. pp. 138–60.

Wolpe, A.-M. (1988) *Within School Walls: The Role of Discipline, Sexuality and the Curriculum*. London: Routledge.

Wright, E. (1985) *Classes*. London: Verso.

Wright, E. (1989) 'Women in the Class Structure', *Politics and Society*, 17: 35–66.

Young, A. (1990) *Femininity in Dissent*. London: Routledge.

Young, I. (1990) *Throwing Like a Girl and Other Essays in Philosophy and Social Theory*. Bloomington: Indiana University Press.

Index